SHAKESPEARE'S FOREIGN WORLDS

SHAKESPEARE'S FOREIGN WORLDS

NATIONAL AND TRANSNATIONAL IDENTITIES IN THE ELIZABETHAN AGE

CAROLE LEVIN AND
JOHN WATKINS

CORNELL UNIVERSITY PRESS
Ithaca and London

First published 2009 by Cornell University Press

Printed in the United States of America

Library of Congress Cataloging-in-Publication Data

Levin, Carole, 1948–
    Shakespeare's foreign worlds : national and transnational
identities in the Elizabethan age / Carole Levin and John
Watkins.
        p. cm.
    Includes bibliographical references and index.
    ISBN 978-0-8014-4741-9 (cloth : alk. paper)
    1. Shakespeare, William, 1564–1616—Characters.
2. Characters and characteristics in literature.   3. Group
identity in literature.   4. National characteristics,
English, in literature.   5. National characteristics in
literature.   6. Aliens in literature.   7. Literature and
history—England—History—16th century.   I. Watkins,
John, 1960–   II. Title.

    PR2989.L438   2009
    822.3'3—dc22
2008044217

PR
2989
.L438
2009

Cornell University Press strives to use environmentally
responsible suppliers and materials to the fullest extent
possible in the publishing of its books. Such materials
include vegetable-based, low-VOC inks and acid-free
papers that are recycled, totally chlorine-free, or partly
composed of nonwood fibers. For further information,
visit our website at www.cornellpress.cornell.edu.

Cloth printing   10 9 8 7 6 5 4 3 2 1

This book is for Michele Osherow, who taught me about Eve Cohan, and for the women of the Bvinovitch clan, especially the young matriarch and the tiniest Bvinovitch girl, who have successfully sojourned in so many foreign worlds
Carole

In memory of my teachers Stuart Sperry and Albert Wertheim
John

❧ Contents

❧ ACKNOWLEDGMENTS

We found working together on this project a wonderful experience that not only heightened our appreciation of each other as scholars but also strengthened our friendship. We would like to thank the many individuals and organizations that made our collaboration possible. We are especially grateful to our editor Peter J. Potter for his enthusiasm and encouragement. Karen Laun, senior production editor, and Martin Schneider, our copy editor, were of great help as the book went to press. Our readers, Phyllis Rackin and Rebecca Lemon, offered generous and helpful advice that inspired numerous points of revision. The undergraduate research program at the University of Nebraska, UCARE, provided us with an excellent and meticulous research assistant in Erica Wright. We are deeply grateful to the UCARE director Laura Damuth and thank Wright for all her hard work. Numerous institutions and societies provided opportunities for us to discuss our work with other scholars as it developed. We would like to thank our friends at the Shakespeare Association of America, the Sixteenth-Century Studies Conference, Shakespeare at Kalamazoo, the Medieval Institute at the University of Western Michigan, the Columbia Shakespeare seminar, the Missouri Valley History Conference, the Center for Early Modern History and the Theorizing Early Modern Studies cohort at the University of Minnesota, Cornell University, and Loyola College of Baltimore. Sections of "The Taming of the Queen," in *High and Mighty Queens of Early Modern England: Realities and Representations,* ed. Carole Levin, Debra Barrett-Graves, and Jo Eldridge Carney (New York: Palgrave Macmillan, 2003) are reproduced with permission of Palgrave Macmillan, and we are very grateful.

Carole Levin's Acknowledgments

I am deeply grateful to Michele Osherow, Jim Shapiro, Lena Orlin, Jo Eldridge Carney, Elaine Kruse, Pamela Starr, and Anya Riehl for their advice and support of this project. In September 2006, I presented a shorter version of chapter 3 at the Columbia Shakespeare seminar. I am most grateful to Katherine Goodland for the kind invitation and to the seminar members for the useful and lively discussion. I particularly want to thank Cristina Alfar for her generous and most helpful and thoughtful comments. I also appreciate all the help and intellectual exchanges from my students, particularly Cassie Olsen Auble, Lindsay Kerns, Nathan Martin, Shannon Meyer, Nate Probasco, Mark Reuter, and Lisa Schuelke. I also thank my colleagues in the Department of History, the Harris Center for Judaic Studies, the Women and Gender Studies Program, and the Medieval and Renaissance Studies Program. Much of the research for my portions of the book was accomplished at the Love Library at the University of Nebraska, the Newberry Library of Chicago, and the Folger Shakespeare Library in Washington, D.C. These superb libraries provided great facilities. I especially want to thank Georgianna Ziegler at the Folger and Kathy Johnson and those at the Interlibrary Loan Department at Love Library for all their help.

For me this project and so much of my intellectual and personal life have been enriched by my relationships with my former students such as Karolyn Kinane, Amy Gant, Tim Elston, Shawn Holderby, and Carolyn Biltoft. I thank them very much.

John Watkins's Acknowledgments

I would especially like to thank Albert Ascoli, Patrick Cheney, Lianna Farber, Valeria Finucci, Shirley Nelson Garner, Roland Greene, Jean Howard, William Kennedy, Rebecca Krug, Marguerite Ragnow, Curtis Perry, Katherine Scheil, and the many Shakespeare students I have taught over the years for their advice and support throughout this project. A summer research grant from the University of Minnesota's Graduate School and a sabbatical fellowship from the American Philosophical Society supported much of my work. My colleagues in Italian Studies at the University of Minnesota, especially Susanna Ferlito and Susan Noakes, inspired two of my chapters, and I am grateful for their help with translations. Our cover illustration was reproduced with the kind permission of Marguerite Ragnow of the James Ford Bell Library. For over twenty years, I have relied on Andrew Elfenbein's incalculable wisdom, intellectual guidance, and patience. His encouragement and our son Dima's infectious joy heartened me throughout the writing of this book. Finally, I cherish memories of the conversations about Shakespeare that I shared with the teachers to whom I dedicate my portions of this volume, Stuart Sperry and Albert Wertheim.

A Note on the Text

Unless otherwise noted, references to Shakespeare's works are to *The Riverside Shakespeare,* 2nd ed., ed. G. Blakemore Evans et al. (Boston: Houghton Mifflin, 1996).

SHAKESPEARE'S FOREIGN WORLDS

Introduction

Portia opens the most famous trial in English literature with a notoriously puzzling question:

I am informed throughly of the cause.
Which is the merchant here? And which the Jew?[1]

Whether we think of this as a moment unfolding in a sixteenth-century Venetian court or on a sixteenth-century London stage, the difference between Antonio and Shylock in *The Merchant of Venice* was presumably apparent. Theater historians tell us that the first Shylock probably wore a shaggy red wig and a hooked nose like the one sported by Judas in the mystery plays.[2] In early modern Venice, the signory insisted that Jews wear a yellow head covering to distinguish them from Christians, or at least respectable ones, since pimps and prostitutes were also supposed to wear yellow.[3] The color symbolism made it patently clear where Jews stood on the social scale. In most

---

1. *The Merchant of Venice,* 4.1.173–74.
2. Toby Lelyveld, *Shylock on the Stage* (Cleveland: Western Reserve University Press, 1960); and Stephen Orgel, *Imagining Shakespeare: A History of Texts and Visions* (Houndmills, U.K.: Palgrave, 2003), 144–46.
3. See Benjamin Ravid, "The Venetian Government and the Jews," in *The Jews of Early Modern Venice,* ed. Robert C. Davis and Ravid (Baltimore: Johns Hopkins University Press, 2001), 21.

European cities with sizeable Jewish populations, distinctive attire—whether gabardines or yellow hats or red turbans—reflected complex interactions involving local custom, Christian ordinance, and Jewish laws. It would be hard to find a place anywhere in sixteenth-century Christendom where a Jewish moneylender might be mistaken for a Christian merchant.

So why does Portia ask this question? A modern judge might begin a trial by asking who is the plaintiff and who is the defendant. But Portia's words are more specific and suggest that the categories of profession, religion, and even race fail to distinguish Antonio from Shylock, at least in ways that would be apparent at first glance. This book began at a conference on Elizabeth I, when the two authors started talking about this passage. We came up with reasons why Portia as a character, or Shakespeare as a dramatist, might pose this seemingly obvious question. Like all scholars who have talked about this passage, we considered how it might not be so obvious after all. Some of our explanations touched on territory long covered by professional Shakespeareans, and some were so farfetched that we quickly retracted them. Some were more historical in focus and others more literary. Did the suggestion that the two characters were not necessarily distinguishable point to anxieties about *conversos* living on the boundaries between the Christian and Jewish communities? Did it point to the interdependence between Jewish money-lending and Christian entrepreneurialism at the dawn of capitalism? Did it remind us of the initial malevolence of the Christian hero who went around spitting on Shylock's gabardine? Did it remind us that racism was less about individuals than a system that demeans the humanity of everyone in it?

The more we talked, the more Portia's questions turned into a metacommentary on our own conversation. If anyone happened to overhear us, they might have found themselves asking, "Which one is the historian here? And which one the English professor?" Like the bargaining and litigation that exposed a common identity between Shylock and Antonio, our conversation identified us as practitioners of a common academic discourse, one more compromised than abetted by our formal disciplinary affiliations. The English professor was no more likely to speak in aesthetic or ostensibly literary terms than the historian, and the historian was no more attuned to questions of social and political context than the professor of English. We shared not only a common point of investigation—the sixteenth-century English past—but a common methodology for generating and defining questions about that past, for resolving them through archival and analytical procedures, and for exploring their ramifications through a common body of cultural theory.

The conversation finally left us with one overriding question: What would happen if we threw out the pretension of disciplinary divergence altogether and began to question the Elizabethan past, not as professors of literature and history but simply as early modernists? What if we were no longer answerable to the canons of institutional and disciplinary affiliation that, at our particular professional moment, seemed more to impede than foster original investigations?

Shakespeare beyond the Disciplines

In many ways, this question could not seem more belated. After all, English professors and historians sometimes seem to have talked about nothing but interdisciplinarity for the last quarter-century.[4] Within early modern literary studies, that discussion has centered most often on debates over the New Historicism, which persists in seeming "new" despite thirty years of contestation and refinement. But the terms of the debate have shifted significantly with the emergence of second and even third generations of historicist readers. The question is no longer whether historical or biographical questions are relevant to the study of literature but rather in what kinds of historical inquiries literary scholars ought to engage. Whether we talk about gender, sexuality, empire, or the material of the book, we are still talking about history. A graduate student who could not talk about social conflict in sixteenth-century London or the political makeup of Elizabeth's privy council would probably fare worse on the current English job market than one who could not say something about Surrey and the invention of English blank verse. The character of the monograph on early modern topics has changed noticeably from the days when Stephen Greenblatt organized *Renaissance Self-Fashioning* as a series of chapters focused on major Renaissance writers like Wyatt, Spenser, Marlowe, and Shakespeare. The newest historicists center

---

4. See, for example, Henry Giroux, David Shumway, Paul Smith, and James Sosnoski, "The Need for Cultural Studies: Resisting Intellectuals and Oppositional Public Spheres," *Dalhousie Review* 64 (1984): 472–86; Stanley Fish, "Being Interdisciplinary Is So Hard To Do," *Profession '89* (New York: Modern Language Association, 1989), 15–22; Julie Thompson Klein, *Interdisciplinarity: History, Theory, and Practice* (Detroit: Wayne State University Press, 1990); David Easton and Corinne Schelling, eds., *Divided Knowledge: Across Disciplines, Across Cultures* (Newbury Park, CA: Sage, 1991); Nancy Easterlin and Barbara Riebling, eds., *After Poststructuralism: Interdisciplinarity and Literary Theory* (Evanston, IL: Northwestern University Press, 1993); Ellen Messer-Davidow, David R. Shumway, and David J. Sylvan, eds., *Knowledges: Historical and Critical Studies in Disciplinarity* (Charlottesville: University of Virginia Press, 1993); Klein, *Crossing Boundaries: Knowledge, Disciplinarities, and Interdisciplinarities* (Charlottesville: University of Virginia Press, 1996); Georg G. Iggers, *Historiography in the Twentieth Century: From Scientific Objectivity to the Postmodern Challenge* (Middletown, CT: Wesleyan University Press, 1997); Tony Jackson, "Questioning Interdisciplinarity: Cognitive Science, Evolutionary Psychology, and Literary Criticism," *Poetics Today* 21 (2000): 319–47; and Tasmin Spargo, ed., *Reading the Past: Literature and History* (Houndmills, U.K.: Palgrave, 2000).

their books on patently historical questions and often spend more time analyzing freshly gleaned archival evidence than reflecting on texts once valued
primarily for their aesthetic interests.[5]

While literary scholars have turned toward history, historians have begun
turning not only toward literature as a primary source but also toward her-
meneutic questions about the knowability and the contingent modeling of
the past.[6] The historiography course typically required for beginning Ph.D.
students in history now features readings by poststructuralist thinkers like
Derrida, Foucault, Bourdieu, Mouffe, and Laclau, the same figures taught
across campus in the "Introduction to Critical Theory" courses taken by
first-year Ph.D. students in English. This engagement with contemporary
cultural theory has revitalized well-worn areas of inquiry like seventeenth-
century politics, where the seeming impasse between revisionists and counter-
revisionists is yielding to Habermasian reflections on the emergence of a
pre-Enlightenment public sphere.[7] New research on reading practices and
the history of the book has proven to be an especially rich point of convergence between early modernists working in English and history departments.
Kevin Sharpe opens his magisterial *Reading Revolutions: The Politics of Reading
in Early Modern England* with a de facto manifesto on the need for historians
to participate in theoretical discussions that were once the domain of literary

---

5. See, for example, Margaret Hannay, *Philip's Phoenix: Mary Sidney, Countess of Pembroke* (Ox-
ford: Oxford University Press, 1990); Kim Hall, *Things of Darkness: Economies of Race and Gender in
Early Modern England* (Ithaca: Cornell University Press, 1994); Laura Lunger Knoppers, *Constructing
Cromwell: Ceremony, Portrait, and Print, 1645–1661* (Cambridge: Cambridge University Press, 2001);
Andrew McRae, *God Speed the Plough: The Representation of Agrarian England, 1500–1660* (New York:
Cambridge University Press, 1996); Nabil Matar, *Turks, Moors, and Englishmen in the Age of Discovery*
(New York: Columbia University Press, 1999); Lena Cowen Orlin, *Private Matters and Public Cul-
ture in Post-Reformation England* (Ithaca: Cornell University Press, 1994); James Shapiro, *Shakespeare
and the Jews* (New York: Columbia University Press, 1996); John Rogers, *The Matter of Revolution:
Science, Poetry, and Politics in the Age of Milton* (Ithaca: Cornell University Press, 1996); Debora Kuller
Shuger, *Political Theologies in Shakespeare's England* (Houndmills, U.K.: Palgrave, 2001); Nigel Smith,
Perfection Proclaimed: Language and Literature in English Radical Religion, 1640–1660 (Oxford: Clarendon Press, 1989); Daniel J. Vitkus, *Turning Turk: English Theater and the Multicultural Mediterranean,
1570–1630* (Houndmills, U.K.: Palgrave, 2003); and Wendy Wall, *The Imprint of Gender: Authorship
and Publication in the English Renaissance* (Ithaca: Cornell University Press, 1993).

6. See Iggers, *Historiography of the Twentieth Century.* See also the essays in Lynn Hunt, ed., *The
New Cultural History* (Berkeley: University of California Press, 1996); and Peter Burke, *The French
Historical Revolution* (Stanford: Stanford University Press, 1990).

7. See Peter Lake and Steven Pincus, "Rethinking the Public Sphere in Early Modern England,"
Journal of British Studies 45 (2006): 270–92; Natalie Mears, *Queenship and Political Discourse in the
Elizabethan Realms,* Cambridge Studies in Early Modern British History (Cambridge: Cambridge
University Press, 2005); David Zaret, *Origins of Democratic Culture: Printing, Petitions, and the Public
Sphere in Early Modern England* (Princeton: Princeton University Press, 2000); and Alexandra Halasz,
The Marketplace of Print: Pamphlets and the Public Sphere in Early Modern England (Cambridge: Cam-
bridge University Press, 1997).

critics. Sharpe identifies several points of convergence between postmodern literary scholarship and what seems to be the most theoretically resistant work in history. For all their attachment to the archive, for example, even the seventeenth-century revisionists share with poststructuralists a skepticism toward teleological narratives of progress. As Sharpe concludes, "Postmodernism has itself historicized the modern perspective, and by returning it (ourselves) to history has enabled us to see that historical meaning resides in particulars not in universals, and helped to free the past from being judged or evaluated by anachronistic, even transhistorical criteria."[8]

Yet the more closely early modern literary and historical studies converge, the more their practitioners sometimes insist in strangely defensive ways that the two disciplines remain distinct. Scholars whose work demonstrates a mastery of the protocols governing research in history and literary studies alike, for example, still voice diffidence in making claims about the past that, in a previous academic generation, would have been reserved for practitioners of the discipline with which they are not institutionally affiliated. More disturbing yet, some scholars adopt a missionary attitude toward the other discipline, as if literary scholars knew nothing about history or historians were incapable of an intelligent engagement with textual evidence. The first generation of historicist critics relied on secondary sources in ways that would have struck a historian as naive, but more recent historicist work rests on an impressive body of primary research as well as a more sophisticated grasp of the historiographical context in which secondary historical sources were written. Even our self-identifications and intellectual practices often lag behind the actual experience of disciplinary convergence in an era in which art historians and literary critics are working in the same archives as political and economic historians. Why should we persist in calling a scholar researching unpublished diaries written by women for clues about the gender politics of the early modern household a "literary critic," as if he or she were making aesthetic pronouncements about the relative merits of *Hamlet* and *The Revenger's Tragedy?*

Perhaps the greatest impediment to a fully integrated investigation of the past lies in the institutional logic of disciplinarity and professionalism itself. For years now, early modern studies has profited from interdisciplinary conferences featuring works by scholars affiliated with departments of history and of the modern languages. These conferences have inspired several noteworthy collections, sometimes edited by two scholars from different

---

8. Kevin Sharpe, *Reading Revolutions: The Politics of Reading in Early Modern England* (New Haven: Yale University Press, 2000), 17.

disciplines. But these occasions and publications have sometimes reinforced, rather than engaged, the assumption of disciplinary prerogatives. Although literary scholars and historians alike attend the North American Conference on British Studies, for example, the conference tends to divide into panels for historians and panels for English professors. Articles in interdisciplinary collections continue to rehearse the sometimes disabling, sometimes aggrandizing *topoi* of disciplinary divergence: "as a historian, I find that," "my perspective as a literary critic allows me to...."

In terms of both form and content, this book attempts to address one aspect of this residual commitment to orthodox disciplinarity. While scholars affiliated with departments of English and history have joined as editors of several noteworthy collections, the collaborative monograph remains a rarity in both fields. On the few occasions when two early modernists have coauthored, they have typically been scholars writing within a single academic discipline. For the authors of this present work, writing a book together fostered our belief that the time has come to abandon as fully as possible the pretensions of disciplinary distinctiveness. As scholars who had published previous cross-disciplinary books on Elizabeth I that had been reviewed in both historical and literary journals, we decided to write a book on Shakespeare that would serve as a metacommentary on the current dialogue between the two fields. We each came to this project with a long history of interdisciplinary cross-dressing. We have organized and participated in interdisciplinary conferences, edited interdisciplinary collections and special issues, taught cross-listed courses and seminars, mentored graduated students in both disciplines, and served on search committees in departments of English and history alike. Above all, our past and current research has taken us beyond the traditional paradigms of research in history and literary studies in ways that heightened our awareness of the permeability of disciplinary boundaries.

We decided to write on the Elizabethan Shakespeare to explore connections between the institutional division of early modernists into historians and literary scholars and the foundational politics of the English nation-state. Shakespeare—the author of the most influential account of the English fifteenth century ever written—has long been canonized as England's greatest writer and a notoriously unreliable historian. Literary types, from poets to English professors, valued him precisely because he was a writer "not of an age, but for all time."[9] In the process, they hailed his apparent distortions of

9. Ben Jonson, "To the Memory of My Beloved, The Author, Mr. William Shakespeare," in *Ben Jonson, A Selection of His Finest Poems,* ed. Ian Donaldson, Oxford Poetry Library (Oxford: Oxford University Press, 1995), 137.

history and his brilliant reworkings of virtually unreadable chronicle history as proofs of his literary genius. Like Sidney's poet refusing to be tied to the restrictions of a brazen world of facts, Shakespeare soared into a golden world of pure creativity. The professionalization of the disciplines in the modern academy exacerbated this tendency. Teachers and editors admitted just enough history to provide an intelligible context for the plays, which were taught almost entirely in the departments of English and Theater Studies. Historians sometimes referred to Shakespeare at the opening of their lectures on the Hundred Years' War or the Wars of the Roses, but only in urging their students to clear their minds of the Shakespearean distortions that might inhibit their confrontation with actual history.

Challenging this disciplinary distinction with respect to Shakespeare was the great legacy of the New Historicism. Within its initial phases, that challenge unfolded almost exclusively within departments of English. But a new generation of historians now regularly includes Shakespearean plays on their syllabuses and in their research as documents offering important insights into the social organization of sixteenth-century English life. A play like *1 Henry VI* may not provide the most reliable account of fifteenth-century dynastic politics, but it can tell us a lot about the way sixteenth-century English men and women thought about sovereignty, religion, gender, and what it meant to be "English" in the first place. Ultimately, the plays can tell us something important about the very notion of a national history and its complex relationship to a national literature.

Shakespeare's Foreign Worlds carries this interdisciplinary conversation further by situating the distinction between historical and literary studies itself at the dawn of the modern era. At first, we imagined a book in which we would each contribute a chapter on each play that represented our own disciplinary perspectives. But the more we wrote, the more we stopped believing in the significance of those distinctions at all. If reading and writing about Shakespeare made us more suspicious than ever of categories like "the English nation" or "the Elizabethan moment," it also made us mistrust the assumption that only an English professor could offer a complex and illuminating reading of a play or that only a historian could pose and resolve questions about the social and political structures of the past. Above all, we began to see more clearly how our disciplinary assumptions bolstered a consensus about an English nation that Shakespeare's plays sometimes celebrated but also called into question.

Instead of writing as a literary scholar and a historian, respectively, we ended up writing as early modernists using Shakespeare's plays as a medium to reflect on the plasticity and permeability of the English nation. While we had different perspectives and scholarly orientations that factored into our work, these differences had little to do with our departmental affiliations. Levin was particularly interested in Shakespeare's responses to marginalized sectors of English society. As a comparatist who writes on France and Italy as well as England, Watkins situated Shakespeare in the context of broadly European historical movements. These complementary interests allowed us to focus the book specifically on an ideological development fundamental to the conception of English nationhood: the emergence of the "foreign" as a portable category that might be applied both to "strangers" from other countries and to native-born English men and women, such as religious dissidents, who resisted conformity to an increasingly narrow sense of English identity.[10]

Shakespeare's Foreign Worlds

Relatively few of Shakespeare's characters are English. Most of his plays take place on the continent, in the ancient and modern Mediterranean, France, Vienna, and Denmark. His most insistently English plays are arguably the Histories, but several of these feature continental characters who propel the plot, like the Dauphin who challenges Henry V with his insulting offer of tennis balls. *King John, Henry V,* and much of the first tetralogy focus on England's relationship with France. *Henry VIII* weaves Katherine of Aragon's fall into an international story of Wolsey's efforts to secure closer ties between France and England by marrying Henry to the Duchesse d'Alençon. *Henry V,* so memorably filmed by Laurence Olivier during the Second World War, is arguably Shakespeare's most English play of all. But its most memorable characters are French, Irish, and Welsh. Henry V himself turns out to be a

---

10. In emphasizing the portability of the foreign as a category that blurs distinctions between insiders and outsiders, the English and the other, our work complements a large body of writing on Shakespeare's representations of the stranger. See Leslie A. Fiedler, *The Stranger in Shakespeare* (New York: Stein and Day, 1972); G. K. Hunter, *Dramatic Identities and Cultural Tradition: Studies in Shakespeare and His Contemporaries: Critical Essays,* Liverpool English Texts and Studies (Liverpool: Liverpool University Press, 1978). See especially Ton Hoenselaars's comprehensive survey, *Images of Englishmen and Foreigners in the Drama of Shakespeare and His Contemporaries* (Rutherford, NJ: Farleigh Dickinson University Press, 1992). Hoenselaars's exploration of the dialectic relationship between "auto-images" of Englishmen and "hetero-images" of foreigners anticipates our interest in the instability of the emergent discourse of national identity. We differ from him in our specific focus on Shakespeare and in the expansion of our inquiry beyond scenes representing Englishmen interacting with foreigners. We believe that exchanges between Jews and Italians in *The Merchant of Venice* or between Paduans and other Italians in *The Taming of the Shrew* offer as much insight into the emergence of a national consciousness as those between French and English nobles in *1 Henry VI.*

Welshman who successfully woos a French princess to become the mother of an heir to both the French and English thrones.

Shakespeare's theater not only focuses on places beyond England but also foregrounds the experience of being an outsider in a dominant culture. At times, that experience is the direct result of national or ethnic displacement. An Irishman finds himself serving in an English army, and a Moor finds himself leading a Venetian one. At other times, the sense of being an outsider has nothing to do with being born abroad but instead reveals habits of mind, character traits, talents, particular stages of life, and manifestations of gender or sexuality that make someone a virtual foreigner within his or her own country. Antonio, in one sense the ultimate Venetian insider, opens *The Merchant of Venice* with a classic statement of alienation: "I know not why I am so sad" (1.1.1). Katherine's seemingly untamable obstreperousness makes her seem not only less ladylike than her sister Bianca but also less Italian. Though a "native here / And to the manner born," Hamlet's intellection sets him so apart from other Danes that he disdains their drinking customs as much as if he were an abstemious foreigner (1.4.14–15). He longs to leave Denmark and return to his studies in Saxon Wittenberg. Prospero's intellection costs him his ducal throne and lands him on an island somewhere between Tunis and Naples or out into the open Atlantic—its geographical imprecision is precisely the point. As a type of international humanist, Prospero's devotion to his books marks him as an outsider, a person without a country and in perpetual exile. Just as Antonio finds himself mirrored in the Jewish Shylock, Prospero finds himself mirrored in Sycorax, the exiled Algerian sorceress.

In Shakespearean drama, every hero internalizes aspects of his or her antagonists. This kind of theater reinforces an exclusionary model of the nation in which those "native here and to the manner born" define themselves as English through the continual castigation of others as foreign. This is always a twofold process involving the stigmatization not only of foreign nationals but also of groups and individuals who do not conform to an idealized set of norms constituting a fundamental but never fully defined Englishness. These include the demographies central to our collaborative investigation: old women, Italians, religious dissenters, Jews, the French, women who refuse to keep silent. The group is strikingly heterogeneous, but that is the point: Shakespeare's England comes about by reducing an almost infinite number of groups and individuals to the general category of the foreign. Shakespeare and his contemporaries refigure this diversity as a simultaneous object of wonder and opprobrium, the foreign other whose multifarious allures make it all the more a threat to a unified experience of Englishness.

The foreign thus defined bears an obvious resemblance to the Oriental in later political and cultural formations associated with the rise of the British Empire and its colonial expansion. Several studies have already addressed Shakespeare's place in the prehistory of Orientalism with respect to his representations of Indians, Moors, and other non-European populations.[11] Our work focuses on another aspect of this prehistory in his invention of the foreigner as a portable category within European society itself. Indeed, in emphasizing the opposition between the European and the non-European other, previous scholars have missed the extent to which the branding of other Europeans as fundamentally different from the English scripted later perceptions of Asians, Africans, and Native Americans. At the same time, most work focused on Shakespeare and the continent has remained frozen in formalist or thematic investigations of his debts to European authors; his imitations of European dramatic and nondramatic forms; and his satirical representations of Germans, Italians, the French, and other national and ethnic groups. Our goal is to bring investigations of such topics into a richer dialogue with history, one that can become part of an ongoing critique of both nation and empire.

In working toward this goal, we have centered our analysis on the years preceding England's expansion into the Atlantic. Instead of looking at the trading adventures that provided an important context for later works like *Othello* (c. 1604) and *The Tempest* (c. 1611), we have concentrated on a series of closely related demographic, legal, mercantile, and cultural developments that occasioned new anxieties about the foreign during the formative years of Shakespeare's career, the final decades of the sixteenth century. Expanding populations, the development of new regional and national markets, and the displacements associated with the continental wars of religion meant that late-sixteenth-century Europeans were more likely than previous generations to find themselves living in close proximity with people who came from elsewhere. As Jean Howard has observed, "London was becoming an

---

11. See Matthew Dimmock, *New Turkes: Dramatising Islam and the Ottomans in Early Modern England* (Aldershot, U.K.: Ashgate, 2005); Andrew Hadfield, *Literature, Travel, and Colonial Writing in the English Renaissance, 1545–1625* (Oxford: Oxford University Press, 2005); Nancy Bisaha, *Creating East and West: Renaissance Humanists and the Ottoman Turks* (Philadelphia: University of Pennsylvania Press, 2004); Ania Loomba, *Shakespeare, Race, and Colonialism* (Oxford: Oxford University Press, 2002); Daniel Vitkus, *Piracy, Slavery, and Redemption: Barbary Captivity Narratives from Early Modern England* (New York: Columbia University Press, 2001); Matar, *Turks, Moors, and Englishmen;* Matar, *Islam in Britain, 1558–1685* (Cambridge: Cambridge University Press, 1998); Kim Hall, *Things of Darkness: Economies of Race and Gender in Early Modern England* (Ithaca: Cornell University Press, 1996); and John Gillies, *Shakespeare and the Geography of Difference* (Cambridge: Cambridge University Press, 1994).

increasingly miscegenated space."[12] A London shopkeeper might find himself selling wares to people who came from a village in Somerset, a farm in Cheshire, a Flemish town, or a city in France. Regardless of where they came from, they did not share with the native Londoner a common history or common attitudes, values, tastes, dress, habits, cuisines, child-rearing practices, or ways of speaking. A newly arrived agrarian worker who had never before seen a city might strike the Londoner as even more foreign than a Huguenot from Paris or Tours. The English spoken in Cumberland or the West Country sounded no less strange than London English spoken with a heavy Dutch or French accent. Everywhere in Shakespeare's London, people were meeting strangers, not all of them from abroad.

The first factor underlying this development was rapid growth in the western European and English populations. Although the nature of sixteenth-century record-keeping makes it difficult to discuss this growth in any precise quantitative way, France, Spain, Italy, the Low Countries, and England all witnessed a post-plague demographic recovery that started in the Late Middle Ages and extended, at least north of the Pyrenees, well into the seventeenth century. The Castilian fiscal censuses, analyzed in conjunction with those of Aragon, suggest that the Spanish population increased from 4,698,000 persons in 1534 to 6,632,000 in 1591.[13] The Italian population climbed steadily from about six million people in the years immediately following the Black Death (1347–48) to about eleven million in 1500.[14] It gained another million over the course of the sixteenth century. The population surge was even more noticeable in France. By the first half of the fifteenth century, disease and war had reduced the population to about ten million people. But a recovery set in around 1450, and by 1500, the population had climbed to fourteen million. By 1560, it had reached twenty million, matching its pre-plague levels as the most populous country in western Europe.[15] Between 1520 and 1580, the English population increased from two million to three and a half million and did not level off until the middle of the next century.[16]

---

12. Jean E. Howard, *Theater of a City: The Places of London Comedy, 1598–1642* (Philadelphia: University of Pennsylvania Press, 2007), 11. In her analysis of London civic spaces, Howard provides an outstanding account of how demographic changes influenced an emergent national consciousness.

13. James Casey, *Early Modern Spain: A Social History* (London: Routledge, 1999), 21.

14. Christopher F. Black, *Early Modern Italy: A Social History* (London: Routledge, 2001), 21.

15. Frederic J. Baumgartner, *France in the Sixteenth Century* (New York: St. Martin's Press, 1995), 65–66.

16. Keith Wrightson, *English Society, 1580–1680* (New Brunswick, NJ: Rutgers University Press, 1982), 122.

The increase did not happen everywhere at the same rate, because some areas proved more capable of sustaining a growing population than others. This meant that the new Europeans were not only more numerous than their ancestors but also more mobile in their efforts to find favorable living conditions. Richer farming districts, especially those with extensive commons for herding and foraging, grew rapidly.[17] But the most striking result of this demographic development was the exponential growth of cities. Eighteen European cities doubled in size during the course of the sixteenth century.[18] In the eighty-year period between 1520 and 1600, the population of London increased fourfold, from about fifty thousand to two hundred thousand.[19]

Sixteenth-century Europeans not only moved from the countryside to towns and cities; they also immigrated across national borders. The year 1492 witnessed the mass expulsion of Jews from Spain, who resettled in Venice, the Low Countries, Morocco, the Ottoman lands, France, and England. Philip II's annexation of Portugal in 1580 led to another large exodus of Iberian Jews. The same years also marked the expulsion of the last Iberian Muslims, who left western Europe altogether and found new homes in the Islamic areas of Africa and the Middle East. The Reformation and Counter-Reformation triggered other waves of religious refugees, with people driven out of one territory seeking asylum elsewhere, either among their coreligionists or in places that at least promised greater tolerance of religious diversity. English Catholics fled to the Spanish Netherlands, and Dutch and French Protestants fled to Switzerland, Poland, Germany, and England. During the reign of Mary I, English Protestants sought asylum in Geneva and Strasbourg.

Sectarian conflict also had a major impact on international trade. The outbreak of the Eighty Years' War in 1568, which pitted Protestants in the Low Countries against the Spanish Catholic overlords, disrupted trading routes between northern and southern Europe that had dated back to the Middle Ages. The English looked for new markets and new ways of obtaining Asian and Mediterranean commodities like silks, spices, and currants. During the 1570s and 1580s, English merchants appeared in places as far as Muscovy and Constantinople. They expanded their trade in both the Baltic and the Mediterranean, where they began to displace the once-formidable Venetians and Genoese. Instead of depending on Italian ships to bring them

---

17. Wrightson, *English Society,* 126–27.

18. Jan de Vries, *European Urbanization, 1500–1800* (Cambridge, MA: Harvard University Press, 1984), 140.

19. Wrightson, *English Society, 1580–1680,* 128. See also Steve Rappaport, *Worlds within Worlds: The Structures of Life in Sixteenth-Century London,* Cambridge Studies in Population, Economy and Society in Past Time (Cambridge: Cambridge University Press, 2002), 61–86.

the luxury goods they desired from the East, the English started going to the eastern Mediterranean ports themselves. The flip side of this sudden appearance of the English in the east was the disappearance of the Italian merchants who once constituted a sizeable émigré population in London. By the time Shakespeare wrote *The Merchant of Venice* (c. 1596–97), the Italians one met in London were more likely to be Protestant refugees than Venetian or Genoese merchants. London itself was poised to become the new Venice.

The demographic displacements occasioned by the fifteenth- and sixteenth-century population explosion, the Spanish *Reconquista,* sectarian conflicts between Protestants and Catholics, and the opening of new markets and new trading routes had an incalculable effect on the way people in Shakespeare's England thought about themselves and their place in an increasingly mobile world. The ships coming into London carried not only silks and currants but also books, immigrants, and returning travelers, all filled with new ideas about politics, religion, warfare, economics, law, diplomacy, gender, sexuality, and property. In such an environment, the question of what constituted Englishness was open. Were the children of Huguenot émigrés, for example, more or less English than a Lancashire Catholic? The country was officially Protestant, and writers like John Foxe, whose magisterial *Acts and Monuments* could be found in every parish, worked hard to make everyone forget that Protestantism itself was a fairly recent foreign import. Like many of his coreligionists, Foxe had developed many of his ideas about religion while living in exile in Strasbourg, Frankfurt, and Basel. A Strasbourg press published the first version of his martyrology in Latin under the title *Commentarii rerum in ecclesia gestarum.* Yet the ideas that Foxe and his coreligionists promoted seemed sufficiently English by the later years of Elizabeth's reign that anyone holding the Catholic faith of his or her ancestors looked disloyal or even downright foreign.

Literature was the primary force in establishing and policing the boundaries between English and foreign identities throughout the Elizabethan period. Shakespeare himself typified the indeterminacy of what counted as England and what counted as foreign. Like so many men and women of his generation, he immigrated to London from a provincial market town and probably spoke English with a heavy Midlands accent. Recent scholars have argued on the basis of some credible evidence that his family was Catholic. With the exception of the English histories, he based most of his plays on foreign sources. Although modern notions of nationhood and authorship make us think of *The Merchant of Venice* as an English play, one could argue that it is at most an English adaptation of a story that remains quintessentially Italian. That argument might sound pretty weak to us now, but that is because in the process of transforming his classical and Italian sources for an English audience, Shakespeare ultimately transformed the very notion of what it means to be English. He also created a lasting place for himself in the canon of world literature as the embodiment of quintessentially English habits of mind and modes of expression.

That transformation is the focus of our project. Building on our complementary interests in the internal diversity of Elizabethan society and in that society's place within an increasingly diverse European community, we analyze Shakespeare's plays in terms of their twofold insistence on the nation's *coherence* and *distinctiveness*. The fiction of coherence denies the fractures within English society that Levin examines in her chapters on Jews, widows and otherwise unmarried women, and religious dissidents. The parallel emphasis on England's distinctiveness denies its embeddedness in a larger European political, economic, and cultural environment. A mythology centered on the break with Rome heightened the sense of absolute national sovereignty that found an iconic focus in the image of the Virgin Queen spurning her foreign suitors. Working together, the fictions of coherence and distinctiveness produced an image of England as a unique social, political, and cultural space—a kind of monad insulated from the rest of Europe and protected from the internal societal conflicts that ruptured late-sixteenth-century Germany and France. Anything that exists outside this idealization is repudiated as foreign. This image of a coherent nation distinct from its foreign enemies continued to hold its power from the immediate post-Armada years, when Shakespeare first devised it, through the Second World War, when Olivier's movie version of *Henry V* rallied the nation in its struggle against Nazi Germany.

The fictions of national coherence and distinctiveness complement each other in almost every play that Shakespeare wrote. But their ideological significance is particularly striking in the three plays we analyze in this book: *1 Henry VI, The Merchant of Venice,* and *The Taming of the Shrew.* Written during the early 1590s, at the height of England's war with Spain, they display an emergent national consciousness based on the denigration not only of non-English Europeans but also of people born in England itself who fail to conform to a narrowing set of normative English behaviors and attitudes. Shakespeare's evocation of foreign and domestic settings in all three plays creates the sense of an English identity continually threatened by a nebulous foreignness both from without and within the country's geographical borders. *1 Henry VI* alternates between scenes in England and scenes in France, and *The Taming of the Shrew* unfolds as an Italian play set within an English frame. The alternation between English and non-English settings provides the most obvious context for reflections on the traits that differentiate the

English character. But as the heightened metadramatic consciousness of *The Taming of the Shrew* makes clear, this is only one of the ways in which the plays foreground the clash between English and foreign identities. Like Petruchio, Katherine, Bianca, and the other Italians in *The Taming of the Shrew,* the French, Italians, Danes, Bohemians, and Illyrians in other Shakespearean plays were acted almost entirely by English men and boys, possibly speaking with fake accents and aping certain stereotypically foreign gestures. Even a play set wholly in Italy like *The Merchant of Venice* thus offered a simultaneous commentary on English and foreign experience. Shakespeare's Venice really is Venice—but it is also London. His play engages the experience of *conversos,* Jewish converts to Christianity, and other "strangers" living in Protestant London as much as it draws on Italian stories about Jews living in Catholic Venice.

The chapters in our first section, "Gender, Punishment, and Peacemaking in *1 Henry VI,*" bring domestic and international perspectives to bear on the single figure of Shakespeare's Joan of Arc. Joan appears simultaneously as a champion of France against England in the Hundred Years' War and as a type of the woman outcast prosecuted in English Assize sessions for crimes like heresy and witchcraft. This double representation engages shifts in legal discourse and practice that heightened the perception of the outsider as a threat to English society as much in the international context of treaty-making as in the local one of criminal procedure. On both levels, striking departures from medieval precedent had an especially pronounced impact on early modern women. Levin's chapter explores how Joan's unsuccessful effort to plead the womb at the end of the play registers a disturbing inconsistency in the way local jurisdictions began to exclude certain women from protections that that they had traditionally held under English law. In the paranoia generated by accusations of witchcraft and heresy, some women went to the stake even though they were pregnant.

The paranoia that Levin explores resulted from the clash between the Reformation and the Counter-Reformation and the attendant construction of the sectarian other as the ultimate foreigner. The sense of an unbridgeable gap between divergent religious cultures also underlies the development in international law that is the focus of Watkins's chapter on *1 Henry VI* and early modern peacemaking. Throughout the Late Middle Ages, diplomats typically resolved conflicts between countries by negotiating marriages between their respective ruling dynasties. Sixteenth-century sectarian divisions, combined with the new ability of the printing press to foment popular outrage, made such arrangements increasingly difficult. Written shortly after the failure of Elizabeth's efforts to marry the Catholic Duke of Alençon,

1 Henry VI dramatizes this crisis in European dynastic history. The Duke of Suffolk orchestrates a diplomatic marriage between Henry VI and Margaret of Anjou at the end of the play. But, writing within this new sectarian context, Shakespeare denigrates the French alliance as a betrayal of fundamentally English interests. He represents Margaret as a malevolent foreigner whose English subjects rightly mistrust her by associating her with the play's other major female figure, Joan of Arc. Shakespeare transforms the deceptive language of both Joan and Margaret into a general indictment of diplomatic discourse as a vehicle for dissolving national boundaries that his own dramaturgy works to strengthen.[20]

Catholicism was not the only religion excluded from the English national imaginary in the sixteenth century. The expulsions of Jews from the Iberian lands created Sephardic refugee communities that lived openly in some countries and clandestinely in others. Our second section of paired chapters, "Aliens in Our Midst: Jews, Italians, and Wary Englishmen in *The Merchant of Venice*," examines Shakespeare's play in light of the contrast between sixteenth-century Venice, an old merchant republic that was relatively tolerant toward its large Jewish community, and Protestant London, in which Jews had less freedom. Levin's chapter focuses on the character Jessica, a Jew who elopes with a Christian and embraces his religion. Levin sees Shakespeare's emphasis on Jessica's isolation as an expression of a pervasive English anxiety about the status of *converso* Jews within the Protestant nation. Reading the play against the archival traces of several Jewish women who converted to Christianity, Levin suggests that the spectacle of celebrated, highly public conversions did not dispel suspicions of an essential Jewishness deemed to be incompatible with English identity. Nothing threatened the coherence of a Protestant national imaginary more than the conduct of a woman like the Bristol émigré Beatriz Fernandes Nuñez, who openly conformed to

---

20. Significantly for a play that focuses so much on the establishment of legitimate boundaries between nationalities and genders, scholars have long debated the legitimacy of *1 Henry VI*'s place in the Shakespearean canon. Critics have pointed to everything from a pervasive dramaturgical crudeness to specific rhetorical and stylistic markers as evidence of its contamination by other playwrights. To the extent that we are less interested in Shakespeare as an individual author than in the contribution that the plays attributed to him made to the production and articulation of what became characteristically English attitudes, we have not directly engaged the question of authorship. But in general, we tend to agree with Michael Hattaway and others that stylistic analysis is insufficient to prove or disprove the authorship of a play that may have been written at such an early period in Shakespeare's career that he was still experimenting with a range of stylistic possibilities. For further discussion of the controversy, see Hattaway's introduction to his edition of *1 Henry VI* (Cambridge: Cambridge University Press, 1990), 41–43.

the English Church but taught new immigrants Jewish prayers and baked matzoh for Passover. Yet at the same time, the *converso*'s irreducible foreignness also gave English national identity a higher value by suggesting that it was something so distinct and precious that the only people who could truly possess it were ones born with it in the first place. In the burgeoning mercantile economy of late Elizabethan England, Englishness itself acquired the aura of the only truly stable and non-vendible commodity.

Watkins's complementary chapter on *The Merchant of Venice* addresses issues of race, religion, and commerce in the context of the decline of the Venetian Republic. Venice was one of the several European cities whose population actually diminished over the course of the late sixteenth century. One set of available figures suggests that between 1563 and 1581, its population declined almost 20 percent, from 168,627 inhabitants to 134,877.[21] Historians continue to debate whether or not such demographic evidence indicates a general stagnation in the Italian economy associated with the rise of London and Amsterdam as global trading centers. But as Watkins suggests in a chapter based on both literary evidence and extant diplomatic correspondence, contemporary Venetians and Englishmen alike *believed* that London's economy was growing at Venice's expense. If Englishmen were happy to reap the economic rewards of becoming the new Venice, they were less sanguine about the impact of this transformation on their country's emerging national identity. *The Merchant of Venice* not only inscribes mounting anxieties about cosmopolitanism but also upholds a cankered image of Venetian life as a warning of what England might become through its economic dependence on foreign trading partners.

People and material goods were not the only things that crossed the English Channel in the sixteenth century. Ideas did as well. In our final section, "Dangerous Reading in *The Taming of the Shrew*," we turn from the role that resident aliens played in the shaping the English national imaginary to the role of foreign ideas about religion, property, and the governance of the household. An older generation of historians analyzed England's sixteenth-century cultural development as the product of complementary intellectual movements that originated in Italy and Germany, respectively: humanism and the Reformation. The relationship of one to the other was a source of continual debate. Instead of replaying those debates, we give the old distinction a new historiographical value in our chapters on *The Taming of the Shrew*

---

21. Black, *Early Modern Italy,* 220.

by examining how both movements challenged a commitment to patriarchy as the basis of a quintessentially English society. Leaving aside the question of their ultimate intellectual compatibility, Protestantism and Italian humanism both had the same practical consequences of offering women a vision of greater independence from male authority, whether yielded by husband, priest, or king. Levin's chapter examines the gradual secularization of a belief in righteous disobedience by uncovering resonances between Shakespeare's play and Foxe's account of Katherine Parr's resistance to the religious policies of Henry VIII. In defending Katherine's objections to the notoriously conservative Six Articles, Foxe effectively qualifies the Pauline insistence on a wife's obedience to her husband. She is only bound to obey him to the extent that he commits himself fully to the Gospel. But what happened once the license to disobey went beyond sacred questions per se? Shakespeare's play recalls the story of Katherine's defiance, so indebted to Foxe's own experiences as an exile living abroad, as a more general challenge to the quintessentially hierarchical English household.

Whereas Levin focuses her reading of *The Taming of the Shrew* on Protestantism, Watkins examines the play as a response to Italian humanism. He begins his chapter with an awkward question: why were there so many more women writers in Italy than in England? The answer lies in the different relationships that Italian and English women had to property. In contrast to English women, Italian women could hold property in their own name. Most importantly, they owned their dowries. Husbands might invest their wives' dowries during their lifetime, but when a husband died, his wife was legally entitled to a full repayment. As Watkins argues, humanist plays would have made English audiences aware of these Italian inheritance practices. The plot of Ariosto's *I suppositi,* on which Shakespeare based the Bianca-plot of *Shrew,* for example, focuses on a father's efforts to cheat his daughter out of her rightful dowry. In adapting the story, Shakespeare turned it into a critique not only of Italian property customs but also of humanist education principles that threatened to destabilize the English Protestant household as effectively as the ardent Protestantism that Levin explores in the previous chapter.

The characters and historical persons we study in *Shakespeare's Foreign Worlds* are liminal, standing on a boundary but not really belonging on either side: the transgender Joan of Arc, the Guernsey women burned for heresy, the Venetian envoy watching English ships unloading their wares in London, Shylock, the obstreperous Katherine, the dissenter queen Katherine Parr, and even Shakespeare himself, the Warwickshire adapter of Italian plays for the London stage. As we traced the careers of these foreigners and outsiders, we found that we increasingly identified with them as surrogates of our own scholarly project. In attempting to move Shakespeare's plays beyond the parameters in which they have traditionally been studied, we have embraced our potentially unsettling identities as "foreigners" within the disciplines that trained us and provide our livelihood. We hope that this experience of disciplinary "alienation" has allowed us to write with greater understanding of Shakespeare's foreign worlds.

✒ PART I

Gender, Punishment, and Peace-Making in 1 Henry VI

From at least as far back as the Norman Conquest of 1066, the story of England's foreign relations was primarily about France. Recent scholarship suggests that as early as the sixth century, the Anglo-Saxon kingdoms were essentially client states of Merovingian Frankia. From 1066 until King John's retreat from France in 1202, the kings of England ruled large areas of French territory in their capacity as dukes of Normandy and spent more time in France than in England itself. Edward II's 1308 marriage to Philip IV's daughter Isabella gave their son, Edward III, a claim to the French throne that he and his successors pursued for over a century in the Hundred Years' War (1337–1453). That war provided the context for most of the history plays that Shakespeare wrote during the reign of Elizabeth I, including the play that we examine in our first two chapters: *1 Henry VI*.

Elizabeth styled herself Queen of France even though England had lost its last continental territory, the city of Calais, just before her 1558 accession. But during her reign, changes in England's relationship to France altered England's understanding of itself as a nation within a wider European community. Throughout the Middle Ages, dynastic interests determined foreign affairs. English kings went to war to assert their claims to French lands and made peace through interdynastic marriages that were supposed to settle disputed territories on an heir descended from both families. By the end of Elizabeth's reign, however, dynastic interests were yielding to a complex of issues that seventeenth-century writers would call "reasons" or "interests of state": trade, national security, and the defense of a Protestant national church.[1] These issues mattered not just to the ruling dynasty and its aristocratic supporters but to every sector of English society as well.

Elizabeth's decision to remain a virgin was symptomatic of the new diplomacy. During her reign, for example, Spain's rise as a major Atlantic power encouraged her to abandon England's centuries-old enmity against France and to pursue instead a tentative alliance with France against Spain. In the Middle Ages, such an alliance would have been sealed with a marriage linking the French and English ruling dynasties. Elizabeth entered into negotiations for such a marriage between herself and the Duke of Alençon during the 1570s, but they failed in the face of popular resistance. A new factor had entered the diplomatic calculus that made the medieval peacemaking apparatus of interdynastic marriage less tenable: religious divergence. Preserving England's Protestant integrity outweighed the advantages to be won through a marriage linking England and France.

Ever since Henry VIII's break with Rome, and especially since Elizabeth's accession, propagandists like John Foxe had worked hard to make Protestantism essentially English. Since Protestantism was a foreign import, this was not easy. As scholars like Liah Greenfeld have argued, Elizabeth's sister and predecessor Mary I, by embracing the nascent Counter-Reformation, inadvertently helped writers like Foxe to make Protestantism a lasting aspect of English national consciousness.[2] The faith that Mary promoted was not the old, indigenous Catholicism that her father and brother had worked to extirpate. She and her advisors insisted on greater diocesan authority, parochial discipline, and a concerted teaching ministry not only to root out Protestantism but also to establish what Eamon Duffy has called "a more scripturally 'correct' emphasis on Christ and his passion" at the expense of regional saints' cults that had been the focus of medieval piety.[3] In this, Mary's practice was conspicuously aligned with that of her unpopular Spanish husband, Philip II. By the end of her reign, her adoption of the Spanish practice of burning large numbers of heretics helped to make Catholicism itself seem foreign.

---

1. Maurizio Viroli, *Dalla politica alla Ragion di stato: La scienza del governo tra XIII e XVII secolo* (Rome: Donzelli, 1994); Maurizio Bazzoli, "Ragion di Stato e interesse degli stati: La trattatistica sull'ambasciatore dal XV al XVIII secolo," in *Stagioni e teorie della società internazionale* (Milan: Edizioni Universitarie di Lettere Economia Diritto, 2005).

2. Liah Greenfeld, *Nationalism: Five Roads to Modernity* (Cambridge, MA: Harvard University Press, 1992), 51–59.

3. Duffy, *The Stripping of the Altars: Traditional Religion in England, 1400–1580* (New Haven: Yale University Press, 1992), 564. See also William Wizeman, S.J., *The Theology and Spirituality of Mary Tudor's Church* (Aldershot, U.K.: Ashgate, 2006).

When Elizabeth came to the throne, she not only reestablished Protestantism as the religion of England but also fashioned herself as its chief defender
and promoter. Like many of her subjects, Shakespeare seems to have come
from a family that was reluctant to adopt the new religion. But in presenting
himself as a national playwright, Shakespeare wrote plays that contributed to
the national fantasy of England as a Protestant space.[4] The Catholicism of
France, Italy, and Spain established their foreignness within the English imagination, a foreignness so pronounced that many English men and women
saw a marriage between their Protestant Queen and a French Duke as an
abomination.

The two chapters in this section examine Shakespeare's *1 Henry VI* as his
earliest and most complex response to the Reformation's impact on English
constructions of the foreign. Since English Protestantism took the form of
a state religion under the monarch's direct authority, the chapters coincide in
their complementary concern with legal developments ascending from the
administration of the local courts to what we now think of as international
law and the regulation of relationships between states. Reading Joan of Arc's
burning at the end of the play against an analogous passage from Foxe's *Acts
and Monuments,* Levin suggests how the perception of heresy as a threat to the
nation's spiritual, legal, and political integrity closed off avenues of defense
once accorded to anyone accused under English common law. Focusing on
Joan's orchestration of a rapprochement between France and Burgundy that
leads to England's loss of the Hundred Years' War, Watkins explores a complementary limitation on avenues of early modern peace-making.

As our common focus on Joan of Arc suggests, we share an interest in gender as a particularly charged site in the emergence of the foreign as a category
of opprobrium defining the English nation. Tainted with sorcery, heresy, and
sexual promiscuity, the transgender body of Joan of Arc opposes the virginal
body of the Protestant English Queen. Joan is everything that Elizabeth,
at least in her iconic role as the epitome of English national glory, is not:
French, Catholic, duplicitous, and double-talking. As the recurrent bawdy
puns on *pucelle* suggest, her virginity is the mirror opposite of Elizabeth's, a
cover for rhetorical, spiritual, and erotic excesses that define the foreign for
Shakespeare and his audience. At the end of the play, Joan has to die not so
much because she is French but because she defies the boundaries between
male and female, sacred and profane, solemn and ludic, that had begun to
define national identity itself in sixteenth-century Europe.

---

4. See Patrick Cheney, *Shakespeare, National Poet-Playwright* (Cambridge: Cambridge University
Press, 2004).

❧ CHAPTER 1

"Murder not then the fruit within my womb"

Shakespeare's Joan, Foxe's Guernsey Martyr, and Women Pleading Pregnancy in English History and Culture

Joan Pleads Pregnancy In *1 Henry VI*

In Shakespeare's play *1 Henry VI* Joan La Pucelle is the driving force of the French victories for much of the action. Her English enemies find her frightening and horrifying. While fighting Joan, Lord Talbot says to her, "Thou art a witch" (1.6.6) and later refers her to as "Pucelle, that witch, that damned sorceress" (3.2.37). He also questions her morality, describing her as "puzzel" (1.5.85), which in the Elizabethan period meant slut. When Joan, having been captured, is brought before the Earl of Warwick and the Duke of York to be condemned at the end of the play, she at first denies her shepherd father and proclaims both her noble birth and her virginity. She claims that she is issue "from the progeny of kings; / virtuous and holy" and adds proudly, "Joan of Arc hath been a virgin from her tender infancy / Chaste and immaculate in very thought" (5.4.38–39, 50–51).[1] These assertions do not, however, impress York and Warwick, who order her to be taken away to her execution. At this point, Joan, panicked at the thought of her imminent death, completely changes her demeanor and makes a very different claim.

An earlier version of this chapter appeared in the journal *Quidditas,* 20 (1999): 75–93.

1. All citations are from William Shakespeare, *The First Part of Henry the Sixth,* ed. Louis B. Wright and Virginia A. Lamar (New York: Washington Square Press, 1966).

Arguing that it is "warrente[d] by law...[as a] privilege" Joan claims, "I am with child, ye bloody homicides: / Murder not then the fruit within my womb" (63–65). But York and Warwick refuse to listen, damning the child for each of its potential fathers as the desperate Joan names one man after another—the Dauphin, Alençon, Reignier. Joan is sent away to be burned, and her last words on stage are her curse to the English. It is important to be explicit: this is Shakespeare's character Joan, not the historical fifteenth-century person, and Shakespeare has this character Joan place saving her life, an attempt that proves futile, above honor and historic glory.

The thought of a pregnant woman being executed is an unsettling one. But though York and Warwick mock Joan once she asserts that she is pregnant, stating "Strumpet, thy words condemn thy brat and thee" (5.4.84), what she demands would actually be hers by right of law in the sixteenth-century Britain in which Shakespeare composed his history play. Many women convicted of capital crimes pleaded pregnancy, and this was one method that kept a number of sixteenth-century women who had been found guilty from being executed.

In this chapter I examine the character Joan's plea within the context of actual women pleading pregnancy to avoid execution in Elizabethan England and Scotland. Pleading pregnancy was a familiar part of the justice system in England in the medieval and early modern period.[2] Many women convicted of felony in Elizabethan and Jacobean England pleaded that they were pregnant, and a number of them successfully maintained that claim, even if in some cases there is real doubt that the women were actually pregnant. Yet we also have several cases of pregnant women being burned as heretics in sixteenth-century England, the most notorious being the Guernsey martyr Perotine Massey. The accusations of harlotry, like those cast at Joan, appear in Massey's case as well. As Watkins argues in the following chapter, the boundary of English nationhood is particularly porous when we examine

---

2. For examples from the fourteenth through the eighteenth centuries, see James Oldham, "On Pleading the Belly: A History of the Jury of Matrons," *Criminal Justice History* 6 (1985): 1–64. See also Sara Mendelson and Patricia Crawford, *Women in Early Modern England, 1550–1720* (Oxford: Clarendon Press, 1998), 54. It continued as a practice well into the twentieth century, until England's abolishment of the death penalty made it superfluous. "A jury composed of matrons empanelled on a writ from Chancery to determine whether a woman was pregnant or not...where a woman was condemned to be executed and pleaded pregnancy as a grounds for delaying execution. From 1931, a pregnant woman would not be sentenced to death but only to imprisonment; she had, however, to satisfy a jury she was pregnant." David M. Walker, *The Oxford Companion to Law* (Oxford: Clarendon Press, 1980), 688. Panels of matrons were also used to determine pregnancy in cases of widows and property dispute where if the widow had a son by her late husband he would inherit. The Earl of Halsbury, *The Laws of England* (London: Butterworth and Co., 1910), XI, 11n.

the Channel Islands, as John Foxe makes evident in the especially barbarous treatment of Perotine Massey and her infant son.

In these cases, the boundaries between law and compassion get confused and moved back and forth because of the sixteenth-century crises of nation-building as portrayed both in drama and religio-political actualities. While in the 1590s Shakespeare's *1 Henry VI* looks back at the remembered crisis of the Hundred Years' War and paints Joan as a woman who uses sorcery to aid the national enemy, in the 1550s Perotine Massey was actually, and illegally, burned as a heretic as Mary I attempted through religious restoration to reclaim the English nation as Catholic. While we might believe that the law ought to apply to everyone, in sixteenth-century England, class played an extensive role in both convictions and type of executions. Men, theoretically only clerics but often any man who was literate, could also plead benefit of clergy; if a woman sentenced to die could show that she was pregnant, she might just escape her fate. Examining the actual cases lends insight into how Shakespeare's audience might have responded to the character Joan, and how women—fictional and actual—related to oppressive state regimes.

Though we in the early twenty-first century may be appalled by the idea of the violent death of a pregnant woman, in early modern England such a death might be perceived as a just punishment for a woman who so visibly stepped beyond the boundary of appropriate behavior. For Elizabethans, Joan, a French woman dressed in masculine attire who consorted with demons, was clearly an uncomfortable, transgressive character. By the sixteenth century, Joan was known as "La Pucelle," almost as a surname. That very title could mean either "virgin" or "slut," the latter meaning first arising in the 1570s. In the same century the word *quean,* which originally meant simply "woman" or "female," came to mean "a bold or impudent woman; a hussy; *spec.* a prostitute." That the word sounds the same as *queen,* a woman who rules, only adds to the complexity.[3]

As Leah Marcus argues, "Joan's crossing of the gender boundaries marking men off from women threatens a whole set of cultural polarities by which the categories were kept distinct." Marcus sees Joan as a fractured image of Elizabeth, a point also made by Barbara Hodgdon: "Figured remarkably like Elizabeth in many attributes, Joan represents a subversive challenge to gender.... Joan, like the Queen whose ghostly image she echoes, functions as a spectacular, and intensely troubling, site of gender display."[4] And around

---

3. *Oxford English Dictionary,* at www.dictionary.oed.com.library.unl.edu (accessed March 15, 2008).

4 Leah Marcus, *Puzzling Shakespeare: Local Reading and Its Discontents* (Berkeley: University of California Press, 1988), 68; Barbara Hodgdon, *The End Crowns All: Closure and Contradiction in*

Elizabeth, as with the character Joan, there were rumors of sexual misconduct and pregnancy; in Elizabeth's case, stories were even told of babies being
burned alive. In the 1580s, both Dionisia Deryck and Robert Gardner were
placed in the pillory for claiming that Elizabeth had illegitimate children
who were burned to death as newborn infants. These stories spread further
as the reign neared its end.[5] Richard Hardin also sees Joan as echoing a queen,
but he posits the parallel with Mary Stuart: both were French, Catholic, violent, and sexually promiscuous. Mary was executed only five years before the
first production of *1 Henry VI*.[6]

Pope Joan

Another figure who stands behind Joan la Pucelle is the other Joan, Pope
Joan. In the twenty-first century, most scholars recognize her to be a legendary character, but many in the sixteenth century believed that she had actually existed centuries earlier. This medieval legend also contained religious
overtones that used cross-dressing and suggested demonic relations. For
sixteenth-century English Protestants such as John Foxe, Pope Joan was
another example not only of the waywardness of women but also of the
contemptible nature of Catholics, since they "to the perpetual shame of
them . . . instead of a man pope elected a whore indeed to minister sacraments,
to saye masses, to geve orders."[7] According to the story, which is alleged
to have occurred around the year 850, Joan—in some versions an English
woman; in others, Dutch—disguises herself as a young man so that she can
travel with her tutor, a young monk who is also her lover. Unfortunately,
Joan's lover dies in Athens. In an effort to forget her grief, Joan, whose
knowledge of the various sciences is masterful, begins to give public lectures.
Her fame as a scholar grows, and eventually she is invited to lecture in Rome,
where her intellectual gifts lead her to being appointed a cardinal and eventually elected pope under the title of Pope John VIII.

Shakespeare's History (Princeton: Princeton University Press, 1991), 55. See also Nina S. Levine,
Women's Matters: Politics, Gender, and Nation in Shakespeare's Early History Plays (Newark: University
of Delaware Press, 1998), 32.

5. See Carole Levin, *The Heart and Stomach of a King: Elizabeth I and the Politics of Sex and Power*
(Philadelphia: University of Pennsylvania Press, 1994), 83–84.

6. Richard F. Hardin, "Chronicles and Mythmaking in Shakespeare's Joan of Arc," *Shakespeare
Survey* 42 (1989): 33.

7. John Foxe, *Acts and Monuments [...]* (1570 edition), 182. All Foxe citations from the Human
Rights Initiative website hriOnline, Sheffield, United Kingdom. Available at www.hrionline.shef.
ac.uk/foxe/, accessed September 27, 2006.

All might have continued well for this remarkable woman but for her sexual appetite. One of the members of her papal retinue—a servant, a chamberlain, even a cardinal, depending on the version—reminds Joan of her dead lover. Soon Joan is all too consoled. Her papal robes hide her pregnancy until, at the most dramatically inopportune moment, she gives birth in the middle of a formal procession in the streets of Rome. It is her pride that undoes her: she had insisted on leading this procession even though she had known she was near her time. In some versions, the Roman mob, furious at the deception, immediately tears her and her infant son to death. Other versions report the authorities hanging her and her child in order to demonstrate her shame. A sixteenth-century German play has Lucifer narrate the story of Pope Joan. At the beginning of the play, he promises her intellect and fame, but at the end she is betrayed to the Roman mob by another devil, who spitefully announces: "The Pope is great with child. He is a woman and no man."[8] Sixteenth-century versions of Pope Joan and Joan of Arc both use the issue of pride and illicit (possible) pregnancy as the way to bring the characters to destruction.

English Views of Joan of Arc

Just as the character of Pope Joan would have been well known to Elizabethans, so, too, would Joan of Arc. Both were portrayed in histories written in the sixteenth century; in the second half of the century there was, argues D. R. Woolf, "an enormous expansion" of public interest in the past.[9] Shakespeare's play about Joan of Arc was immensely popular; in 1592 Thomas Nashe stated that at least ten thousand spectators had seen 1 Henry VI. Phyllis Rackin and Jean Howard argue that this is actually a conservative estimate: Philip Henslowe's receipts for the play's initial run suggest a figure closer to

---

8. The information about the play comes from Lucy de Bruyn, *Woman and the Devil in Sixteenth-Century Literature* (Tisburg, U.K.: Compton Press, 1979), 153–54. This is her translation. I am deeply appreciative of the help offered to me by Barbara Krep on the lines of the play. For more information on the legend of Pope Joan, see C. A. Patrides, "The Fable of Pope Joan," in *Premises and Motifs in Renaissance Thought and Literature* (Princeton: Princeton University Press, 1982), 152–81; Emily Hope, *The Legend of Pope Joan* (Carlton, South Victoria: Sisters Publications, 1983); Rosemary Anne Pardoe, *The Female Pope: The Mystery of Pope Joan* (New York: Sterling, 1988); Peter Stanford, *The Legend of Pope Joan: In Search of the Truth* (New York: Henry Holt, 1999); and especially Craig Rustici, *The Afterlife of Pope Joan: Deploying the Popess Legend in Early Modern England* (Ann Arbor: University of Michigan Press, 2006).

9. D. R. Woolf, "Genre into Artifact: The Decline of the English Chronicle in the Sixteenth Century," *The Sixteenth Century Journal* 19 (Fall 1988): 331.

twenty thousand, and only one other play Henslowe produced earned more than this Joan of Arc play.[10] Joan's plea, echoing the pleas of actual women in the courts, would have been heard by many playgoers.

In the world of the play of *1 Henry VI* one might wonder if Joan is indeed pregnant.[11] At the beginning of the play she cautions the Dauphin that she cannot think about love while it is her duty from the Virgin Mary to expel the English: "I must not yield to any rites of love, For my profession's sacred from above: When I have chased all thy foes from hence, Then will I think upon a recompense" (1.2.113–16). Although Joan and Charles do enter together in Act II, scene 1, when they flee Rouen in the middle of the night and the English later refer to her paramours, there is no explicit evidence that Joan has taken any lovers, much less that she is pregnant.

Her pregnancy has the same problematic quality as the child of Lady Macbeth, another Shakespearean character who also calls forth spirits. In a number of ways Joan is Lady Macbeth's "predecessor," as Catherine Belsey points out.[12] Lady Macbeth may have "given suck," but she has no child during the course of the play. Some scholars argue that we have no evidence that Lady Macbeth ever had a child. So, too, Joan's claim of pregnancy was much more likely to be specious, an attempt to avoid execution, just as actual women who were not pregnant made the claim in attempting to save their lives. Given Lady Macbeth's murderous behavior and call to the spirits to "unsex" her—an echo of Joan's anguished offer to the spirits—the thought of Lady Macbeth as a mother is troubling, especially when the child is only mentioned in the context of her boast that had she promised to do so, she would dash the child's brains out to keep the oath. So, too, the active Joan who fights the English, talks back to the Dauphin, negotiates with the Duke of Burgundy while showing her contempt for him only to the audience, the Joan who offers "body, soul, and all" (5.3.22) to fiends from hell if they will

---

10. Jean Howard and Phyllis Rackin, *Engendering a Nation: A Feminist Account of Shakespeare's English Histories* (London: Routledge, 1997), 22.

11. A number of scholars are skeptical. For example, David Bevington refers to her "desperate and fallacious confession of pregnancy to avoid execution." "The Domineering Female in *1 Henry VI*," *Shakespeare Studies* 2 (1966): 51. Bevington has also, however, stated, "Joan's sexuality is not only demonic but also obsessive in its promiscuity and seeming insatiability," suggesting that the men she named were indeed her lovers. Bevington, ed., *Complete Works of Shakespeare*, 5th ed. (New York: Longman, 2003), 499.

12. "Predictably, these creatures who speak with voices which are not their own are unfixed, inconstant, unable to personate masculine virtue through to the end. Lady Macbeth sleepwalks, compelled to utter what she may not speak by day, and so betrays the truth. La Pucelle, deserted by her familiars, frantically asserts her innocence and then her pregnancy to escape the death she deserves." Belsey, *The Subject of Tragedy: Identity and Difference in Renaissance Drama* (London: Methuen, 1985), 183–84.

aid her in battles, is a highly problematic mother figure, certainly troubling to all those who watched from the audience.[13]

The idea of a Joan claiming pregnancy was not new to Shakespeare. It seems to have first emerged in the 1460s in an anonymous English chronicle that stated: "And then she said that she was with childe, whereby she was respited A while; but in conclusion it was found that she was not with child, and then she was [burned]."[14] In the 1460s, the decade after the Hundred Years' War finally ended, the French held the second trial that would rehabilitate Joan's character. Presenting Joan as lying about a pregnancy and fearful of death would be another way for the English to destroy her reputation and credibility.

This presentation of the lying, fearful Joan was further developed in the sixteenth century. In his history of England written during the reign of Henry VIII, Polydore Vergil explained that after she was condemned for wearing men's clothing and for witchcraft, "the unhappie Maide...fained herselfe to be with childe, to thende she might eyther move her enemies to compassion, eyther els cause them to appoynt some more milde punishment." When "her surmise [was] found false, she was burned not withstanding." Vergil did not celebrate Joan's fate, calling the sentence "the hardest that ever had been remembred" and questioning why this woman of "martiall manly prowesse" who had been defending her country was deemed ineligible for mercy.[15]

This is a very different portrait from that presented by Edward Hall in his *Chronicle,* published in 1548. Hall described Joan as "a rampe of suche boldness" who would do things "that other yong maidens bothe abhorred & wer ashamed to do." Hall called Joan "a monster," though he does not mention her false claim of pregnancy.[16] John Stow and the editors of *Holinshed's Chronicle* continued Hall's characterization, and they also repeated the story of the pregnancy. *Holinshed's Chronicle* describes Joan as "shamefullie rejecting hir sex abominablie in acts and apparell to have counterfeit mankind." The authors also described her as "a pernicious instrument to hostilitie and bloudshed in divelish witchcraft and sorcerie." Once she was sentenced to death, she claimed pregnancy to avoid execution and this claim won her a

13. Her contemptuous aside is "Done like a Frenchman: turn, and turn again!" (3.3.85).

14. Cited in W. T. Waugh, "Joan of Arc in English Sources of the Fifteenth Century," in *Historical Essays in Honor of James Tait,* ed. J. G. Edwards and V. H. Galbraith (Manchester, 1933), 394. Caxton published this chronicle in 1483 as *The Chronicles of England with the Fruit of the Times.* See Marina Warner, *Joan of Arc: The Image of Female Heroism* (New York: Knopf, 1981), 107.

15. Polydore Vergil, *Three Books of Polydore Vergil's English history, comprising the reigns of Henry VI, Edward IV, and Richard III from an early translation, preserved among the mss. Of the old royal library in the British museum,* ed. Sir Henry Ellis (London: Camden Society, 1844), 38.

16. Edward Hall, *Hall's Chronicle,* ed. Henry Ellis (London: Printed for J. Johnson, 1809), 148.

stay of nine months. The authors of *Holinshed's Chronicle* were convinced that this was pretense. They did not doubt her virginity but declared it shameful that she would pretend she was not a virgin in an attempt to save her life: "Yet seeking to eetch out life as long as she might... [she] confesse[d] herself a strumpet, and (unmarried as she was) to be with child... [but in this] found as false [and] wicked [as] the rest."[17] In the *Annales of England* (1592), John Stow called Joan a "monstrous woman" who pretended pregnancy to try and save her life. He had no sympathy for her that this bid failed.[18]

Elizabethan Women Pleading Pregnancy

In sixteenth-century England, a number of women actually did plead pregnancy in an attempt to avoid execution. The judges then ordered them to be examined by a board, or jury, of matrons. These were usually married women of good character, "discreet women" whom the sheriff had asked to serve. Quite possibly these women were already in the audience at the court and were thus impaneled. Married women were considered to have sufficient knowledge in matters of pregnancy and childbirth; midwives were not specifically put on such juries. James Oldham tells us that "the use of the jury of matrons was a settled practice throughout England in the sixteenth and seventeenth centuries."[19] Those the board explicitly proclaimed were not pregnant were indeed executed, but according to the law even ones found to be pregnant were to have their sentence merely deferred, though in some cases the sentence was then never carried out. While juries of matrons reported that most of the women they examined were not pregnant, as we will see, there were a number of cases where the women may or may not have been pregnant but were reprieved.[20] There is no such chance for the character Joan.

Men found guilty of capital crimes in the medieval/early modern period could claim benefit of clergy, the commonest method of avoiding execution. Benefit of clergy was available to literate laymen in all cases of murder and felony. The convicted man, claiming benefit, was then asked to read a prescribed passage from a Psalter. Laymen could make this claim only once; to

---

17. *Holinshed's Chronicles of England, Scotland, and Ireland,* ed. Henry Ellis (London: Printed for J. Johnson, 1807–1808), III, 170–71.

18. John Stow, *Annales of England* (London: Ralfe Newbery, 1592), 597, 600.

19. Oldham, "On Pleading the Belly," 3, 15.

20. Garthine Walker, *Crime, Gender, and Social Order in Early Modern England* (Cambridge: Cambridge University Press, 2003), 198.

prevent them from attempting to use it a second time, a statute passed in 1490 had such felonious "clerks," as distinguished from actual priests, branded on the left thumb with a T (for thief) or M (for manslayer).[21]

Women did not have this option in the sixteenth century. They were granted limited rights to benefit of clergy for minor crimes only in 1623. If, however, they were found guilty in a capital offense, they could claim they were pregnant; indeed, if they could sustain this claim, the sentence was supposed to be deferred until the child was born. A pregnancy plea was supposed to be accepted only if the woman was "quick" rather than "young" with child, but in fact this distinction was often not made. Theoretically, a woman would within a month of the child's birth be executed, but in fact some were not.[22] The 1559–1625 figures for the home circuit, the most populous judicial region in England, show that over 1,600 women were accused of felonies. Of the 44 percent of these women found guilty, one-third pleaded pregnancy. As with men and benefit of clergy, this was a plea that could only be made once. In *The Complete Justice* (1637), it states: "Women arraigned for felony, may only for one time have the benefit of their belly."[23] *The Laws Resolution of Women's Rights* augments this argument: "If after such respite when she is once delivered, she become great againe, and object to prolong her life, the Judge ought to command execution, presently, for this benefit shall bee claimed but once. If the judge inquire further of it, it must be but to set a fine on the Marshall or Sheriffe for looking no better to her."[24]

For some women this claim saved their lives, but during the sixteenth century this varied in different courts at different times. And some were indeed executed after giving birth, particularly if they were found guilty of murder or infanticide. As Garthine Walker cogently puts it, "Benefit of clergy was used as a standard method of mitigating the death sentence; benefit of belly

---

21. J. S. Cockburn, *Calendar of Assize Records: Home Circuit Indictments Elizabeth I and James I: Introduction* (London: HMSO, 1985), 114; and J. H. Baker, "Criminal Courts and Procedure at Common Law, 1550–1800," in *Crime in England, 1550–1800*, ed. J. S. Cockburn (Princeton: Princeton University Press, 1977), 41–42. See also Luke Owen Pike, *A History of Crime in England* (London: Smith, Elder, and Co., 1873), I, 297–303.

22. Baker, "Criminal Justice at Newgate," 314, cited in Cockburn, *Calendar of Assize Records...: Introduction*, 121; J. A. Sharpe, *Crime in Early Modern England, 1550–1750* (London: Longman, 1984), 147; and C. L'estrange Ewen, *Witch Hunting and Witch Trials* (London: Kegan Paul, 1929), 33.

23. *The Complete Justice. A Compendium of the particulars incident to Justices of the Peace, either in Sessions or out of Sessions* (London, 1637), 292. See also Matthew Hale, *Pleas of the Crown*, 5th ed. (London: Printed for D. Brown, J. Walthoe, and M. Wotton, 1716), 272.

24. T. E., *The laws resolutions of womens rights: or, The laws provision for woemen. A methodicall collection of such statutes and customes, with the cases, opinions, arguments and points of learning in the law, as doe properly concerne women. Together with a compendious table, whereby the chiefe matters in this booke contained, may be more readily found* (London: Printed by Miles Flesher, 1632), 207.

was not."[25] The servant Agnes Barns murdered her newborn child in August 1559, was found guilty the following March but remanded because she was pregnant. This only delayed her execution until July 1561. In July 1576 Joan Bretton was found guilty of drowning her infant daughter but successfully pleaded pregnancy. She was, however, hanged a year later, in July 1577. In 1562 Emily Pott, wife of Valentine Pott, attacked Edward Chapman with an axe and killed him. Her successful pregnancy plea delayed her execution for two years. In 1592, Eleanor Iden, a spinster, poisoned her relative Thomas with arsenic and was remanded because she was pregnant, but she was hanged a year later. In 1622 Katherine Read's claim of pregnancy was validated but she was hanged after her child was born. The same happened to Elinor Ratcliffe in 1623 and Anne Dickenson, alias Sarah Merrett, in 1664. Garthine Walker discovered in cases she examined in Cheshire in the 1620s that twenty-four women claimed to be pregnant. The matrons confirmed the claims for only four of the women; the other twenty were hanged. Of the four who were not hanged because of their pregnancies, two were executed after the babies were born.[26] A number of those reprieved on the grounds of pregnancy, however, were eventually released. For example, in 1550, Alice Cowland of Tottenham in Middlesex pleaded pregnancy after pleading guilty to the theft of goods worth £2, which made it a capital crime. The judge pardoned her.[27] But it could also be a lengthy wait. Women remanded to await pardon or for corroboration of a plea of pregnancy might stay in jail for a very long time; some, like Isabel Naylor in 1627, though reprieved, died there. Several women were detained for up to seven years, either before or after their pregnancies were verified.[28]

A woman who claimed pregnancy was examined in private by the specially appointed panel of twelve matrons, who then reported her condition to the court. As Cynthia Herrup points out, this examination was "more complex, more humiliating and probably less open to manipulation than the test administered for benefit of clergy."[29] Moreover, successful benefit of clergy

25. Walker, *Crime, Gender and Social Order,* 200.

26. J. S. Cockburn, ed., *Calendar of Assize Records: Essex Indictments, Elizabeth I* (London: Her Majesty's Stationery Office, 1978), 882; J. S. Cockburn, ed. *Calendar of Assize Records: Kent Indictments, Elizabeth I* (London: Her Majesty's Stationery Office, 1979), 53, 87, 174; J. S. Cockburn, ed. *Calendar of Assize Records: Sussex Indictments, Elizabeth I* (London: Her Majesty's Stationery Office, 1975), 1361; and Walker, *Crime, Gender, and Social Order,* 198.

27. Anne Lawrence, *Women in England, 1500–1700* (London: Weidenfeld and Nicolson, 1994), 269.

28. Cockburn, *Calendar of Assize Records…: Introduction,* 35; and Walker, *Crime, Gender, and Social Order,* 199.

29. Cynthia Herrup, *The Common Peace: Participation and the Criminal Law in Seventeenth-Century England* (Cambridge: Cambridge University Press, 1987), 143n16.

was achieved because of a skill; a successful pleading of the belly was due to a biological condition. If the matrons found a woman who pleaded was indeed pregnant, the judge was bound to stay the execution until after the child was born. But the means of verification, especially of early pregnancy, is to our twenty-first-century minds sometimes questionable, suggesting that on some occasions the judges may have used this ground as a way of commuting sentences or pardoning condemned women. James Oldham suggests that for the most part these juries of matrons were conscientious, a point also argued by Patricia Crawford, who states that in all instances in which matrons were impaneled to judge the condition of other women, "society expected that women's responsibility to tell the truth, according to their office and licence, would override any moral obligation to other women."[30] The "fore Matron" of the jury had to take an oath when she was sworn in: "You as fore Matron of this Jury shall swear, That you shall search and try the Prisoner at the Bar, whether she be quick with Child, and thereof a true Verdict shall return: So help you God." After she was sworn in, the rest of the jury of matrons also had to take the same oath.[31] Yet it seems that at least some of the village matrons wished to give condemned women every possible opportunity. In a number of cases, judges either delayed the examination of the women for six to twelve months or, if the matrons were not sure of the woman's condition, ordered that she be reexamined some months later. Even though according to the law, the woman had to be "quick" rather than "young" with child, in some cases women were able to plead pregnancy even early into their term. Early pregnancy was not always easy to confirm, however, so the plea in a woman of childbearing age might well win her at least a measure of delay.[32]

While by law the execution was not to be postponed if the woman became pregnant while in custody, whenever a woman was remanded to await examination—often for several months—this was always a possibility, and in the early modern period there was serious concern that many women became impregnated in prison while awaiting their trials. Monsieur Misson, a French visitor to England in the late seventeenth century, heard that every prison had a few men there just to "help out" women. Female arrivals were advised "that if they are not with child already, they must go to work

30. Oldham, "Pleading the Belly," 19; Patricia Crawford, "Public Duty, Conscience, and Women in Early Modern England," in *Public Duty and Private Conscience in Seventeenth Century England,* ed. John Morrill, Paul Slack, and Daniel Woolf (Oxford: Clarendon Press, 1993), 64.

31. Richard Garnet, *The Book of Oaths and the Several Forms thereof, Both Ancient and Modern,* 2nd ed. (London: H. Twyford, 1689), 250. My thanks to Valerie Wayne for bringing this reference to my attention.

32. Barbara Rosen, ed., *Witchcraft in England, 1558–1618* (Amherst: University of Massachusetts Press, 1991), 294n55.

immediately to be so, that in case they have the misfortune to be condemned they get time, and perhaps save their lives." He adds, perhaps a bit cynically, "Who would not hearken to such wholsom Advice?"[33] By the early eighteenth century, Captain Alexander Smith saw other abuses in the system, claiming that prisoners had their own matrons on hand to assert they were quick with child whether they were or not.[34]

Certainly there are highly suspicious cases in the sixteenth century as well. Mary Osborne pleaded pregnancy in July 1581 but was not examined until March 1582, when she was said to be quick with child. Her son was not baptized, however, until September 1584, making one wonder exactly when he was conceived and when born. Osborne was in prison until at least July 1585. Elizabeth Munsloe was remanded on plea of pregnancy in March 1562, was found to be pregnant in July 1563, and finally released in 1569. Margaret Judge was convicted of infanticide at the Maidstone Assizes in July 1560 and remanded because of her plea of pregnancy. She was examined, but the decision was deferred until a second examination a year later in July 1561, when a jury of matrons found her to be pregnant. The judge sent her back to jail; two years later, in July 1563, she was again examined and again found to be pregnant. She remained in prison until the judge pardoned her in 1565. As J. S. Cockburn argues, this suggests a judicially conscious fiction—or else an amazingly long and convoluted pregnancy. He states, "Whether or not the women concerned in such cases actually gave birth—or indeed, whether or not they were ever pregnant—remains uncertain."[35] In at least some cases, such as that of Petronella Hayward, convicted March 1583 of poisoning her husband, found pregnant July 1583, pardoned 1587, Cockburn argues that the trial judge pardoned her because he was convinced of her innocence, and the pregnancy was a deliberate fiction used to save her.

J. A. Sharpe suggests that in a number of cases men whose literacy was doubtful were coached so that they could claim benefit of clergy; so, too, some women were declared pregnant and those in control deliberately closed their eyes to the immutable realities of biology. Certainly in sixteenth century England many people were concerned with the severity of punishments prescribed for crimes. Even the fact of bringing a prosecution to law was

---

33. Maximilien Misson, *M. Misson's Memoirs and Observations in his Travels over England with Some Account of Scotland and Ireland. Dispos'd in Alphabetical Order. Written originally in French,* trans. Mr. Ozell (London: Printed for D. Browne, 1719), 329–30.

34. Capt. Alexander Smith, *The History of the Lives of the Most Noted Highwaymen, Foot-pads, House-breakers, Shop-lifts and Cheats, of Both Sexes, etc.* 2nd ed. (London, 1714), II, 185, cited in Oldham, "Pleading the Belly," 17.

35. Cockburn, *Calendar of Assize Records ...: Introduction,* 122–23.

selective. As Penry Williams points out, the decision to prosecute depended on a number of issues: the reputation of the offender, the attitude of the victim, local opinion, and communal pressure for conciliation or arbitration. Many people were arraigned because of their reputations for notorious bad character or persistent misconduct.[36] And once there was a prosecution, jurors regularly undervalued stolen goods to ensure that the crime would not be a capital one.[37] Humanists debated the merits of capital punishment. Earlier in the century, Thomas More pursued the question in his *Utopia,* which was translated from the original Latin into English in 1551. More argued against capital punishment for thieves, having Raphael state, "Surely, my lord, I think it not right nor justice, that the loss of money should cause the loss of man's life: for mine opinion is, that all the goods in the world are not able to countervail man's life."[38] The plea of pregnancy allowed at least some judges some latitude about fulfilling the rigors of the law on convicted women, though this was far more unusual than the illiterate man coached well enough to avoid execution.

Just as with Joan, some women found guilty of witchcraft in early modern England pleaded pregnancy and in some cases managed to avoid execution. The matrons on the jury examining women who pleaded pregnancy were often the same women who looked for witchmarks.[39] In July 1564 Elizabeth Lowys, wife of John Lowys, a husbandman, was indicted for murder by witchcraft. The indictment stated that she had murdered an infant and two adult men. She was found guilty on all counts but was remanded because she claimed pregnancy. The next March a jury of matrons examined her along with three other women. One of the other women was found to be pregnant but not Lowys, who was executed.[40] The spinster Avis Cunny, convicted of

---

36. Penry Williams, *The Later Tudors: England, 1547–1603* (Oxford: Clarendon Press, 1995), 218–19.

37. Cockburn, *Calendar of Assize Records...: Introduction,* 123; Cockburn, ed., *Calendar of Assize Records: Kent,* 202; and Sharpe, *Crime in Early Modern England,* 67–68. Goods valued at less than £2 meant it was not.

38. Thomas More, *A most pleasant, fruitful, and witty work, of the best state of a public weal, and of the new isle called Utopia,* trans. Ralph Robinson, ed. Rev. T. F. Dibdin (London: The Shakespeare Press, 1808), 74.

39. Jim Sharpe, "Women, Witchcraft, and the Legal Process," in *Women, Crime, and the Courts in Early Modern England,* ed. Jennifer Kermode and Garthine Walker (Chapel Hill: University of North Carolina Press, 1994), 106–24; and Oldham, "Pleading the Belly," 8.

40. Cockburn, *Calendar of Assize Records: Essex,* 31, 35. Anne Barstow claims that she was indeed pregnant and executed anyway, but I cannot find any confirmation of that. Barstow, *Witchcraze: A New History of the European Witch Hunts* (San Francisco: Harper San Francisco, 1995), 134. Apparently Elizabeth Lowys exclaimed before her execution, "Christ, my Christ, if thou be a saviour come down and avenge me of my enemies, or else thou shall not be a saviour." Cited in Keith Thomas, *Religion and the Decline of Magic* (New York: Charles Scribner's Sons, 1971), 123. See also Ewen, *Witch Hunting and Witch Trials,* 117–18.

using witchcraft to murder Richard Franck and to make Jeremiah Browne lame, successfully pleaded pregnancy in 1589 but was executed in 1590 after the child was born.[41] But Elizabeth Lightbone was found guilty of witchcraft in 1614, successfully pleaded pregnancy, and was pardoned two years later.[42]

Alice Samuel was also found guilty of witchcraft and was mocked when she attempted to plead pregnancy. In 1593 Alice, by then an elderly woman, was put on trial for witchcraft with her husband and daughter; all were found guilty.[43] The case had started four years earlier when the daughters of Robert Throckmorton, the wealthiest man in the village of Warboys, began to have strange fits. The doctors suspected witchcraft, and the afflicted daughters accused one of their neighbors, Alice Samuel, a poor older woman of the village of bewitching them. Alice was forced repeatedly to come to the Throckmortons' house and eventually to live with them. At first she accused the girls of "wantonnesse"—of making it all up—but after years of being told she was a witch who was causing these problems, she confessed to bewitching the children and causing the death of Lady Cromwell, the wife of the landlord who had paid a sympathy visit to the Throckmortons. When Alice returned to her own home, her husband and daughter were appalled and at their urging convinced her to recant her confession. This so outraged Throckmorton that he had not only the mother arrested but her daughter Agnes as well, whom the girls then claimed was a far worse witch than her mother ever was. Though both were indicted and jailed, Throckmorton bailed Agnes out and forced her to live in the family home, where she was constantly questioned and harangued. The spirits the girls said possessed them also told the children to scratch and beat Agnes.

At the trial, Alice Samuel, her daughter Agnes, and Alice's husband John, who had also been accused, were all found guilty. Alice pleaded pregnancy. Since Alice was quite elderly and clearly past the age of childbearing, the

---

41. Rosen, *Witchcraft in England,* 182; Marion Gibson, *Reading Witchcraft: Stories of Early English Witches* (London: Routledge, 1999), 65; and Ewen, *Witch Hunting and Witch Trials,* 164, 166, 168. Cockburn's Assize records, however, only state that she was found pregnant, not the later order for execution. *Calendar of the Assize Records: Essex,* 2006, 2008, 2029, 2039, 2096.

42. Ewen, *Witch Hunting and Witch Trials,* 33.

43. *The Most strange and admirable discoverie of the three Witches of Warboys, arraigned, convicted, and executed at the last Assises at Huntington, for the bewitching of the five daughters of Robert Throckmorton, Esquire and divers others persons, with sundrie Divelish and grievous torments: And also for the bewitching to death of the Lady Crumwell, the like hath not been heard of in this age* (London, 1593). All quotations are from this text. For more on the case, see Gibson, *Reading Witchcraft,* 62, 65–66, 105–7, 122–25; Rosen, *Witchcraft,* 239–97; and R. Trevor Davies, *Four Centuries of Witch-Beliefs* (London: Methuen, 1947), 32–39. Barstow refers to this case as "another example of class prejudice," while Belsey discusses Agnes Samuel's testimony in terms of silence and language. See Barstow, *Witchcraze,* 193; and Belsey, *The Subject of Tragedy,* 188–90.

entire court burst out in laughter. The judge told her to give up that plea, but Alice insisted on being examined by a board of matrons. "A Jury of women were empaneled, and sworne to search her: who have up their verdite, that she was not with childe, unlesse (as some saide) it was with the divell." Another prisoner suggested to Agnes that she also make this plea, which given her age would have been more believable. Just as she had always maintained her innocence to the charge, neither would she attempt to save her life by this means, stating, "It shall never be sayd, that I was both a Witch and a whore."[44] Mother, father, and daughter were all hanged.

One woman who apparently could have pleaded pregnancy, which would have at least saved her until after the birth of her child, but refused to do so was Margaret Clitherow. She was drawn to stories of Catholics who had suffered heroically because of their beliefs and she herself converted to Catholicism in York in 1574, though her husband John remained a churchgoing Protestant. As a convert, Margaret hid fugitive priests and thus provided her recusant neighbors with access to the Catholic sacraments. She was imprisoned three different times for her nonconformist activities (1577–78, 1580–81, 1583–84). Even after harboring a Catholic priest became a capital crime in 1585, Margaret continued to do what she thought was right. On March 10, 1586, Margaret, pregnant at the time, was arrested for harboring a priest. On March 14, before the Assizes, after repeatedly being asked to plead, she refused. If someone refused to plead guilty or not guilty, the trial could not proceed. By law such a person would be laid out on the ground with weights put on top of them until they either pleaded or were pressed to death. For a week after her refusal, Margaret was kept in prison as members of her family and various Protestant preachers begged her to plead—or at least to admit that she was pregnant and thus obtain a stay of execution. Margaret refused this advice; on March 25, 1586, she was pressed to death. She probably wished to protect other recusants who had aided her, as they would most likely have been named at her trial. But her early biographer, the priest John Mush, also described her as attracted to martyrdom.[45]

Margaret Clitherow acted both with courage and a desire for martyrdom, in opposition to Shakespeare's Joan, who claimed to be pregnant in an effort to avoid death. Even more impressive in her courage, as she clearly had no

44. Gibson points out that our source for this is the pamphlet. "This is a suspicious piece of noble eloquence perhaps, but it is not in the interests of the pamphleteer since it presents the witch sympathetically, and thus it may be true." *Reading Witchcraft,* 66.

45. Claire Walker, "Clitherow, Margaret [St Margaret Clitherow] (1552/3–1586)," *Oxford Dictionary of National Biography,* Oxford University Press, 2004, available at www.oxforddnb.com/view/article/5692, accessed October 16, 2006.

desire for death, Agnes Samuel also stands in contrast to the fictional Joan. We know Agnes's words from the pamphlet about the case, obviously written from a hostile point of view, which makes it all the more likely that the brave statement Agnes made was accurate. Agnes Samuel's statement from the heart demonstrated her awareness of the enormous damages to reputation that pleading pregnancy could bring. Shakespeare's portrayal of Joan of Arc at the end of *1 Henry VI* was another evident example.

Pleading Pregnancy in Scotland

There were a number of cases of witches in Scotland pleading pregnancy in this period as well. In 1624, a commission was established by the Privy Council of Scotland to search for, apprehend, and detain a number of witches, including Isobel Falconer, who was suspected of being a witch, specifically of having "used sindrie diviliishe practiseis aganis / sindrie of our goode subjectis prejudiciall and hurtfull to thair lyves." There had previously been a commission granted against Isobel Falconer; everything had been prepared for her trial, when she "most subtilie and falslie alledgeit, and confidentle and impudentlie affirmed, that sho wes with chyld, and upoun hat falce infformatioun procured any warrand frome our Counsaill for continewing of hir tryall till sho wer delyverit of hir birthe; quhilk as yitt now after mony yeiris is not donne," and meanwhile "she continewis in hir divilishe practiises."[46]

At the very time that *1 Henry VI* was being performed in London, the English people were also learning about a massive witchcraft scare in Scotland. Large numbers of people in Scotland were tried for treason accomplished through sorcery in trials that began in November 1590, and James VI himself was at the center of the trials. The letters from English ambassador Robert Bowes to William Cecil, Lord Burghley, are filled with details of the various cases. From this vantage point it is impossible to say exactly what happened. During the course of the trials it was alleged that over three hundred witches had gathered to try to destroy the king through raising storms while James and his bride Anne of Denmark were at sea and by melting his effigy in wax. The witches were accused of indulging in obscene rituals in churches. More than a hundred suspects were examined, a large number of whom were executed. One of the focuses of the trial was Francis Stewart, Earl of Bothwell, a relative of the king whom James perceived as a dangerous

---

46. *The Register of the Privy Council of Scotland: 1622–1625,* edited and abridged by David Masson (Edinburgh: H. M. General Register House, 1896), XIII, 460–61.

political enemy. In January 1591 two suspected witches accused Bothwell of consulting with other witches to discover the date the king would die.[47]

James was intensely interested in the trials; indeed, several times he personally exhorted the jurors to convict. By the spring of 1591 it was the king's impetus that kept the trials going. The one in which he showed the greatest interest and commitment was that of Barbara Napier, wife of burgess Archibald Douglas, who was arrested for being part of the conspiracy to encompass the death of James and for the successful murder of Archibald, Earl of Angus, through magic. James VI was particularly concerned about Napier, because she was known to be a friend of Bothwell. Napier claimed to be with child, which caused James in April 1591 to write to one of his advisors, Sir William Maitland, "Trye by the medicinairis' [oaths] gif Barbara Napair be with bairne or not. Tak na delaying ansour. Gif ye finde she be not, to the fyre with her presentlie." But even if she were pregnant, James pushed for the full punishment of the law. The jury, in part because of Napier's pregnancy, was reluctant to convict her and acquitted her of attempting to destroy the king or of being implicated in the death of Angus. They were even reluctant to find her guilty of consulting with witches. Christina Larner suggests that the clause in Scotland's Witchcraft Act of 1563 that imposed death for merely consulting with witches had never before been enforced, so the jury may well have felt it difficult to find her guilty when such a verdict could easily lead to her execution. It appears that Napier's connection with Bothwell was what made James feel so vindictive toward her. James was appalled that the jury did not convict Napier and commanded them to return so that he could argue the verdict, stating, "God hath made me a King and judge." But his harangue had no effect: "He was deeply mortified by the presumption of this jury in acquitting a woman he believed to be guilty of treason."[48] The 1591 pamphlet *Newes from Scotland* said of Napier and another woman arrested with her that until the accusation they were "reputed... as civill

---

47. Christina Larner, "James VI and I and Witchcraft," in *The Reign of James VI and I,* ed. Alan G. R. Smith (London: Macmillan, 1973), 79; and Rob Macpherson, "Stewart, Francis, first earl of Bothwell (1562–1612)," in *Oxford Dictionary of National Biography,* ed. H. C. G. Matthew and Brian Harrison (Oxford: Oxford University Press, 2004).

48. William K. Boyd and Henry W. Meikle, eds., *Calendar of State Papers, Relating to Scotland and Mary, Queen of Scots* (Edinburgh: H. M. General Register House, 1936), X, 497, 506, 510, 514–15, 518, 520, 523–25; and Larner, "James VI and I and Witchcraft," 80–83. See also Godfrey Watson, *Bothwell and the Witches* (London: Robert Hale, 1975), 130–43; and Edward J. Cowan, "Darker Visions of the Scottish Renaissance: The Devil and Francis Stewart," in *The Renaissance and Reformation in Scotland: Essays in Honour of Gordon Donaldson,* ed. Ian B. Cowan and Duncan Shaw (Edinburgh: Scottish Academic Press, 1983), 125–40.

honest women as any that dwelled within the Citie of Edenbrough, before they were apprehended."[49]

The Guernsey Martyrs

So, within a year of the presentation on stage in London of *1 Henry VI,* a woman accused of witchcraft did escape conviction and thus execution because of her pregnancy and the compassion shown by the jury. And meanwhile, in England, a number of women convicted on a number of capital crimes were able to plead pregnancy. Clearly Shakespeare's audience would have been well aware when Joan made her plea on that stage that she was right—she had the law on her side. Audience members would have known of actual women who successfully made this plea. But they would also have known about other women in sixteenth-century England who were pregnant and were burned to death anyway. These cases appeared in John Foxe's *Acts and Monuments.* Many of the martyrs whose stories Foxe dealt with so movingly were women. Certainly one of the most horrific of his stories was that of Perotine Massey. As Megan Hickerson points out, "The story of the Guernsey martyrs is notorious for its gruesomeness."[50] Foxe himself was certainly aware of the special nature of this particular example: "Among al and singular histories touched in this booke before, as there be many pitifull, diuers lamentable, some horryble & tragicall: so is there none almoste to bee compared to thys cruell and furious facte of the homicide Papists, done in the Isle of Garnsey upon three wemen and an infant."[51]

The background to the story is straightforward. In May 1556 Vincent Gosset, whom Foxe described as "a noughty woman," stole a goblet and attempted to pawn it with Perotine Massey, "a very honest woman."[52] Massey lived with her sister, Guillemine Gilbert, and her mother, Katherine Cawches or Cowchen. Massey recognized the goblet and suspected that it was stolen; she tried to restore it to its rightful owners, but in the subsequent investigation she, her sister, and her mother were all arrested for harboring stolen goods. At their trial their neighbors reported that the three women were neither "theves, nor evil disposed persones, but lyved truly and honestly,

49. G. B. Harrison, ed., *Newes from Scotland (1591)* (London: The Bodley Head, 1924), 11.

50. Megan L. Hickerson, *Making Women Martyrs in Tudor England* (New York: Palgrave Macmillan, 2005), 97.

51. John Foxe, *Acts and Monuments [...]* (1563 edition), 1541.

52. John Foxe, *Acts and Monuments [...]* (1563 edition), 1542.

as became christian women." On July 1 they were found "not gilty of that they were charged with," but it was also discovered that the three women had not always been obedient to the holy church and had not been attending regularly. They were returned to prison for a new trial. In the trial for heresy on July 17, they were convicted and condemned to be burned "until they be consumed with ashes" the following day. In the 1563 edition Foxe reported that the women, terrified, were willing—even desperate—to start attending Catholic services but were illegally executed anyway. Perotine, "beyng great with childe," from the heat of the fire, gave birth to a goodlye man chylde," which was rescued, but "the cruell tormentours...threw most spightful-lye the same chylde into the fyre agayne, wher it was burned with the sely Mother, Graūdmother, and Aunt, very pitifully to behold." Foxe's reference to Massey as "sely," meaning "silly," was in no way pejorative. In the sixteenth century, according to the Oxford English Dictionary, in addition to having the meaning the word does now, the word also meant "deserving of pity, compassion, or sympathy," or "helpless, defenseless, especially women and children," and this is no doubt how Foxe was using the term. Foxe added, "Oh cruel papists, that ever suche a foule murther upon earth should be committed." Hickerson argues that in the 1563 edition Foxe's reason for giving such details about the Guernsey women was to "demonstrate the ex-traordinary behaviour of the Catholic authorities, particularly in murdering the child born so violently to Perotine Massey in the flames." While Foxe sympathized with the horrors Perotine, "a goodly woman," endured, he did not call her either a saint or a martyr.[53]

Foxe admitted that the "horrible straungenes" of what happened might mean that some readers would hardly believe it "but rather thoughte to bee foreged, or els amplified." He explained how he had heard the story from witnesses who were there, including Perotine's uncle, Matthew Cawches. As part of his evidence, Foxe included a letter of complaint from Cawches to Elizabeth I's commissioners. As Steven Mullaney points out, "In remote Guernsey, only a handful of people witnessed the death of Perotine, her fam-ily and child." Foxe had to tell the story for it not to be lost to history.[54]

Foxe's instincts were absolutely correct. Such a story did draw criticism; over the next four decades, Thomas Harding, Cardinal William Allen, and

---

53. Hickerson, *Making Women Martyrs,* 121.

54. John Foxe, *Acts and Monuments [...]* (1563 edition), 1544–45; and Steven Mullaney, "Re-forming Resistance: Class, Gender, and Legitimacy in Foxe's *Book of Martyrs,*" in *Print, Manuscript and Performance: The Changing Relations of the Media in Early Modern England,* ed. Arthur F. Marotti and Michael D. Bristol (Columbus: Ohio State University Press, 2000), 241.

the Jesuit Robert Parsons all challenged Foxe's veracity in telling the story of the Guernsey martyrs.

In 1567 Thomas Harding attacked Foxe's representation of the facts of the case. In 1547, Harding, a regius professor of Hebrew at Oxford, clearly had some Protestant leanings, as he resigned his chair to become the chaplain to Henry Grey, Marquis of Dorset, and thus was in the same household as Grey's famous and devoted Protestant daughter Lady Jane. Within a year of the accession of Mary, however, Harding turned his back on Protestantism, which so distressed the by-now-imprisoned Jane that she wrote him a letter of her surprise that he was "the unshamfast pararmour of AntiChrist... a cowardly runaway" who now preferred "the stinking and filthy kenel of Sathan." Foxe published the letter in the 1563 edition of *Acts and Monuments,* but he did not name Harding, describing him instead as "a certayne learned man, whome both I knowe, and coulde also here nominate, if I were disposed," but he decided not to name him, "trustinge and hopyng of some better towardnes of the partie hereafter."[55] This hope proved to be a vain one. Soon after Elizabeth became queen, Harding left England for Louvain and during the 1560s engaged in series of polemical pamphlet wars with John Jewel, bishop of Salisbury, in which he also argued against the veracity of Foxe.

Harding's first line of attack was to suggest that birth and delivery back into the flames of Perotine's child never happened since Foxe "tolde us in his false martyrologue, a thousand mo lyes then this." But even if Foxe's story were true, Harding proclaimed, the fault lay with Massey herself. Harding accused the "prattling parrot Perotine" of heresy, theft, whoredom, and murder. He argued that Perotine, her sister, and her mother were willing accomplices to theft, even though Foxe had declared them vindicated on this charge. Harding went on to say that Perotine was a whore, since "of the childes Father, there is no woorde spoken." If she were not ashamed of being pregnant, she would have pleaded pregnancy to escape punishment. As she did not do so, Harding argued, Perotine herself was the actual murderer of her child. Since she "claimed not the benefite of the Lawe, and so now not only like an harlot or Heretique, but like a Murtherer went desperately to the fier, and murdered bothe her selfe, and her childe conceived within her."[56] This argument was further expounded in 1587, the year Foxe died, by Cardinal William Allen

---

55. John Foxe, *Acts and Monuments [...]* (1563 edition), 920.

56. Thomas Harding, *A Rejoindre to M. Jewels Replie against the Sacrifice of the Masse* (1567; repr. Menston, U.K.: Scolar Press, 1970), 184, 185. For a general discussion of contemporary Catholic response to Foxe, see Glyn Parry, "John Foxe, 'Father of Lyes', and the Papists," in *John Foxe and the English Reformation,* ed. David Loades (Aldershot, U.K.: Scolar Press, 1997), 295–305.

in his *A True, Sincere, and Modest Defense of English Catholics*. Allen argued that since Perotine Massey hid her pregnancy, did not claim "the benefit of her belly," she alone was responsible for her child's death. Allen suggested piously, "Almighty God discovered her filth and shame, where she looked for the glory of a saint and of a virgin martyr." There is no evidence whatsoever that Perotine wished to be glorified as a virgin martyr; indeed, as a pregnant woman near term dying an agonizing death, this was probably the furthest thought from her mind.[57]

Around the time of the death of Elizabeth and the accession of James, a Jesuit named Robert Parsons published the three-volume *Treatise of Three Conversions of England from Paganisme to Christian Religion* (1603–1604), which contained a lengthy and venomous attack on *Acts and Monuments* and specifically the Perotine Massey case. Parsons maintained that Foxe told this story "to make Catholiks hatefull in the beginning of the late Q. raigne," of which there is certainly an element of truth. Less accurate is Parson's description of his own approach, when he claims that "we come with moderation and temperate discretion, to weigh the substance & circumstances of this story, we shall find in this, as in infinite other matters that Foxe and his fellows have little conscience in their sayings . . . and no regard of truth and sincerity." Parsons described Perotine as a "secret strompett, not confessinge her selfe to be with child" and in any case, the boy "that fell out of the said Perotines belly when she was burned . . . was borne dead." He later went on to discuss the Harding and Foxe controversy in more detail, arguing how accurately Harding, that "learned and pious man," labeled Perotine a whore and a murderer. Parson described Foxe as "most wonderfully troubled," saying that he "maketh the most fond and childish discourses, therby to defend [Perotine], and the honour of his ghospell, that ever perhaps man did, that was in his right witts."[58]

In his 1570 edition, Foxe responded to Harding's criticisms. On the charge that Perotine was having an illegitimate child, Foxe stated that she was married to a man named David Jores, who was known as a Protestant, and also gave the name of the minister, Noel Regnet, who married them. D. M. Ogier names Jores as one of the Huguenot ministers who had fled to Guernsey during the reign of Edward VI. Once there he met and married Perotine but then fled to Normandy earlier, during Mary's reign, leaving his pregnant

---

57. William Allen, *A True, Sincere, and Modest Defense of English Catholics*, ed. Robert M. Kingdon (Ithaca: Cornell University Press, 1965), 104.

58. Robert Persons, *A Treatise of Three Conversions*, vol. 3 (1604; repr. London: Scolar Press, 1976), 91. My great thanks to Megan Hickerson for her help with this reference.

wife with her mother.[59] Foxe also was much more effusive in his praise of Perotine and her family, calling them "holy Saintes of God" and describing their burning as the way "they should consummate their Martyrdome." He also went into even more detail about the death of the child. "The infant being a fayre man child, fell into the fire, and eftsoones being taken out of the fire by one W. House, was layde upon the grasse. Then was the child had to the Provost, and from him to the Bailife, who gave censure, that it should be carried backe agayne and cast into the fire."[60] Foxe assured his readers that they "thus have you the true narration of this history." Foxe went on to suggest that "we have herein to wonder at M. H. . . . goeth about, first to deny the story, terming it to bee a fable"; according to Foxe, once Harding admitted the truth, "seeking by all meanes to cleare the Clergie from the spotte of crueltie, transferreth the whole blame onely upon the women that suffered, but principally upon poore Perotine: whom he specially chargeth with . . . whoredome and murder."[61]

Foxe assured his readers that Perotine was no whore—after all, she was married. More importantly, to label someone as "the murderer of her owne infant" is to make her "more then a monster." How can one call her the murderer of her child, he asked? She did not put herself and the child at risk. She did not "purposely and wyttyngly thrust her selfe in jeopardy, to the destruction of her childe, when she needed not, as Pope Joane, when she might have kept her bed, would needes adventure forth in procession, where both she her selfe, and her infant perished in the open streete." Foxe's contrast of Massey with Pope Joan while demonstrating their difference also ties them together, giving us further evidence of the ease of linking the charge of inappropriate sexuality and danger. As to the charge that she murdered her child because she did not plead pregnancy, Foxe suggested she did not know the law. Besides, argued Foxe, even if she were ashamed, would shame have kept her from saving her life? Even if Massey had pleaded pregnancy, Foxe argued, we do not know if this might have saved her. As Foxe pointed out, "How is Master Harding sure of this?" Foxe remarked that Lady Jane, whom Harding himself knew, was "thought to be with childe" at the time of her execution in 1554, a fact that did not save her. While this statement has dubious historicity, it makes the execution of the innocent, heroic Jane, whom Harding had known personally, even more horrific. Another woman, the wife of Bradbreges, burned as a heretic at Canterbury in June 1557 "was

---

59. D. M. Ogier, *Reformation and Society in Guernsey* (Woodbridge, U.K.: Boydell Press, 1996), 53.

60. John Foxe, *Acts and Monuments [...]* (1570 edition), 2128.

61. John Foxe, *Acts and Monuments [...]* (1570 edition), 2131.

thought to be with childe." A closer parallel to the Massey case is that of Elizabeth Pepper, a married woman of about thirty, also described in Foxe, who was burned to death in June 1556 at Stratford the Bowe near London. At the time of her execution, she was about eleven weeks pregnant "as shee testified to one Bosomes wyfe, who then vnloosed her neckerchiefe." When Bosome's wife asked Elizabeth Pepper why she did not tell her judges she was pregnant, she answered, "Why quoth she, they know it well enough." In June 1557 the widow of Bradbreges was burned even though "Thys Bradbreges wife was thought to be with childe."[62]

Foxe finally concluded of Perotine Massey, "whatsoever the woman was, she is now gone." As for Harding, "to byte so bitterly against the dead" shows little decency. "Charitie would have judged the best. Humanitie would have spared the dead. And if he could not foord her hys good word, yet he might have left her cause unto the Lord, which shall judge both her and him."[63] Foxe was not the only Protestant appalled by Massey's fate—or who saw the anti-Catholic propaganda value of the case. William Cecil's 1586 work *The Execution of Justice in England* related the atrocities committed during Mary's reign, including "lamentably destroyed... women, some great with child, [and one] out of whose body the child by fire was expelled alive, and yet also cruelly burned."[64]

Certainly Protestant propagandists were horrified by the fate of Perotine and especially of her child. Early in Elizabeth's reign, the sheriff in charge of the execution was charged and found guilty with murder for the death of the baby boy; however, Elizabeth, as part of her effort to heal the religious divides, pardoned him.[65] Also, in 1563 the English authorities dismissed Helier Gosselin, the bailiff who had ordered the baby to be thrown back in the fire, from office. But, as D. M. Ogier points out, the people of Guernsey appeared not to be so distressed over what Gosselin had done to the baby boy. Two years later, the Guernsey's *États,* as the government is known there, elected him one of the twelve jurats who constituted the island's Royal Court.[66]

There are certain resonances between Joan's story and that of Perotine Massey's. Shakespeare's Joan is very much of an outsider. As Ogier points

---

62. John Foxe, *Acts and Monuments [...]* (1570 edition), 2144, 2167.

63. John Foxe, *Acts and Monuments [...]* (1570 edition), 2132–33, 2167; and John Foxe, *Acts and Monuments [...]* (1583 edition), 1916.

64. William Cecil, *The Execution of Justice in England,* ed. Robert M. Kingdon (Ithaca: Cornell University Press, 1965), 20. For more on Cecil's pamphlet and Allen's response to it, see Wallace T. MacCaffrey, *Queen Elizabeth and the Making of Policy, 1572–1588* (Princeton: Princeton University Press, 1981), 136–39.

65. Jasper Ridley, *Bloody Mary's Martyrs* (New York: Carroll and Graf, 2001), 152, 215.

66. Ogier, *Reformation and Society in Guernsey,* 69.

out, so was Perotine. She was a Protestant in a community that was almost entirely Catholic. And her husband was not only a Protestant, but also a foreigner who was absent. Just as the English feared in Joan a woman who was not under the control of any man, there was no man in the household in which Perotine lived.[67]

Not Saved Through Pleading Pregnancy

English Protestants of the sixteenth century would have been aghast at the accounts in Foxe. But as audience members at Shakespeare's play, would they have had the same sympathy to a French woman labeled a "witch" and a "strumpet"? Nina Levine finds the ending "complicated and troubling" particularly since an Elizabethan audience might regard York and Warwick as "aspiring noblemen whose interests are clearly against those of the nation at large." If the building of English nationhood is one key to the play, as Watkins argues in the next chapter, York and Warwick complicate and sabotage that goal, so that even though the character Joan has called on demons to fight the English, we are not comfortable with the men who destroy her. Donald Watson, however, argues that the audience's response to Joan "begins and ends with derisive laughter. . . . The derisive laughter at Joan's expense returns in the unmasking of her final scene . . . [the] virtuous saint is reduced to revealing her pregnant state to save herself." Yet, as was discussed earlier, we cannot assume with any certainty that the character Joan is telling the truth when she claims to be pregnant, and this certainly does *not* save her. While Hardin suggests that this final scene with Joan "would have greatly amused a mostly male audience," Gabrielle Jackson "wonders what an English audience would have made of . . . Warwick's call for plenty of faggots and extra barrels of pitch for Joan's stake." She adds, "It is altogether difficult to be sure how an Elizabethan audience might have reacted to Joan's punishment. Opinion on witches in 1591 was by no means monolithic."[68] Nor do we

---

    67. Darryl Ogier, "New-born Child Murder in Reformation Guernsey." I greatly appreciate Dr. Ogier sharing this research with me in manuscript.

    68. Levine, *Women's Matters,* 45; Donald G. Watson, *Shakespeare's Early History Plays: Politics at Play on the Elizabethan Stage* (Athens: University of Georgia Press, 1990), 44, 45; Hardin, "Chronicles and Mythmaking," 31; and Gabrielle Bernhard Jackson, "Topical Ideology: Witches, Amazons and Shakespeare's Joan of Arc," *ELR* 18 (1988): 62, 63.

know if it was a mostly male audience. Andrew Gurr suggests that women eagerly came to the theater almost as much as men.[69]

There was a whole range of opinions on witches in 1591. While many were convinced of the reality of women using supernatural power to harm others, only a few years earlier, Reginald Scot in *The Discoverie of Witchcraft* (1584) had scoffed at those who held such beliefs. The fear of witches seems to have increased in the last decade of the sixteenth century and the first decades of the next. Certainly more women were put on trial. Still, as Sharpe points out, there was certainly popular skepticism, and "educated people in Elizabethan and early Stuart England were able to hold a number of intellectual positions on witchcraft."[70] And opinion on Joan of Arc in the sixteenth century, from Polydore Vergil to John Stow, was not uniform either. Many of those who argued that she claimed pregnancy were also convinced that it was a desperate ruse to save her life, an attempt the historical Joan never made. At the end of *1 Henry VI*, the character Joan claims pregnancy and thus allows herself to also be called a strumpet. The criticisms Harding, Allen, and Parsons directed at Perotine Massey echo in our ears here, as does Agnes Samuel's passionate declaration that they might label her a witch but not a whore. Pleading pregnancy saved the lives of a number of women in early modern England, but it seems particularly in witchcraft and heresy cases that the labeling of women as illicitly sexual could also be used to destroy them and their reputations.

Perhaps the greatest irony is that it is not out of the question that the historical Joan was pregnant at the time she was burned. As Anne Barstow and Marina Warner argue, she may well have been raped during her time in prison. In the trial to rehabilitate her character twenty-five years after her death, Guillaume Manchon testified that Joan had several times complained that "one of her guards had tried to rape her." Thomas Marie heard Joan state that "she would rather die than stay any longer in the company of these Englishmen."[71] If Joan indeed had been sexually assaulted, it could at least theoretically have led to a pregnancy. If we today are uncomfortable with a

---

69. Andrew Gurr, "The Theatre and Society," in *The Oxford Illustrated History of Tudor and Stuart Britain,* ed. John Morrill (Oxford: Oxford University Press, 1996), 168. See also Richard Levin, "Women in the Renaissance Theatre Audience," *Shakespeare Quarterly* 40, no. 2 (Summer 1989): 165–74.

70. James Sharpe, *Instruments of Darkness: Witchcraft in England, 1550–1750* (London: Hamish Hamilton, 1996), 56, 165.

71. Anne Barstow, *Joan of Arc: Heretic, Mystic, Shaman* (Lewiston, NY: Edwin Mellen Press, 1986), 115; Warner, *Joan of Arc,* 106; and Regine Pernoud, *The Retrial of Joan of Arc: The Evidence at the Trial for her Rehabilitation, 1450–1456,* trans. J. M. Cohen (New York: Harcourt, Brace, and Co., 1955), 186.

possibly pregnant character Joan being burned at the end of Shakespeare's play, how much more heartrending and tragic to consider the experience of the historical nineteen-year-old Joan of Arc, burned to death in 1431, or, less well known but equally horrific, the burning death of Perotine Massey and her infant son in 1556. Massey never pleaded pregnancy. Shakespeare's Joan did, but it was not enough to save her.

CHAPTER 2

Shakespeare's *1 Henry VI* and the Tragedy of Renaissance Diplomacy

Historicist critics have awarded Shakespeare's *Henry VI* plays a privileged place in the drama of English nation-building. Leah Marcus, Annabel Patterson, and Richard Helgerson hail the features that galled earlier critics—the plays' alleged inconsistencies, stylistic discrepancies, crude depictions of character, and jingoism—as symptoms of the contradictions on which the absolutist state rested.[1] In representing a feudal crisis, Shakespeare seems to have voiced populist positions, such as Jack Cade's, that anticipate the mid-seventeenth-century abrogation of monarchy, or perhaps its constitutional containment in the Glorious Revolution. Critics debate whether Shakespeare's earliest history plays endorse, qualify, repudiate, contain, or exclude the popular discourse that they ventriloquize. But almost everyone agrees that Shakespeare foregrounds conflicts among Crown, aristocracy, and commons that were central to England's rise as a sovereign power.

---

1. Leah S. Marcus, *Puzzling Shakespeare: Local Reading and Its Discontents* (Berkeley: University of California Press, 1988), 51–105; Annabel M. Patterson, *Shakespeare and the Popular Voice* (Oxford: Basil Blackwell, 1989), 32–51; and Richard Helgerson, *Forms of Nationhood: The Elizabethan Writing of England* (Chicago: University of Chicago Press, 1992), 195–245.

As much as this insight has enhanced our understanding of Shakespeare's theater as a national institution, it casts the story of the developing English state as an *intra*-national one. As Deanne Williams notes:

> The constant presence of French kings and princesses in Shakespeare's history plays, and the many references to 'French' customs... in the comedies, have achieved surprisingly little scholarly attention. The afterlife of the seventeenth-century notion of a free, democratic Anglo-Saxon society, recoverable by embracing England's Germanic roots, has instead produced readings of the history plays that, for all the attention that they pay to their portrayal of the emergence of English nationhood, remain strangely blind to the fact that English national identity was underwritten by the legacy of conquest, and produced out of an ongoing dialogue with France.[2]

This tendency is synecdochic of a larger problem in English literary and historical studies: scholars who have addressed the question of early modern nationalism have written as if England's emergence as a nation depended on a synthesis among competing sectors of English society. Yet this insular analysis is precisely what Shakespeare's first tetralogy resists, because it treats *civil* conflicts that have attracted so much attention as the consequence of a prior *international* conflict involving France, England, and their allies.[3]

This international focus has contributed to the first tetralogy's unpopularity. Despite all of their familiar Francophobic jingoism, the diplomatic landscape that they depict is more foreign than the one that Shakespeare later created in *Henry V.* In *Henry V,* national boundaries are more clearly drawn, and the conflict between France and England appears more like one between modern states. The play opens with the two kingdoms confronting each other on opposite sides of the channel. Although the justification for Henry's strike against the French depends on an English claim to French territory, the Salic law speech drives recollections of a shared Angevin identity so far into

---

2. Deanne Williams, *The French Fetish from Chaucer to Shakespeare* (Cambridge: Cambridge University Press, 2004), 184. Williams's chapter on Shakespeare is the most recent and useful treatment of his engagement with the French. See also the essays collected in two special journal issues, "France in the English and French Theatre of the Renaissance" (*Renaissance Studies* 9, 1995) and "Shakespeare and France" (*Shakespeare Yearbook* 5, 1994).

3. Like other historians of diplomacy, I use the term *international* with considerable hesitation in reference to relationships among premodern powers. As Daniela Frigo cautions, it "presupposes the existence of nations, or at least of 'homogeneous' political organizations, which establish relationships with each other." Frigo, "Introduction," *Politics and Diplomacy in Early Modern Italy: The Structure of Diplomatic Practice, 1450–1800,* ed. Frigo (Cambridge: Cambridge University Press, 2000), 8.

the medieval past that they look like a trumped-up excuse. Shakespeare ends the play before he has to imagine the political and dramatic consequences of a channel-spanning empire.

Yet that was the task that he took on almost a decade before when he wrote *1 Henry VI,* a play that opens with Henry V's funeral and the union of French and English crowns in the person of his infant successor. Boundaries are blurrier and personal loyalties less distinct than in the second tetralogy. Shakespeare never fully assimilates the parcelized geographies of fifteenth-century feudalism to the neater outlines of the sixteenth-century French and England nation-states. Instead, he captures both countries at a moment of contingency in their development. The England that he imagines on the basis of his chronicle sources was not the England in which he lived. Late medieval France, divided into competing apanages, bore even less resemblance to late-sixteenth-century France.

By approaching *1 Henry VI* as a play about the Hundred Years' War as well as the Wars of the Roses, as a story not just about England but also about France, Burgundy, and their interactions, I will de-nationalize the history that dominates our understanding of the English sixteenth century. *1 Henry VI* scripts England's story as a struggle between competing sectors of English society. But it embeds this struggle within an international one that overdetermines seemingly indigenous English politics. The play is unique within Shakespeare's canon in its response to shifts in diplomatic practice that contributed directly to the rise of the absolutist and, later, bourgeois states in England, France, and ultimately throughout Europe. Some of its most puzzling theatrical moments—Joan of Arc's corruption of Burgundy and Margaret of Anjou's sudden appearance as Joan's posthumous surrogate—acquire new clarity when we read them as a repudiation of older images of how to establish alliances between warring powers.

Marcus and others have taken the play's misogynistic focus on Joan and Margaret as symptomatic of an ambivalence toward female sovereignty that centered on Elizabeth I. But misogyny in *Henry VI* has less to do with sovereignty per se than with modes of diplomacy that were falling into disrepute— in part because of their association with women. Women bore much of the cost of the transition to a state-centered diplomacy. As an absolute monarch, Elizabeth and her late-sixteenth-century peers—Mary Tudor, Mary Stuart, Elisabeth of Valois, and Catherine de' Medici—occupied an uncertain territory between a Europe centered on the feudal dynasty and a Europe centered on the nation-state. Women played a primary role in traditional dynastic diplomacy, with its focus on interdynastic marriage as a means of sealing alliances. Queens consort often intervened in international disputes, and some, such as Marguerite de Navarre, served as negotiators. The old forms were still in place during Elizabeth's lifetime, but particularly in merchant London, men were beginning to imagine a new practice that bypassed dynastic prerogatives in favor of imagined national interests. Shakespeare's *Henry VI* reinforced the misogynistic underpinnings of this new patriotism and the foreign policy that it espoused.

Rival Diplomacies and the Early Modern State

In their recounting of the *dynastic* rivalry between the Plantagenets and Valois, Shakespeare's *Henry VI* plays fostered a culture of *national* rivalry that outlasted the constitutionalization of monarchy in England and its extirpation in France. Writing after the death of feudal diplomacy but before the flowering of modern diplomacy in the early nineteenth century, Shakespeare captured the drama of evolving attitudes toward what was becoming—but had not yet become—a European community of nations. His plays enact an archaeology revealing aspects of at least three important moments in international relations theory and practice. They recall a period when negotiations unfolded primarily under the aegis of canon law, still revered as a body of common European opinion. But that consensus was already eroding during the period that Shakespeare represents in his first tetralogy and had yielded by his time to a balance among rival absolute monarchies that recognized no common authority. By the late 1590s, moreover, that dominant absolutist model was yielding in England to an even later configuration that separated the interests of the Crown from those of the imagined political nation so that the last traces of feudal diplomacy—treaties sealed by royal marriages and the like—were falling into disrepute.

As David Aers has argued, any discussion of the early modern period as a transition between medieval and modern worlds risks oversimplifying, even sentimentalizing, medieval life.[4] To reduce that risk, I emphasize that any codification of diplomatic theory stands in a vexed relationship to actual diplomatic practice. Trumpeting their commitment to a European *res publica Christiana* in the face of endemic warfare, theorists from Gulielmus Durandus, writing in the thirteenth century, to Bernard du Rosier, writing during the Hundred Years' War, can sound naively idealistic. The more they claimed

---

4. David Aers, "A Whisper in the Ear of Early Modernists; or, Reflections on Literary Critics Writing the 'History of the Subject,'" in *Culture and History, 1350–1600: Essays on English Communities, Identities, and Writing,* ed. Aers (Detroit: Wayne State University Press, 1992), 177–202.

that an ambassador's primary commitment was to the peace of Europe, the more that actual ambassadors fought for the particular governments they represented. Theorists envisioned an ordered society descending from Pope and Emperor working together for the good of Christendom.[5] But nothing was more common in medieval diplomacy than conflict between popes and emperors. Despite some of the most idealistic statements about the sanctity of the ambassador's office ever written, actual ambassadors engaged in Machiavellian intrigue long before Machiavelli.[6]

But even if there was no simple correspondence between medieval reflection on diplomacy and the work of ambassadors and princes, the theory was not irrelevant. Although popes and emperors were never above the political fray, appeals to papal and imperial mediation could pave the way to effective negotiations, truces, and treaties. Innocent III, for example, resolved a seemingly intractable imperial election of 1208 in favor of Otto IV and arbitrated a conflict between France and Denmark when Philip Augustus tried to divorce his Danish wife.[7] Perhaps even more significantly, the belief that the peace of Christendom mattered more than the interests of its individual components elevated the tone of diplomatic conversation and established parameters for seeking neutrality.

The argument that an ambassador's first commitment was to the peace of Europe never completely died, but with the consolidation of nation-states it lost much of its force. During the Italian Renaissance, when the Pope's identity as yet another prince was felt with particular acuity, theorists downplayed the *res publica Christiana* and touted instead the ambassador's allegiance to his employer. The Venetian Ermolao Barbaro, for instance, urged in *De officio legati* that an ambassador must follow orders without question and should never consider himself wiser than his superiors.[8] For Barbaro and other Renaissance writers, loyalty to the state defined diplomatic responsibility.

---

5. See J. N. Figgis, *From Gerson to Grotius* (Cambridge: Cambridge University Press, 1923), 31–54; R. W. and A. J. Carlyle, *A History of Medieval Political Theory in the West* (London, 1936), 6:111–71; and Garrett Mattingly, *Renaissance Diplomacy* (1955; repr. New York: Dover, 1988), 15–22. Durandus's diplomatic reflections and du Rosier's 1436 *Ambaxiator brevilogus prosaico moralique dogmate pro felice et prospero ducato circa ambaxiatas insistencium excerptus* are both available in Vladimir E. Hraber, *De Legatis et legationibus tractatus varii* (Dorpat, 1906).

6. See John Watkins, "Introduction: Toward a New History of Medieval and Early Modern Diplomacy," *Journal of Medieval and Early Modern Studies* 38 (2008): 2–3.

7. See Jane Sayers, *Innocent III: Leader of Europe, 1198–1216* (New York: Longman, 1994), 41–93.

8. Ermolao Barbaro, *De coelibatu—De officio legati* (1489–91), ed. Vittore Branca (Florence: Olschki, 1969). See also Douglas Biow's discussion of Barbaro in *Doctors, Ambassadors, Secretaries: Humanism and Professions in Renaissance Italy* (Chicago: University of Chicago Press, 2002), 108–20.

Ideas like Barbaro's bore their greatest fruit north of the Alps, where they reinforced monarchical centralization. In Tudor England and late Valois France, the notion that the ambassador's highest loyalty was to his king superseded claims of his more general duties to Christendom. In England, the ideal of a pan-European *res publica Christiana* was last voiced, and last adopted as the basis of diplomatic policy, by Henry VIII's Catholic chancellors, Thomas Wolsey and Thomas More. After the break with Rome, it acquired distinctly conservative, even reactionary, associations. A new discourse of international relations prevailed, one that transferred epithets and recriminations once reserved for the Turk to the Pope and, more broadly, to Catholic Europe.[9]

Henry VIII was happy to encourage any discourse that reinforced his independence from a repudiated papacy. But an apocalyptic view of international affairs threatened to wrest diplomatic initiative from the same monarchs who had only recently broken the pope's claim to speak for an international *consensus fidelium*. Propagandists like John Bale and later John Foxe made the new discourse for discussing foreign affairs available to popular audiences. Throughout the Middle Ages, neither the commons in England nor their representatives in Parliament had much to say, at least officially, about international policy.[10] Although this was still comparatively true throughout the Tudor period, under Elizabeth Parliament began meddling more in international matters—provided the perceived importance was high enough. Almost every time Elizabeth clashed with her House of Commons—over her leniency toward Mary Stuart, her reluctance to marry, or her refusal to name a successor—the conflict involved England's relationship with foreign powers. From Elizabeth's perspective, nothing stood more outside the liberties of Parliament than discussions about the marriage and succession settlements through which the Crown aligned itself with foreign powers.

By the time Elizabeth and her leading parliamentarians fell out over her possible marriage to the Duke of Alençon, a radically Protestant view of England's place in Europe, one with apocalyptic overtones, had coincided with the parliamentary assumption of a right to debate the nation's foreign policy.[11] The condemnation of Catholic Europeans as agents of the Antichrist was virtually inseparable from Parliament's determination to engage

9. See Mattingly, *Renaissance Diplomacy,* 164–78.

10. See P. S. Crowson, *Tudor Foreign Policy* (London: Adam and Charles Black, 1973), 33–36; John Ferguson, *English Diplomacy, 1422–1461* (Oxford: Clarendon Press, 1972), xviii–xxi; and H. G. Richardson, "The Commons and Medieval Politics," *Transactions of the Royal Historical Society,* 4th series, vol. 28 (1946): 21–45.

11. See Susan Doran, *Monarchy and Matrimony: The Courtships of Elizabeth I* (London: Routledge, 1996), 130–94.

questions previously reserved to the monarch and privy council. The parliamentarians who were most vocal in urging Elizabeth to marry, to name a successor, or to execute her Scottish cousin were the ones most committed to the Protestantization of Europe. The most extreme awaited the day when England might lead a crusade against Rome itself.[12]

As threatening as Elizabeth found Jesuit assassins and Spanish armadas, she knew that she also had much to lose from a parliamentary seizure of diplomatic initiative. As the next century demonstrated, Parliament's increased involvement in affairs of state signaled a dramatic reorientation in the country's foreign policy. Dynastic imperatives yielded to the interests of the nation at large, interests that were increasingly imagined to conflict with the monarch's private ambitions. During the Hundred Years' War, for example, the relationship between France and England followed from that between the Houses of Valois and Plantagenet. England went to war against France to assert its claim to lands presumably inherited from the interdynastic marriages of English kings to Eleanor of Aquitaine and Isabelle of France. During Elizabeth's reign, several dynastic marriages, including two with the Valois, failed to materialize because Elizabeth subordinated her dynastic interests to other considerations, including the preservation of her country's Protestant integrity. One obvious consequence of this relegation of dynastic considerations to second or even third place in national foreign policy was the extinction of the House of Tudor itself upon Elizabeth's death.

In terms of foreign policy, Elizabeth's virginity mattered not simply as a way of dodging entanglements in the conflict between the Habsburgs and the Valois. More generally, Elizabeth's decision not to marry contributed, indirectly, to the emergence of a diplomacy centered on national rather than dynastic interests.[13] For centuries, marriages between heads of states or their heirs had been the lynchpin of negotiations between allies and belligerents alike. In 1559, for example, Henri II and Philip II sealed the most important European treaty of the sixteenth century—the treaty of Cateau-Cambrésis conceding domination of the Italian peninsula to Spain—through Philip's marriage to Henri's daughter Elisabeth.[14] Since Elizabeth I acceded to the English throne only a few months before the treaty was finalized, diplomats throughout the continent wondered whether the balance between Spanish

12. See Fulke Greville's account of Sidney's internationalist vision in his so-called *Life of Sidney*, that is, *A Dedication to Sir Philip Sidney*, in *The Prose Works of Fulke Greville, Lord Brooke*, ed. John Gouws (Oxford: Clarendon Press, 1986), 69–71.

13. See Doran, *Monarchy and Matrimony*, 210–18.

14. See R. J. Knecht, *The Rise and Fall of Renaissance France, 1483–1610*, 2nd ed. (Oxford: Blackwell, 2001), 230–45.

Habsburg and French Valois interests would survive Elizabeth's likely marriage into one or the other royal houses.[15] As things turned out, Elizabeth
kept aloof from both, in the process changing the fundamental nature of
European politics.

Elizabeth herself seems to have feared that her decision indirectly abetted
parliamentary, and even popular, encroachments on her diplomatic prerogatives. In insisting on her right to choose or to reject particular suitors, and
ultimately to reject marriage altogether, she repeatedly asserted the monarch's
centrality in foreign affairs. She vented her especial distaste for popular discussion of England's relationship with foreign countries on men like John
Stubbs, who lost his hand for arguing that national religious interests *ought*
to prevail over the queen's private wishes.[16] Elizabeth was happy enough to
talk about her sacrifices for the welfare of the English nation. But she always
saw those sacrifices as instances of monarchical grace rather than duty or
obligation. She certainly did not see them as concessions to a foreign policy
scripted in Commons or, worse yet, in pulpits, pamphlets, conventicles, and
theaters.

Throughout Elizabeth's reign, few things tested the boundaries of what
the queen thought of as legitimate and illegitimate venues for discussions
about foreign affairs as much as the perennial question of a foreign marriage. Whenever a match between Elizabeth and a foreign suitor seemed
likely, writers across the spectrum of literate society admonished her about
her duties to her country. Elizabeth pursued an interdynastic marriage most
earnestly during the years 1579–81, when it seemed that she might actually
wed the Duke of Alençon to block Habsburg aggression in the Netherlands
and in the Atlantic. Sir Philip Sidney opposed the alliance in a *Letter to Queen
Elizabeth Touching Her Marriage to Monsieur,* and Edmund Spenser challenged
it in the political allegory of *The Shepheardes Calender.*[17]

Although the Armada and the outbreak of war with Spain aligned Elizabeth's diplomatic agenda with the aspirations of left-leaning Protestants like

---

15. See John Watkins, "Elizabeth through Venetian Eyes," *Explorations in Renaissance Culture* 30
(2004): 121–38.

16. See Ilona Bell, "'Souereaigne Lord of lordly Lady of this land': Elizabeth, Stubbs, and the
Gaping Gvlf," in *Dissing Elizabeth: Negative Representations of Gloriana,* ed. Julia M. Walker (Durham:
Duke University Press, 1998), 99–117.

17. See Paul E. McLane, *Spenser's* Shepheardes Calender: *A Study in Elizabethan Allegory* (Notre
Dame: University of Notre Dame Press, 1961); David Norbrook, *Poetry and Politics in the English
Renaissance* (London: Routledge and Kegan Paul, 1984), 69–90; and Annabel Patterson, *Pastoral and
Ideology: Virgil to Valéry* (Berkeley: University of California Press, 1987), 118–27. See also Marcus's
discussion of the Alençon incident with specific reference to *1 Henry VI* in *Puzzling Shakespeare,*
71–74.

Spenser, the conflict between dynastic and nationalist interpretations of foreign policy haunted the literature of the 1590s. These years witnessed the emergence of the Elizabethan history play as a distinctive theatrical genre. Although historicist critics have treated these plays as expressions of domestic anxieties over succession, the queen's gender, and rivalries between competing ranks and regions, they have not have not accounted for these plays' concern with England's place in a European order. With their retrospective glance at the preconditions, troubled course, and humiliating conclusion of the Hundred Years' War, tragedies from Marlowe's *Edward II* to Shakespeare's epic Lancastrian cycle served as one of the first popular media for developing, representing, and disseminating opinions about foreign policy. A single production of one of these plays probably reached a wider audience than any political pamphlet or courtly allegory written during the period. Cutting across the country's divisions of rank and occupation, they allowed even illiterate theatergoers to participate at least in the fantasy of deliberations about their country's security.[18]

At least one early modern ambassador, Sir Henry Wotton, expressed dismay over the spectacle of common players staging affairs of state before artisans and their apprentices:

> The Kings' players had a new play, called *All is true,* representing some principal pieces of the reign of Henry VIII, which was set forth with many extraordinary circumstances of pomp and majesty, even to the matting of the stage: the Knights of the order with their Georges and garters, the Guards with their embroidered coats, and the like: sufficient in truth within a while to make greatness very familiar, if not ridiculous.[19]

Wotton was anything but idealistic with respect to his own profession. In a famous quip, he defined the ambassador as a "man sent to lie abroad for his country's good."[20] He realized that successful negotiation entailed deceit. But he also recognized that such an urbane, Machiavellian insight was the

---

18. See Alfred Harbage, *Shakespeare's Audience* (New York: Columbia University Press, 1941); Ann Jennalie Cook, *The Privileged Playgoers of Shakespeare's London, 1576–1642* (Princeton: Princeton University Press, 1981); Andrew Gurr, *Playgoing in Shakespeare's London,* 2nd ed. (Cambridge: Cambridge University Press, 1996); and Louis Montrose, *The Purpose of Playing: Shakespeare and the Cultural Politics of the Elizabethan Theatre* (Chicago: University of Chicago Press, 1996), 41–52.

19. Letter to Sir Edmund Bacon, July 2, 1613, in *The Life and Letters of Sir Henry Wotton,* ed. Logan Pearsall Smith (Oxford: Clarendon Press, 1907), 2:32–33.

20. *"Legatus est vir bonus peregre missus ad mentiendum Reipublicae causa,"* attributed to Wotton by Isaac Walton. See Mattingly, *Renaissance Diplomacy,* 274n7.

prerogative of the highest social ranks. Nothing was more unsettling to him than this performance of Shakespeare's *Henry VIII,* with its public exposition of struggles involving kings, popes, emperors, and cast-off consorts. Perhaps his recollection of the play's title as *All is true* reveals the heart of his anxiety. Although he condemned the play as an act of grotesque feigning, what most alarmed him was its proximity to truth. The actors dressed up in clothes probably once sported by actual aristocrats did not misrepresent "greatness"; the players represented the truth of state so well that the humblest viewer could become as familiar with it, and as cynical about it, as Wotton himself.

By making "greatness very familiar, if not ridiculous," Shakespeare's history plays occupy a troubled space between an older order in which the monarch's dynastic interests counted for everything and an emerging one in which they would count for nothing. At their most radical, the plays raised the possibility that a monarch might act against his or her country's interests by managing military and diplomatic affairs. This concern lends itself to the representation of the reign of Henry VI, during which the Hundred Years' War finally ended with a decisive English defeat. That defeat—which looms proleptically even over plays treating earlier Plantagenet reigns—seemed to expose all the dangers inherent in the older, dynastically driven foreign policy that the plays repudiate. Shakespeare attributes England's disgrace to the apparatus through which medieval dynastic diplomacy had been conducted: the relaxation and reassertion of feudal obligations, marriage alliances between former belligerents, and submission to the international authority of the Roman Church.

Early in the play, *1 Henry VI* inscribes an intertextual trace of departures from medieval diplomatic culture. When the English beat back the French from the walls of Orléans "with Great loss," the Duke Alanson notes that the English have shown such valor from the beginning of the century-long conflict:

> Froissard, a countryman of ours, records
> England all Olivers and Rolands bred
> During the time Edward the Third did reign.
> More truly now may this be verified,
> For none but Samsons and Goliases
> It sendeth forth to skirmish. (1.2.29–34)

By noting that the English are still formidable, Alanson asserts continuity between the reigns of Edward III and Henry VI. But his lines themselves belie that claim. Froissart's generosity toward the English belongs to a lost chivalric past, when the French and English could admire each other's martial accomplishments even at the height of battle. In referring to the English soldiers as latterday Olivers and Rolands, Froissart paid them the highest French compliment, since Oliver and Roland, the heroes of the *Chanson de Roland,* were prototypical Frankish heroes.[21] His admiration points to a common aristocratic culture that transcended ethnic and national difference. According to its codes, any Englishman who fought valiantly was worthy of being a Roland.

Yet the moment Alanson recalls Froissart's compliment, he degrades it in ways that reinforce the play's emphasis on an irreconcilable enmity between the English and the French. In his updated version of the original comparison, Roland and Oliver yield to Samson and Goliath as the prototypes of the English soldiers. The exchange cancels out the suggestion that a modern Englishman could ever be as valiant as one of the great Frankish heroes of the *chansons de geste.* At the same time, the new biblical allusions are drastically doubled-edged. Although Samson was an Israelite hero, he was known not only for his strength but also for his fatal and scandalous attachment to his Philistine wife. The Bible does not present Goliath as a hero but as the champion of the Philistines, a people condemned for their incursions against the Israelites. Early Christian exegetes allegorized Goliath's confrontation with David as a type of Satan's battle against the Church.[22] Both allusions associate the English, who are fighting to maintain their occupation of France, with Philistine oppression of Israel. Within the larger context of the play, the reference to Samson foreshadows Henry VI's destructive foreign marriage to Margaret of Anjou at the end of the play.

Alanson's passing memory of Froissart's international chivalry thus evaporates into the nationality-based invective and mutual recrimination that pervades the play. After all, the same Alanson has already mocked the famished English as "mules" who must have their "provender tied to their mouths, / Or piteous they will look like drowned mice" (1.2.10, 11–12). Nor does Shakespeare suggest that a return to the more chivalrous, internationalist perspective of Froissart is in order. The English speak just as coarsely of the

21. As recent scholarship has suggested, Froissart's attitudes toward the English changed throughout his career with his changes in patronage. Shakespeare would have known Froissart primarily through the English translation by John Bourchier, Lord Berners, *The chronycles of Englande, Fraunce, Spayne,* 2 vols. (London: Richarde Pynson, 1523–25). This translation made predictably good use of the earlier, pro-English versions of the *Chroniques.* See Peter Ainsworth, "Jean Froissart: A Sexcentenary Reappraisal," *French Studies* 59 (2005): 364–72; and J. J. N. Palmer, *Froissart, Historian* (Woodbridge, U.K.: Boydell Press, 1981).

22. See Raymond-Jean Frontain and Jan Wojcik, eds., *The David Myth in Western Literature* (West Lafayette, IN: Purdue University Press, 1979).

French as the French do of the English. Talbot, arguably the play's hero, first broaches the puns on "*dauphin*" and "*pucelle*" through which the English ridicule the French court and Catholic faith:

> Pucelle or puzzel, Dolphin or dogfish,
> Your hearts I'll stamp out with my horse's heels,
> And make a quagmire of your mingled brains. (1.4.107–9)

Chivalry descends to violence in Talbot's fantasy. Throughout the play, such vilification of the French, rather than any expressed devotion to king and country, marks the true-blooded Englishman.

Instead of presenting the French and English as equal participants in a pan-European chivalric culture, Shakespeare portrays them as quintessentially different with respect to religion, warfare, government, gender, sexuality, and personal ethics. The English are Protestants before their time. They have a simple and sincere faith in God, best expressed by Talbot's plainspoken oaths by "God and Saint George" (4.2.55). The French, on the other hand, practice a Catholicism that quickly degenerates from Joan of Arc's ostensibly superstitious and spurious devotion to the Virgin to open sorcery. The English win battles through manly displays of courage; the French win through subterfuge. Unlike Talbot, who rebuffs the Countess of Auvergne's Delilah-like efforts to seduce him, the French wallow in sensuality. By the time Joan of Arc goes to her execution, she confesses to sleeping with so many Frenchmen that we can have no idea who fathered her unborn child. Wanton sexuality and a promiscuous transgression of gender boundaries mark an indelible foreignness that distinguished the French from the trustworthy English.

Given these irreconcilable differences, the only acceptable relationship between the two states is warfare. The diplomatic overtures that would have been possible in the days of Froissart no longer work. The play discredits any rapprochement between the two realms as a threat to English integrity. Above all, diplomatic outreach threatens to infect the English with the effeminacy and cowardice that defines the foreign for Shakespeare and his Elizabethan audience.

The Repudiation of Peace: Shakespeare and the Treaty of Arras

When Elizabeth I delivered her final speech to Parliament on December 19, 1601, she surveyed her conflict with Spain in words that probably fell short of satisfying the hawks in her audience. The landing of four thousand Spanish troops in Ireland had encouraged the members to grant one of the reign's most generous subsidies, but it had also unleashed a tide of rhetoric painting the conflict as one between absolute good and evil. Addressing the queen on the last day of the session, Speaker Croke condemned Spaniards and English Catholics alike as agents of Antichrist: "Were not their eyes more than blind, they might see the hand of God against them, and His protecting arm toward you . . . even His angel to stand in the way against them, and God Himself to withstand them."[23] Throughout the second half of the Tudor century, this was familiar rhetoric. Like other Protestants, Croke painted his queen as a defender of the Reformation in the face of Catholic perfidy. In one sense, Philip III's continuation of his father Philip II's crusade against England gave assertive Protestants just what they wanted: an international Catholic menace that could unite Protestant Europe.

A costly, long-lasting, and multi-front war was the last thing the frugal Elizabeth ever wanted. Even though the Queen was grateful for the subsidy, her response to Croke implicitly criticized his rhetoric and its apocalyptic view of foreign affairs. Instead of painting the presence of Spanish troops as the Antichrist's encroachment, she condemned it as the betrayal of dynastic ties that dated back to the Late Middle Ages and that she herself had respected:

> For to let you know what is not perhaps understood by any other than such as are conversant in state matters and keep true records of dealings past, even that potent prince the king of Spain (whose soul I trust be now in heaven), that hath so many ways assailed both my realm and me, had as many provocations of kindness by my just proceedings as by hard measure he hath such returned.[24]

Even when the United Provinces had begged Elizabeth to champion them against Philip II's alleged tyranny, Elizabeth held back: "I was so far from forgetting that old league that had lasted long between the race of Burgundy and my progenitors and the danger that might grow to many states by giving countenance or encouragement to opposition against the prince in one, as I dissuaded."[25] Elizabeth downplayed Croke's emphasis on the sectarian

23. Quoted in J. E. Neale, *Elizabeth I and Her Parliaments, 1584–1601,* 2 vols. (New York: St. Martin's Press, 1958), 2:424.

24. "Queen Elizabeth's Final Speech Before Parliament," Version 1, in *Elizabeth I: Collected Works,* ed. Leah S. Marcus et al. (Chicago: University of Chicago Press, 2000), 348.

25. "Queen Elizabeth's Final Speech," 349.

basis of the conflict with Spain. Even though the Dutch rebels shared her Protestantism, she was reluctant to aid them out of loyalty to the European monarchical system.

More specifically, she resisted supporting the rebellion out of her respect for "that old league that had lasted long between the race of Burgundy and my progenitors." The reference to Burgundy confuses modern readers, who associate Burgundy with a region of France southeast of Paris. But for Elizabeth's original audience, the phrase recalled the ties that bound England to the Dukes of Burgundy during the Hundred Years' War. Although technically vassals of the French king, the Burgundian dukes were enormously powerful. Their demesne included not only large portions of modern-day France but also Belgium and the Netherlands. As they consolidated these holdings into a single administrative unit, they wielded so much diplomatic influence that modern historians still refer to the period from 1363 to 1477 as "the Burgundian century." When Mary of Burgundy married the future Habsburg Holy Roman Emperor in 1477, the union of Burgundian and Habsburg lines set the stage for Elizabeth I's greatest diplomatic challenge: the Spanish king's claim to the Netherlands in his capacity as duke of Burgundy. As Philip II's name reminded everyone, he was the heir and descendent of Philip the Good, the same duke of Burgundy who figures as a pivotal character in Shakespeare's *1 Henry VI.* From Elizabeth's perspective, England's confrontation with Spain and its troubles over the Netherlands were chapters in a story of Anglo-Burgundian diplomacy dating back to the early fifteenth century.

This perspective countered those painting England's war with Spain as an apocalyptic showdown. Instead of concentrating on the opposition between Roman and Reformed religion, Elizabeth reminded her audience that England and the Burgundians who ruled Spain had long been allies. Without Philip the Good's support, for example, England would never have wrested the concessions from Charles VI of France that Shakespeare commemorated at end of *Henry V.* Throughout much of the fifteenth century, Elizabeth's Plantagenet "progenitors" had depended on their Burgundian alliance to counter France.[26] According to Elizabeth, she had tried to honor this alliance as long as possible, even if it meant overlooking the sufferings of her coreligionists. Her priority was clear: respect for the dynastic alliances that had developed over centuries. In her speech, she approached the current war

---

26. See Ferguson, *English Diplomacy,* 1–34; Crowson, *Tudor Foreign Policy,* 47–58; and Marie-Rose Thielemans, *Bourgogne et Angleterre: Rélations Politiques et Economiques entre les Pays-Bas Bourgignons et L'Angleterre, 1435–1467* (Brussels: Presses Universitaires de Bruxelles, 1966).

not with the zeal of an apocalyptic crusader but with the reservation of a prince committed to the rights and dignities of her fellow monarchs. She even expressed her hope that the soul of her old enemy, Philip II, "be now in heaven," a wish that may have unsettled her more zealous auditors (348).

The rhetorical tension between Elizabeth and Croke reflected a conflict between rival diplomatic visions and divergent historiographies. Elizabeth saw Europe in terms of dynastic loyalties that had been honored, strengthened, disregarded, forgotten, and, in recent history, tragically broken. But her words left open the possibility of peace between belligerent parties, and she never demonized the fellow monarch whose soul she hoped rests in heaven. The sincerity of that wish was beside the point. What mattered was her public assent to an older diplomatic model, in which all Europeans were imagined to be capable of working toward peace in common hope of salvation. Her words could not have contrasted more emphatically with Croke's sense of England as engaged in a religious war that precluded a diplomatic resolution.

In *Henry VI,* Shakespeare anticipates Elizabeth's effort to see Europe in terms of fifteenth-century alliances. Whereas Elizabeth recalled a friendship recently betrayed by Philip II and his son, however, Shakespeare concentrates on a bitter moment in England's century-long rapport with the Dukes of Burgundy: the 1435 treaty of Arras, in which the Burgundian duke Philip the Good aligned himself with Charles VII of France against his former English allies. The treaty concluded what was arguably the first peace conference in European history. It was also indecisive. Philip the Good's alliance with France was half-hearted at best; within three years, he was ready to approach England for a possible reconciliation. Philip ultimately favored the Yorkists in their struggle for the English throne, and the Yorkist victory of 1467 ensured a strong relationship between the realms.[27]

Shakespeare's treatment of Philip the Good's defection is one of his most salient revisions of the historical record in the chronicles. To appreciate most fully how he transformed it into an indictment of the unreliability of dynastic alliance, and arguably of diplomacy itself, we need to recall the circumstances that gave rise to the treaty. Regardless of how enthusiastically Henry V's eulogists hailed his consolidation of the French and English monarchies in

---

27. See Joycelyne Gledhill Dickinson, *The Congress of Arras, 1453: A Study in Medieval Diplomacy* (Oxford: Clarendon Press, 1955); Thielemans, *Bourgogne et Angleterre,* 65–107; Robin Neillands, *The Hundred Years War* (London: Routledge, 1990), 266–72; Richard Vaughan, *Philip the Good* (1970; repr. Woodbridge, Suffolk: Boydell Press, 2000), 98–126; and Bertram Wolffe, *Henry VI* (1981; repr. New Haven: Yale University Press, 2001), 81–83.

the treaty of Tours, the trans-Channel imperium was impossible to maintain with the resources available to any fifteenth-century monarch. By 1435, the war was costing £170,000 a year, roughly six times the English king's annual revenue.[28] The French were no better off. Much of the war had been fought on French soil, and Charles VII was having problems financing his efforts to regain the lands conquered by Henry V. Nor were the belligerents the only Europeans invested in peace. Pope Martin V actively encouraged peace negotiations, not least because he wanted to focus Catholic powers on suppressing heresy in Bohemia.

When Philip the Good finally convened the council at Arras in July, he hosted representatives not only from France and England but also from Norway, Denmark, Sicily, the Holy Roman Empire, the Church, and other European states. It was a spectacular, and in great part futile, testimony to the belief that all Christendom had a stake in the peace of Europe. Since the English representatives were given no room to negotiate over the question of their king's claim to the French throne, they soon withdrew from the conference and left the field to Philip and Charles, who came to terms, even if they did not fully resolve their differences. England's Henry VI, who was only thirteen, was stunned to learn that Philip had made a separate peace with Charles.[29] Londoners took up their king's outrage. In early 1436, they captured some Burgundian merchants returning from Portugal to Bruges and confiscated their goods. In even more aggressive defiance of international law, the English imprisoned two Burgundian ambassadors and confiscated their letters. According to a French chronicle, the ambassadors—who had been entrusted by Philip the Good to persuade Henry VI's government to accept Charles VII's terms for peace—barely escaped with their lives.[30]

The first English chroniclers, whose work had a direct bearing on Hall's, Holinshed's, and ultimately Shakespeare's interpretations of these events, roundly condemned Burgundy's Philip the Good as an opportunist who had betrayed his English overlord. Certainly Philip stood to profit from the peace, although modern historians agree that he was ultimately duped by Charles VII, who seems to have made several promises he had no intention of fulfilling. But the chronicles never take issue with the principal reason for the congress's failure to achieve a lasting peace: the English representatives' refusal to compromise on their king's claim to the French throne. England put itself in a terrible position, one that was soon to get much worse. Although it did

28. Neillands, *The Hundred Years War,* 276.
29. See Wolffe, *Henry VI,* 83.
30. See Ferguson, *English Diplomacy,* 21.

not have the resources to win a decisive victory against Charles VII, it also refused to enter into a meaningful diplomatic conversation. The acts that followed its defection from the Congress of Arras—especially its attack on the Burgundian ambassadors—signaled its repudiation not just of traditional diplomatic conventions and immunities but of any commitment to the peace of Europe as the basis for foreign relations as well.

By the time Shakespeare inherited the chroniclers' biased account of Arras, he used it to transform a fifteenth-century dynastic conflict into a sixteenth-century drama of national consciousness. In the late sixteenth century, England's diplomatic and military objectives—with the major exception of its colonizing relationship with Ireland—were primarily defensive. It had to ward off Habsburg aggression in Spain, and it feared the threat of an expansion of French Valois power in the Netherlands. England's position was diametrically opposed to what it had been a hundred fifty years earlier, when it played the aggressor in France. Shakespeare's play transfers the urgency of England's situation in the post-Armada years back to the Late Middle Ages.

Throughout the play, the "good" characters—Bedford, Gloucester, Talbot—speak as if an encroachment on the English *occupation* of France were tantamount to an attack on England itself. As a loyal messenger laments in informing the English regency council of French revolt against English rule, "Cropp'd are the flower-de-luces in your arms, / Of England's coat one half is cut away" (1.1.80–81). From his perspective, which all true Englishmen endorse, the fleur-de-lis in the English coat of arms represents sovereignty over French territory as an immutable aspect of England's own national integrity. Those who even consider the possibility of a negotiated settlement—Winchester, Suffolk—come off as traitors. In the play's jingoistic historiography, any rapprochement so damages England that civil war becomes inevitable.

The play's ultimate traitor is the English ally, Philip of Burgundy. But as Shakespeare reduces the complexities of Arras to a forty-line encounter involving Burgundy, Charles VII, and Joan of Arc, he adapts the historical record to make national loyalty dangerous. Up to this point in the play, Burgundy has appeared as a proponent of the English cause who upbraids Charles for his "treason" against Henry and quips in hearty English fashion about Joan's cross-dressing (2.1.19–24). But as soon as Joan calls him to parley, her words strip away this English veneer and create in him an identity as a patriotic Frenchman. Ironically sounding like a Tudor tract against the evils of civil war, she accuses him of betraying his own nation:

Look on thy country, look on fertile France,
And see the cities and the towns defac'd

By wasting ruin of the cruel foe.
As looks the mother on her lowly babe
When death doth close his tender-dying eyes. (3.3.44–48)

In a magnificent projection of her own ambiguous gender onto her spell-bound interlocutor, she invites Burgundy to look on France with the eyes of a mother watching her child's death. As he yields to her, a maternal bond to the soil, cities, and towns of suffering France supplants his martial, masculinist alliances with the Englishmen and makes them seem—at least to him—superficial: "I am vanquished. These haughty words of hers / Have batt'red me like roaring cannon-shot / And made me almost yield upon my knees" (3.3.78–80).

Shakespeare's fantasy rests on a distortion of history. Joan died in 1431, four years before the Congress of Arras. Her capture by Burgundian soldiers and transfer into English hands marked a salient instance of Philip's cooperation with the English. By suppressing Burgundy's complicity in her tragedy and making him instead her dupe, Shakespeare discredits everything that was accomplished at Arras by treating it as a result of Joan's bewitching rhetoric.[31] The deliberations that unfolded for several weeks during the summer of 1435, involving representatives from several European powers, are entirely forgotten. All that remains is an indictment of persuasive speech itself, the essence of any diplomatic exchange. Throughout the brief scene, each character directs attention to the seductive power of Joan's language:

> [CHARLES]: Speak, Pucelle, and enchant him with thy words. (3.3.40)
> [BURGUNDY]: Either she hath bewitch'd me with her words,
>   Or nature makes me suddenly relent. (3.3.58–59)

As a substitution for the first European peace conference, the scene discredits diplomacy by linking it with women, diabolism, effeminacy, and the seductions of language against the martial valor of men like Talbot, Bedford, and other champions of the English occupation.

Situated at the center of the play itself, in the third scene of the third act, Burgundy's defection repudiates the assumptions of diplomatic theory expounded by Durandus, du Rosier, and other medieval commentators. But it also exposes the contradictions on which the emergent system of nation-states would ultimately rest. In the sixteenth century, loyalty to country replaced a commitment to European peace as the ambassador's cardinal virtue—a shift

---

31. Williams notes that Joan's seductive language reinforces an opposition that runs throughout the play, and generally throughout Shakespeare's histories, between an effeminate French verbosity and a masculine English commitment to action. Williams, *The French Fetish,* 189–93.

that surely advanced the interests of heads of states involved. Yet it also introduced a diplomatic Hobbesianism that made conflict between rival states inevitable. If every subject or citizen was bound to defend his or her national interests, who was authorized to judge the actions of states themselves? The repudiation of the *consensus Christianus* created a discursive vacuum easily filled by sectarianism and xenophobia. In *1 Henry VI,* Joan's appeal to Burgundy as a son of France complicates the play's endorsement of patriotism as a virtue: love of country is an admirable quality in Englishmen like Bedford and Talbot; in a Frenchman or woman, it is a medium of seduction.

By imagining a Europe atomized into competing national interests, the play casts doubt on the possibility of diplomatic exchange. Burgundy's defection warns England to be wary of even its allies. His re-alliance with France may have been a nod to the former Protestant Henri IV's 1593 conversion to Catholicism, a move that jeopardized his friendship with Elizabeth.[32] Hopes of advantage might compel a foreign power to forge an alliance with England, but there was no guarantee that it would remain loyal when other military or diplomatic advantages appeared. The case was especially problematic when the ally in question had dynastic, economic, ideological, or historical ties with a hostile power. As Shakespeare's Joan of Arc recognizes, Burgundy's identity as a Francophone member of the Valois extended family compromised his reliability as an English ally. The play's diplomatic skepticism threatens the basis of any agreement between states, since the national interests of any powers can never coincide fully enough to establish complete trust. What replaces that trust is xenophobia: the good guys are English, the foreigners are bad, and any Englishman who works to overcome their mistrust is a knave or a fool.

The Evils of a French Marriage: Shakespeare and the Truce of Tours

Joan's death in *1 Henry VI* coincides with the first appearance of Margaret of Anjou, Henry VI's consort, who assumes Joan's role as the French woman who jeopardizes England's war effort.[33] Margaret also takes over Joan's role as a demonic embodiment of diplomacy, both as the bride in an interdynastic marriage between Valois France and Plantagenet England and as a queen who strives to resolve the conflict. In terms of the play's portrayal of

32. See Hattaway's discussion of this connection in his gloss to 3.3.85 in his New Cambridge edition of *1 Henry VI* (Cambridge: Cambridge University Press, 1990).

33. See Marcus, *Puzzling Shakespeare,* 89–90; and Leslie A. Fiedler, *The Stranger in Shakespeare* (New York: Stein and Day, 1972), 48.

all diplomacy as betrayal of English interests, this makes her an archvillain. Shakespeare so powerfully articulated the old Yorkist attack on Margaret that historians and biographers are only now beginning to separate the Shakespearean myth from fifteenth-century evidence.[34]

Shakespeare's defamation of Margaret, like his earlier attack on Joan, follows from and reinforces a shift in European diplomacy that made the fact of her defamation all but invisible until the age of Maastricht and the new Europe. By the late sixteenth century, a marker of an emergent, parcelized national consciousness was an increasing resentment of the role that women had played in earlier diplomacy. John Knox's *The First Blast of the Trumpet Against the Monstrous Regiment of Women* (1558), for example, brought nationalist and misogynistic discourses together in a combination that implicitly discounted the achievements of women like Isabeau de Bavière, Eleanor of Aquitaine, and the Empress Matilda.

Although the accession of Elizabeth I complicated the Knoxian model, propagandists continued to reserve some of their most bitter rhetoric for Catholic queens like Mary Stuart and Catherine de' Medici. Nor was female sovereignty their only target. They also resented interdynastic marriages that seemed to subject their country to foreign influence. Mary Tudor's marriage to Philip II drove Sir Thomas Wyatt into rebellion against her in 1554, and nothing came closer to alienating Elizabeth from left-leaning Protestants than her marital negotiations with the Duke of Alençon (1572–81).

Henry VI's union with Margaret of Anjou provided a perfect instance of the marital diplomacy that unsettled Elizabeth's nationally self-conscious subjects. After the Congress of Arras failed to achieve a lasting peace, affairs worsened for the French, the English, and the Burgundians. England and France were split by internal factions, and Philip of Burgundy's advisors suggested that only a universal peace would stave off rebellion among his Flemish subjects.[35] Statesmen throughout Europe urged Charles VII and Henry VI to make peace and to spare the continent further suffering. Edward Hall's *The Union of the Two Noble and Illustre Famelies of Lancastre and Yorke* (1548), a principal source for Shakespeare's play, summed up the general European longing for peace:

Thus, while Englande was unquieted, and Fraunce sore vexed, by spoyle, slaughter, and burnyng, all christendom lamented the continuall

---

34. Helen E. Maurer, *Margaret of Anjou: Queenship and Power in Late Medieval England* (Woodbridge, U.K.: Boydell Press, 2003), 1–2.

35. Vaughan, *Philip the Good,* 104.

destruccion of so noble a realme, and the effusion of so much Christen bloud, wherfore to appeace the mortall warre, so long contineuyng betwene these twoo puyssaunt kynges, all the princes of Christendom, so muche labored and travailed, by their orators and Ambassadors, that the frostie hartes of both the parties, wer somewhat mollified, and their indurate stomackes, greatly asswaged.[36]

On the English side, the 1444 peace effort was led by the king's great-uncle, the Cardinal Beaufort; the Cardinal's nephew Edmund, Duke of Somerset; and William de la Pole, Earl of Suffolk. Despite setbacks and opposition from the pro-war party of Humphrey, Duke of Gloucester, Beaufort and the pacifists finally joined their French counterparts for a peace conference at Tours in 1444. Suffolk, who led the English delegation, was a veteran of the French wars who had honed his diplomatic skills under Beaufort's guidance at Arras.[37] Although the belligerents could not agree to a lasting peace, they achieved a two-year truce sealed by Henry VI's marriage to Margaret of Anjou, Charles VII's niece and the daughter of the Valois Duke of Bar and Lorraine and titular king of Naples. Despite the charges of later Yorkist chroniclers, Henry's betrothal to Margaret did not thwart a possible marriage to one of Charles VII's own daughters. The last thing Charles VII would have wanted was another marriage to strengthen the English claim to the French throne. Margaret was the perfect compromise; she was close enough to the French royal family to strengthen an alliance between the two houses, but her offspring would have no place in the French succession.[38]

The festivities that accompanied the marriage on both sides of the Channel underscored the people's hopes for an end to the war. The eight pageants that accompanied Margaret's entry into London centered around peace.[39] Just before she crossed over London bridge from Southwark, allegorical representations of Peace and Plenty assured Margaret that through her "grace and highe benignite / Twixt the reawmes two, Englande and Fraunce, / Pees shal approche, rest and unite." Other pageants compared her to the dove that brought Noah the olive branch signaling the end of the Flood and to the Virgin Mary, figured as the supreme intercessor between heaven and earth. There is no reason to discount these displays as royalist propaganda, especially

---

36. Hall, *The Union of the Two Noble and Illustre Famelies of Lancastre and Yorke* (London, 1548), 146.

37. See "William de la Pole, First Duke of Suffolk," in *The Oxford Dictionary of National Biography* (Oxford: Oxford University Press, 2004–2007).

38. Wolffe, *Henry VI*, 159–61.

39. Maurer, *Margaret of Anjou*, 17–23. I am indebted to Maurer's analysis of Margaret and Henry's nuptial pageantry.

in light of recent research suggesting that they represented the work of civic pageanteers rather than courtly artists like John Lydgate.[40] Since London merchants and tradespeople stood to profit from a cessation of hostilities, they welcomed a quick end to a war that, even if it had gone well for the English, would have benefited the nobility far more than the common people.

Once Margaret arrived at Henry VI's court in 1445, she worked tirelessly to expand the Truce of Tours into a comprehensive peace. Although Yorkist propagandists condemned her efforts as intrusions into her husband's affairs, medieval queens were expected to take on the role of intercessor between their husbands and other parties, both foreign and domestic. As Paul Strohm, David Wallace, and Helen Maurer have argued, the queen's intercessory office was a smokescreen that allowed kings to negotiate and compromise without seeming weak.[41] Queen Philippa, for example, pleaded with Edward III for the burghers of Calais in 1347, and Anne of Bohemia interceded with Richard II for the alienated citizens of London in 1392. Many generations later, Catherine of Aragon begged Henry VIII to spare the perpetrators of the 1517 Evil May Day riots against foreign merchants and artisans. In seeking a reconciliation between her uncle Charles VII and her husband Henry VI, Margaret was taking on a peacemaking role linked to the precedents of the Virgin Mary and the biblical Esther.

Extant sources make it difficult to assess a given queen's agency when she mediated between her husband and his enemies. In some cases, the chronicles are likely recounting spontaneous instances of intercession; in others, they may recall more calculated scenarios in which the queen was acting a role scripted by her husband and his councillors. We will probably never know who initiated what Shakespeare condemns as one of the pacifists' greatest crimes, the cession of Maine and Anjou to Margaret's father, René, Duke of Anjou and titular King of Naples. A couple of royal letters suggest that Margaret, only a teenager at the time, may have encouraged Henry VI to follow through with the proposal. Even if she did, she was simply acting in the intercessory role played by previous medieval consorts.

Yorkist writers emphasized that the loss of England's French possessions followed the cession of Maine and Anjou. Arguing *post hoc ergo propter hoc,* they suggested that Henry's exchange of land for an extended truce had

---

40. Maurer, *Margaret of Anjou,* 22.

41. Maurer, *Margaret of Anjou,* 35; Strohm, *Hochon's Arrow: The Social Imagination of Fourteenth-Century Texts* (Princeton: Princeton University Press, 1992), 95–119; and Wallace, *Chaucerian Polity: Absolutist Lineages and Associational Forms in England and Italy* (Palo Alto, CA: Stanford University Press, 1997), 363–76.

precipitated the disaster. Even modern historians concede that Charles VII probably used the truce to muster his resources for the assault on Normandy and Gascony.[42] But fifteenth-century propagandists tied the French marriage, the cession of Anjou and Maine, and the loss of France into a single case of treasonous intrigue, with Margaret and the Duke of Suffolk, the primary architect of the Truce of Tours, as the villains. By the time Robert Fabyan completed his *New Chronicles of England and France* in 1504, he charged that Henry's marriage to Margaret caused later English civil wars. Once Tudor chroniclers like Polydore Vergil, Grafton, Hall, and Holinshed incorporated Fabyan's views, the stage was set for Shakespeare's condemnation of Margaret as the "she-wolf of France" (*3 Henry VI,* 1.4.111).

Since almost all the English sources on Henry's marriage and its consequences are contaminated by Yorkist bias, it is difficult to separate Margaret from her myth. Instead of making the case that she was not instrumental in bringing about England's disasters, I want to examine how the myth immortalized by Shakespeare—like his treatment of Joan of Arc—brings together misogyny, xenophobia, and nationalist paranoia as the basis of a new theory of diplomacy. Fabyan and the chroniclers may have felt that the Valois marriage led to England's disasters, but that would not have been obvious to negotiators at Tours or even to the parties who engineered the subsequent cession of Anjou and Maine. What the peace party probably did think was something that Edward III had learned in the early fourteenth century: England would never have the resources to achieve the absolute conquest of France. In light of that inevitability, the exchange of land for peace was not necessarily a bad move. It might have kept open, for example, the possibility of compromises that could have preserved English interests in territories like Normandy and Gascony, where the English claim predated the Lancastrian conquest.

Traditional historiography has little place for speculation about what might have happened. But in cases like this, where the war party pointed to Charles VII's violation of Tours as evidence that the truce should never have been made, it is important to recover the contingency of events as they unfolded. There is no need to see Margaret, Suffolk, Winchester, or any other supporters of the truce and of the cession of Anjou and Maine as a villain plotting England's destruction. In making that charge, their detractors have implicitly, or even explicitly, endorsed the assumptions of the pro-war faction: that England's claims to France were legitimate, that maintaining those claims was a point of national honor, that total victory was possible, and that

---

42. See Wolffe, *Henry VI,* 169–83.

no English party should have conceded anything to the French themselves or to any other continental power. Such assumptions precluded any grounds for compromise and arguably for negotiation with the French king.

These assumptions dominated the discussion when Parliament tried Suffolk for treason in 1450. The trial looms large in the medieval diplomatic history because it marked an unusual parliamentary intrusion in foreign policy. Specifically, Parliament charged Suffolk with exceeding the powers specified in his commission when he consented to the cession of Maine and Anjou.[43] But this was only a cover. What was really at stake was the future of diplomacy as an alternative to war as a means of resolving disputes between England and France. Like attacks on the Burgundian ambassadors after the Treaty of Arras, Suffolk's prosecution and subsequent murder attest to changing assumptions about an ambassador's duties, rights, freedoms, initiatives, and immunities.

By the time Shakespeare took up the Truce of Tours, England was again embroiled in a continental war and xenophobia was running high. *1 Henry VI* adopts the assumptions of the war party about the dangers of negotiation and frowns on dynastic marriages that bring de facto foreign agents into the king's bedroom. The play concludes with a three-scene burlesque of the Truce of Tours in which diplomatic arrangements go from bad to worse. In Act V, scene 3, the Duke of Suffolk falls in love with Margaret of Anjou and decides to marry her to Henry VI in order to keep her near him. In Act V, scene 4, Charles VII and the Duke of York wrangle over the terms of a truce, presumably without knowing Suffolk's plans. Finally, in Act V, scene 5, Suffolk successfully persuades Henry VI of Margaret's virtues so that the marriage proceeds over the objections from the Duke of Gloucester. The play ends with Suffolk's Iago-like boast that "Margaret shall now be Queen, and rule the King; / But I will rule both her, the King, and realm" (5.5.107–8).

The *entrelacement* of Suffolk's scheming with the public conversation between Charles VII and the Duke of York constitutes a two-tiered critique of the marital diplomacy that led to numerous late medieval peace treaties. On a general level, the exchange between York and Charles indicts any peacemaking process that thwarts total victory for either side. The Suffolk scenes then embed this general issue within a wider exposé of marriage diplomacy as a mixture of high politics, household intrigue, and sexuality. The conversation between Charles and York centers on the peacemakers' efforts

---

43. Ferguson, *English Diplomacy*, 161–63; and Wolffe, *Henry VI*, 220–28.

to convince their compatriots to accept the settlement. In a burst of patriotic fervor, York argues that anything short of a total victory makes a mockery of English losses:

> Is all our travail turn'd to this effect?
> After the slaughter of so many peers,
> So many captains, gentlemen, and soldiers,
> That in this quarrel have been overthrown
> And sold their bodies for the country's benefit,
> Shall we at last conclude effeminate peace? (5.4.102–7)

Recalling the deaths of Salisbury, Bedford, Talbot, and Talbot's son, which have dominated much of the previous action, York's words take on a dramatic authority that cannot be dampened by Warwick's assurances that the only peace the English will accept is one "with such strict and severe covenants/ As little shall the Frenchmen gain thereby" (5.4.114–15).

The French king, meanwhile, barely accepts the "strict and severe covenants" that the English propose:

> 'Tis known already that I am possess'd
> With more than half the Gallian territories,
> And therein reverenc'd for their lawful king.
> Shall I, for lucre of the rest unvanquish'd,
> Detract so much from that prerogative
> As to be call'd but viceroy of the whole? (5.4.138–43)

Although dismissed as an "insult" by York (147), Charles's lines expose the absurdity of what the play imagines as an honorably negotiated settlement. Charles has a point: what would he have to gain by conceding his royal title? After all, the English control only half of the French territory, while the other half acknowledges Charles as its sovereign. The settlement that the English propose, in which Charles would renounce his crown and serve as a viceroy for Henry VI, would be accepted only by a country that had suffered total defeat, not by one still possessing half of its territory. What the English offer is less a set of terms for a truce than conditions for a full surrender, one that the French have no reason to honor. Taken together, the speeches of York and Charles suggest the absurdity of any negotiated settlement when both parties are capable of further fighting.

York's charge that any peace in lieu of total victory is "effeminate" provides a powerful gloss on the second aspect of Shakespeare's defamation of Tours, the indictment of interdynastic marriage as a means to resolve hostilities. As the action unfolds, Margaret's physical beauty becomes a metaphor for the seductions of diplomacy itself, imagined as a bewitching power that catches statesmen off their guard and renders them susceptible to foreign betrayal. In one of the most suggestive pairings of entrances and exits in all Shakespeare, York carries off the captured Joan of Arc one line before Margaret first appears to step into Joan's role as the embodiment of French duplicity. Suffolk announces that she too, like Joan, is a "prisoner" (5.3.45). But with his protestations of love in the next line, it becomes clear that he is now *her* prisoner and that she is poised to play a major role in future Anglo-French politics. Since Suffolk is already married, he concocts the plan to marry Margaret to Henry over political objections simply because that is the best way to keep her near him. As the scene progresses, his lusts subvert whatever devotion to king and country he may have ever possessed: "I'll win this Lady Margaret. For whom? / Why, for my king. Tush, that's a wooden thing!" (5.3.88–89). The antecedent of the word "thing" here is unclear, and editors have glossed it as a reference either to Suffolk's plot or to the king. But the general point is unmistakable: Margaret's marriage to a notoriously weak, gullible, and sexually unappealing king will allow Suffolk to enjoy access to her.

In traditional dynastic diplomacy, marriage between scions of rival states symbolized the peace, reconciliation, and renewed commitment to common aspirations that was imagined to reign between the former belligerents. Nothing could be further from that ideal than Shakespeare's representation of Margaret's marriage to Henry. In the subsequent plays, the affair between Margaret and Suffolk develops into an alliance through which Margaret outstrips Joan in her destructive power. Henry VI's already weakened credibility collapses when his magnates discover that the marriage bargain entailed the surrender of crucial English territories, Maine and Anjou. She destroys Duke Humphrey, drives the country to civil war, and, by participating in the brutal murder of York, earns her epithet as the "she-wolf of France."

In Shakespeare, Henry VI's union with an overbearing, deceptive, and adulterous consort suggests that diplomacy is, at best, warfare by other means. From his staunchly francophobic perspective, Margaret was France's best weapon, one that managed not only to lure Henry into surrendering his French kingdoms but also to precipitate England's own decline into civil war. Far from achieving peace and reconciliation, this dynastic marriage leads to English humiliation on the international stage and mounting discord at home.

1 Henry VI and Elizabeth I

The post-Armada years were a confusing time in English diplomatic history. Although the medieval commitment to the peace of Christendom—always an elusive aspiration at best—was now extinct, the concept of a European balance of powers would not be fully articulated for another two centuries. The emergence of powerful monarchies in the late fifteenth and early sixteenth centuries, coupled with new military and technological developments, raised the specter of war on a larger, more destructive scale than ever before. The old religious consensus was broken, but religious ideology persisted in ways that exacerbated conflicts between states divided along sectarian lines. In England, new voices were entering diplomatic conversations, as the Crown and the nobility began to lose their monopoly on foreign policy. Not coincidentally, these were the same voices most committed to sectarian views of England's role in European affairs.

Elizabeth I faced the shift in changing diplomatic attitudes with ambivalence. Her predecessors had contributed directly to the atomization of Europe into competing national states that acknowledged no limits on their individual sovereignty. The Tudors' efforts to diminish the country's hereditary aristocracy had even paved the way for a broader discussion of foreign affairs by entrusting ambassadorships to men of humble backgrounds. Henry Beaufort, the cardinal who crafted Henry VI's foreign policy, was the king's great uncle; Richard Wolsey, the cardinal who crafted Henry VIII's, was probably the son of an Ipswich butcher. The men who crafted, debated, and negotiated Elizabeth's foreign policy were almost all Tudor "new creations"—men of relatively humble background raised to positions of power—and diplomats throughout Europe commented on their low birth.

At the same time, Elizabeth guarded her prerogative in affairs of state and did everything in her power to honor the dynastic rights, obligations, and alliances that had long shaped the diplomatic map of Europe. As her last speech to Parliament suggests, she interpreted contemporary events more in the light of Plantagenet history than in the apocalyptic rhetoric popular in the House of Commons and even with some of her own privy councilors. Instead of seeing England pitted against a unified Catholic opposition, she recalled the old rivalry between Burgundy and France that Henry V had exploited in the fifteenth century. That recollection provided her with the historical basis for her own manipulation of the conflict between Valois France and Habsburg Spain.

Nevertheless, as her final speech also suggested, the rules had changed in bewildering ways. Burgundy—recast as Philip II—was the enemy, and to counteract that threat, she now had to pursue an alliance with the traditional Plantagenet enemy, France. The difficulties that she faced making this transition were compounded by the emergence of a popular discourse that cast France and Spain as agents of the Antichrist. More than anything else, the new sectarianism of the sixteenth century limited the freedom with which medieval monarchs had forged and sealed alliances through dynastic marriages. Popular outcries against the Alençon negotiations reminded Elizabeth that, however useful she may have found an alliance with France as a counterweight against Spain, her people may no longer have greeted a French consort with the enthusiasm that their ancestors had showered on Margaret of Anjou, at least in 1445.

As a retelling of the same Plantagenet past that Elizabeth evoked in her final speech to Parliament, *1 Henry VI* seems unambiguously committed to the popular nationalism, even isolationism, that complicated Elizabeth's relationship with other European dynasts. When she needed a close relationship with France to ward off Spanish aggression, the play revived all the old Plantagenet hostilities between the two realms. More significantly, it cast doubts on the feasibility of any European alliance by imagining a world in which no other country could be trusted. Glancing over the importance of the Burgundian alliance to England throughout most of the fifteenth century, it transformed one particularly dark moment in that relationship into an admonition about the unreliability of all continental Europeans. Shakespeare's Burgundy becomes a prototype of both France and Spain in the Protestant imagination, a direct ancestor of Philip II and a model for the religious treachery of Henri IV. Finally, Shakespeare's brutal characterization of the Truce of Tours contributed to a paranoia about interdynastic marriages that would explode a decade or so later, when James I tried to negotiate a marriage between his son and the Spanish Infanta. Elizabeth herself warded off her subject's outrage by abandoning a French marriage. Her successors were not so lucky. Something of the hostility that Shakespeare showed Margaret of Anjou would come back to haunt Anne of Denmark, Henrietta Maria, Catherine of Braganza, and Mary of Modena, the women whose identity as foreign consorts contributed to the downfall of the Stuart dynasty.

PART II

Aliens in Our Midst

Jews, Italians, and
Wary Englishmen in
The Merchant of Venice

The Black Death of 1347–51 killed a third of Europe. Nothing on that scale affected European demographics in the sixteenth century. But the changes that took place had a dramatic impact on the way people began to think of themselves as belonging to a nation with a coherent and distinct culture. By the time Shakespeare moved to London from Stratford sometime in the late 1580s or early 1590s, he joined an urban community in which numerous residents had come from somewhere else. This was an unsettling experience for everyone. Often speaking languages or even forms of English that were not intelligible to their new neighbors, immigrants were prey to swindling, extortion, exploitation, and a pervasive xenophobia.

Fortunately, events like the Evil May Day of 1514, in which a thousand apprentices looted and vandalized homes of foreigners living just north of St. Paul's, were rarer in London than in some continental cities. But on a daily basis, immigrants were subjected to the petty crimes and extortions that writers like Robert Greene recorded in cony-catching pamphlets:

I remember a mery iest done of late to a welchman, who being a meer stranger in London, and not wel acquainted with the English tongue, chanced amongst certaine conicatchers, who spying the gentleman had monie, they so dealt with him, that what by signes and broken English, they got him in for a conie, and fleest him of euerie peny that he had, and of his sword: at last the man smoakt them, and drew his dagger vpon them at Ludgate, for therabout they had catcht him, and would haue stabd one of them for his mony, but people stopt him, the rather because they could not vnderstande him, though he had a card in one hand, and his dagger in the other, saying as wel as he could, a card, a card, mon dien. In the mean while the conicatchers were got into pauls, and so away, The welchman folowed them seeking there vp and down in the church til with his naked dagger and the card in his hand, the gentlemen maruele what he meant thereby: at last one of his countri-men met him, and enquired the cause of his choler, then he told him how he was cosened at cards, and robd of al his monie, but as his losse was voluntarie, so his seeking for them was meere vanitie, for they were stept into some blind alehouse to deuide the shares.[1]

This passage captures the vulnerability of the new arrival lacking the lin-guistic, cultural, and legal resources to defend himself against urban criminals determined to profit from his ignorance. The Welshman becomes the ideal coney. He is simultaneously wealthy and untutored in the urban codes that might have enabled him to "smoak" out the cozeners' trap before he fell into it. Above all, his inability to communicate with anything but "signes and broken English" enhances his susceptibility and then prevents him from soliciting help. By the time a presumably bilingual fellow Welshman comes to his aid, the coney-catchers have escaped and are safely dividing his money in "some blind alehouse."

What a modern reader might find most disturbing in Greene's account is his lack of sympathy for the Welshman. To some extent, this is a charac-teristic of the coney-catching genre, which, in its fascination with crimi-nal ingenuity, tends to downplay sympathy for victims. But in this passage, Greene's status as a university-educated, assimilated Londoner compounds his emphasis on the absurdity of the Welshman's situation. Greene identifies less with victim or perpetrator than with the befuddled Londoners trying to figure out exactly what a Welshman is doing holding a card and a dagger and running up and down the aisles of St. Paul's: "The gentlemen maruele what he meant thereby."

---

1. Robert Greene, *A Notable Discouery of Coosenage. Now daily practised by sundry lewd persons, called connie-catchers, and crosse-byters. Plainely laying open those pernitious sleights that hath brought many ignorant men to confusion.…With a delightfull discourse of the coosenage of colliers* (London, 1592), n.p.

An outraged foreigner wielding a dagger and babbling in broken English is at once menacing and ridiculous. He is the product of a discourse of the foreign that cast new immigrants not only as thieves, murderers, conspirators, sodomites, and misers but also as bunglers, clowns, and fools. When these roles combined in ways that challenged generic decorum, the result was tragicomic. Whether portrayed as villain or victim, the foreigner was always a potential object of ridicule. Even writers like Thomas Dekker, who cast the foreigner as a hero, made him and his strange speech an object of mirth, however good-hearted.

The foreigner's absurdity and excess established a normative Englishness grounded in moderation, good taste, reserve, common sense, and a common— albeit not yet standardized—language.[2] In Greene's account, that English level-headedness belongs to the London bystanders and to Greene's own narrative voice. We hear it most emphatically in the final pronouncement against the Welshman: "But as his losse was voluntarie, so his seeking for [the perpetrators] was meere vanitie, for they were stept into some blind alehouse to deuide the shares." Greene casts the pronouncement in ethical and pragmatic terms. The Welshman really does not deserve to get his money back, because he got himself into this "voluntarie" mess in the first place. Besides, the scoundrels who tricked him have absconded into some "blind alehouse" and could not be caught and brought to justice even if the Welshman had a legitimate case. The final sentence might offend a modern sense of justice, but Greene suggests that it is good enough for a knife-wielding Welshman.

A similar consciousness of an alien trespassing social boundaries underlies Greene's notorious description of Shakespeare as

> an vpstart Crow, beautified with our feathers, that with his Tygers hart wrapt in a Players hyde, supposes he is as well able to bombast out a blanke verse as the best of you: and beeing an absolute Iohannes fac totum, is in his owne conceit the onely Shake-scene in a countrey.[3]

Greene embedded this attack in one of his last works, the pamphlet *A Groats-worth of Wit Bought with a Million of Repentance*, in which he casts himself as a reprobate playwright urging his readers to use their wit for more wholesome

---

2. For further discussion, see Ton Hoenslaars, *Images of Englishmen and Foreigners in the Drama of Shakespeare and His Contemporaries: A Study of Stage Characters and National Identity in English Renaissance Drama* (Rutherford, NJ: Farleigh Dickinson University Press, 1992).

3. Greene, *A Groats-vvorth of Witte, Bought with a Million of Repentance. Describing the follie of youth, the falshoode of makeshifte flatterers, the miserie of the negligent, and mischiefes of deceiuing courtezans. Written before his death, and published at his dyeing request* (London, 1592), n.p.

and profitable ends. In a section urging young men not to become playwrights, he castigates Shakespeare not only for being a plagiarist who has beautified his works with other writers' feathers but also for aspiring to write at all. As a university man, Greene imagines a hierarchical social order in which players depend on learned playwrights for their scripts. The contemporary London theater provokes his outrage by disregarding this distinction and championing an uneducated newcomer like Shakespeare, who acts and writes. From Greene's perspective, the "vpstart Crow" from Warwickshire's attempt to "bombast out a blanke verse" is almost as linguistically preposterous as the knife-wielding Welshman's attempt to explain the injustice he has suffered to the Londoners around St. Paul's. Like the Welshman, Shakespeare is an outsider whose behavior—specifically his egregious appropriation of "*our* feathers"—establishes a sense of superior community linking Greene, the witty gentlemen he addresses, and the pamphlet's larger audience. It even allows Greene to dispel the effects of his own previous self-presentation as someone who has made a profit for himself in the theatrical underworld. Throughout the pamphlet, he has confessed to blasphemy, drunkenness, womanizing, and general debauchery. Castigating Shakespeare reintegrates him at least partially into the respectable world whose conventions he has so often flouted. As bad as Greene has been, he is still good enough to condemn an unschooled writer and a plagiarist.

At first, this construction as a privileged insider at the expense of someone else denigrated as alien may seem only abstractly related to questions of national identity. But in condemning Shakespeare as a parvenu with a "Tygers hart wrapt in a Players hyde," Greene alluded to the *Henry VI* cycle, the anti-French jingoism of which was already creating for Shakespeare a reputation as the consummate English playwright. In fact, the line echoes York's castigation of Henry VI's consort, Margaret of Anjou, as a "she-wolf of France," a foreigner opposed to fundamental English interests: "O tiger's heart wrapp'd in a woman's hide!" (*3 Henry VI,* 1.4.111, 137). Trying to portray Shakespeare as a playwright whose outsider status would always be obvious to the cognoscenti, Greene focuses on the very passage through which Shakespeare presents himself as the ultimate insider, a spokesperson for a fundamental Englishness threatened by aliens like Margaret of Anjou.

Even as the "vpstart Crow" charge probably tells us more about Greene's jealousies than about Shakespeare, Greene may have been onto something about his new rival for the attention of London playgoers. Shakespeare's plays repeatedly create an identity for their author as English by displacing anxieties about origins onto patent foreigners like Margaret of Anjou and Joan of Arc. Our next two chapters focus on one of his earliest and most complex interrogations of the possibility of the outsider's assimilation within English society, *The Merchant of Venice*. Greene's image of the knife-wielding Welshman trying in vain to recover his property before an unsympathetic and uncomprehending group of London onlookers bears an uncanny resemblance to Shylock, the knife-wielding Jew who pleads for justice before an unsympathetic cast of scoffing Christians. Like the Welshman, Shylock too loses his money to a group of conspirators. When he discovers the theft, he too charges through the streets speaking words that are barely intelligible to anyone who is not already privy to the precise nature of the crime that has befallen him:

> I never heard a passion so confus'd,
> So strange, outrageous, and so variable
> As the dog Jew did utter in the streets:
> "My daughter! O my ducats! O my daughter!
> Fled with a Christian! O my Christian ducats!
> Justice! the law! my ducats, and my daughter!" (2.8.12–17)

In each case, the spectacle forces us to balance what empathy we feel for the foreigner against our fears of him as a potential threat to civic society. Like the Welshman, Shylock cannot use the courts of the dominant culture to his advantage, in part because he too seems to be responsible for bringing his disasters onto his own head. Shakespeare's characterization of him as an object of fear, sympathy, and ridicule is tragicomic in ways that continue to baffle readers. Like the spectacle of the Welshman pursuing the conspirators who have outsmarted him, Shylock's doom forces us to balance what empathy we feel for him as an outsider against our fears of him as a threat to civic society.

In *The Merchant of Venice*, the question of the foreigner's relationship to the dominant culture is bound up with religious conversion, the theme of Levin's chapter on Shylock's daughter Jessica. Reading the play against the traces of actual Jewish women living in Shakespeare's England, Levin suggests that their stories, like Jessica's, exposed the persistence of a fundamental Jewishness that could never fully assimilate to English society. Not even baptism could turn a Jewess into an Englishwoman. This insistence on a racial and cultural alterity worked to validate Englishness itself as an inalienable right of those born to English parents.

Whereas Levin focuses on the anxieties attending the conversion of the individual, Watkins examines those associated with the conversion of English society itself in the wake of mercantile expansion. The spectral outsider that haunts his reading of the play is not the *conversa* but the Venetian merchant. The Italian merchants who once populated the docks and custom houses of the East End were becoming infrequent visitors to Shakespeare's England. After the 1580s, the goods that had once been transported from ports of the eastern Mediterranean on Venetian and Genoese vessels were more likely to arrive on English ones. Italians were well aware of the expansion of the English trade at their own expense. But as *The Merchant of Venice* suggests, the English were anxious about their rapid transformation into the Venice of the North Atlantic: would assuming the Venetian mantle also mean that England would one day experience its own version of the Venetian decline? Was England converting itself into a foreign country in its pursuit of foreign trade?

CHAPTER 3

Converting the Daughter

Gender, Power, and Jewish Identity
in the English Renaissance

Jessica, Abigail, and Jewish Women in Renaissance Drama

Jessica, the daughter of Shylock in William Shakespeare's *The Merchant of Venice,* disobeys her father by eloping with Lorenzo and converting to Christianity. Scholars have traditionally either blamed her as a disobedient daughter or lauded her as a loyal Christian wife.[1] But what is most striking about Jessica

---

Some of the material in this chapter was addressed in my essay, "Shakespeare and the Marginalized 'Others,'" in *Concise Companion to English Renaissance Literature,* ed. Donna Hamilton (Malden, MA: Blackwell, 2006), 200–16. The edition of *The Merchant of Venice* used in this essay is edited by David Bevington and David Scott Kastan (New York: Bantam, 2005) and the edition of *The Jew of Malta* is edited by James R. Siemon, 2nd ed. (New York: W. W. Norton, 1994).

1. For a good discussion of the different scholarly perspectives, see Austin C. Dobbins and Roy Battenhouse, "Jessica's Morals" *Shakespeare Studies* 9 (1976), 107–20; and Camille Slights, "In Defense of Jessica: The Runaway Daughter in *The Merchant of Venice,*" *Shakespeare Quarterly* 31 (1980): 357–68. More recently, Lyn Stephen sees Jessica as having a choice: staying with Shylock, "apparent loyalty and soul-death," or going with Lorenzo, "apparent treachery and life." "'A Wilderness of Monkeys': A Psychodynamic Study of *The Merchant of Venice,*" in *The Undiscover'd Country: New Essays in Psychoanalysis and Shakespeare,* ed. B. J. Sokol (London: Free Association Books, 1993), 121. Very valuable is Mary Janell Metzger, "'Now by My Hood, a Gentle and No Jew': Jessica, *The Merchant of Venice,* and the Discourse of Early Modern England Identity," *PMLA* 113 (1998): 52–63. I found Lisa Lampert's analysis in her study *Gender and Jewish Difference from Paul to Shakespeare* (Philadelphia: University of Pennsylvania Press, 1994) especially useful. See also Sharon Hamilton, *Shakespeare's Daughters* (Jefferson, NC: McFarland and Co., 2003).

is her isolation as a Jewish woman. We do have the representation of a Jewish woman in both *The Merchant of Venice* and Christopher Marlowe's *The Jew of Malta*.[2] In both plays the daughters convert, but to the other non-Jewish characters, both women are still considered to be Jews rather than Christians, thus keeping them isolated. This isolation leads us to question whether a non-Christian woman in early modern England could ever truly become a Christian one, whether a Jew could ever truly stop being a Jew. Examining Jessica, Abigail, and actual female conversions allows us to see the different definitions of identity, the significance of gender in these definitions, and the ways that other citizens in early modern England could contribute to the identification of the self. A pamphlet written by a Christian bishop that describes the conversion of Eve Cohan almost a century after these plays echoes some of the major events involving Jessica and Abigail. Because there are few sources about Eve Cohan except the pamphlet, we do not know the extent to which her life really did parallel these fictional depictions; perhaps the cultural ideas were strong enough to alter the depiction of Eve's life. Jessica, Abigail, and Eve attempt to cross one of the most difficult borders of the early modern world: religious identity. Their failure to do so with complete success shows them to be caught in a liminal space in which they belong in neither one realm nor the other.

Shakespeare's play ends in Belmont with Antonio, Portia and Bassanio, Nerissa and Gratiano, Lorenzo and Jessica all celebrating not only Antonio's escape but also the added wealth that Lorenzo shall have as the husband of Shylock's daughter. Jessica, unlike her earlier counterpart Abigail, is not killed, but at least some productions of *The Merchant of Venice* end with an utterly isolated Jessica.

Both Jessica and Abigail are depictions of Jewish women, created by non-Jewish *male* playwrights of the late Elizabethan age. I am suggesting that we must remember that Jessica and Abigail were created characters who emerged from a culture with specific values and attitudes toward Jews and, more specifically, toward Jewish women. While these are the fictional creations of male non-Jewish playwrights, there also were some Jewish women living in England at the time of Shakespeare and Marlowe, though we do not know if any were personally known to either of the men. Janet Adelman argues that "whether or not Shakespeare and his audience knew" of the presence of Jewish *conversos* in London, "Jessica's entrance into Belmont and

---

2. For more on Abigail, see Jeremy Tambling, "Abigail's Party: 'The Difference of Things' in *The Jew of Malta*," in *In Another Country: Feminist Perspectives on Renaissance Drama,* ed. Dorothea Kehler and Susan Baker (Metuchen, NJ: Scarecrow Press, 1991), 95–112.

her would-be entrance into Christianity provokes a response that would have been entirely familiar to the conversos themselves."[3] Jessica and Abigail may reflect aspects of the reality of lives of Jewish women; far more, however, they represent the dominant cultural anxiety over gender and difference.

Medieval Background

From the early medieval period, the established Christian Church had often described Jews as being responsible for the crucifixion of Jesus; in the following centuries throughout Europe, Jews came to be associated with everything demonic and immoral, including sorcery, poisoning, and the ritual murder of Christian children. Often they were blamed for outbreaks of the plague because many were convinced that they had poisoned the drinking water. In the eleventh century the Church called for people to join the first Crusade; many in continental Europe, especially France, came to wonder why they should go all the way to the Holy Lands to slay the Infidel when they could do it so conveniently right at home; a number of Jews fled to England. But England's reputation as a haven of tolerance soon proved illusory. For the coronation of Richard I in 1189, the new king called for the exclusion of all women and Jews from the ceremony. According to Matthew Paris, Richard made this order "because of the magic arts which Jews and some women notoriously exercise at royal coronations."[4] Certainly violent, militaristic, misogynistic Richard feared that the presence of Jews and women at such a sacred ceremony would be polluting and dangerous, no doubt a Jewish woman doubly so. Some Jewish leaders came anyway to profess their loyalty. Word soon spread, though falsely, that in retaliation, Richard ordered the extermination of all Jews in England. This rumor led to the slaughter of many Jews including in 1190 the deaths of about one hundred and fifty Jews in York at Clifford's Tower. To focus more attention on Jews, Richard stated that "by publique edict commaunded bothe the Iewes and their wyues not to presume eyther to enter the church or els his palace," according to John Foxe's sixteenth-century account of Richard's coronation and its aftermath.[5]

3. Janet Adelman, "Her Father's Blood: Race, Conversion, and Nation in *The Merchant of Venice*," *Representations* 81 (2003): 4.

4. Matthew Paris, Hist. Angl. 2:9 cited in Sharon Achinstein, "John Foxe and the Jews," *Renaissance Quarterly* 54 (2001): 97.

5. John Foxe, *Acts and Monuments [...]* (1570 edition), 182. Human Rights Initiative website hriOnline, Sheffield, U.K. Available at www.hrionline.ac.uk/johnfoxe/main/4_1570_0300.jsp, accessed March 10, 2008.

A century after Richard's reign, Edward I, having first confiscated their wealth, ordered that all Jews who did not convert to Christianity leave England on pain of death, taking with them only what each could carry. As a result, virtually all Jews, roughly two thousand of them, left England in 1290; not legally allowed to return as Jews until 1656—well after Shakespeare's death—although small numbers of them began to return in the late fifteenth and early sixteenth centuries, many of them living outwardly as Christian.[6] But even if Jews converted to Christianity, the English often did not accept them as "true Christians," fearing that their mere presence in the country would weaken the Christian faith and cause people to convert to Judaism. We will see the lack of acceptance of a converted Jew in the late seventeenth century in the case of Eve Cohan later in the chapter.

In the centuries after the expulsion, while there were few or no actual Jews in England, the image of the Jew as a dangerous monster only continued to grow. By the thirteenth century, the term *Jew* had become part of the English vocabulary as a catchall term of abuse, often directed at other Christians. "I hate thee as I do a Jew," someone might say. A 1580 murder pamphlet by Anthony Munday describes a cruel woman, Amy Harrison, who regularly beat her young godchild who was living in her house as her servant. Harrison demanded far more than a child her age could perform, "so that often her unhabilitie caused her to be whipt, beaten, tiranically tormented." Harrison treated the child "very Jewishly," finally beating her so badly that she died.[7]

Especially at times of great social and cultural change, one of the ways for a group to define itself is to exclude all who are—or have characteristics of—difference. And for most Elizabethans, religion in late sixteenth century England was tumultuous indeed. Their grandparents had turned from Rome to the Church of England under Henry VIII, while their parents might have reverted to Catholicism under Mary, before changing their faith again with the accession of Elizabeth. As James Shapiro points out, in the decades after the break with Rome in the 1530s and the establishment of the Reformation, "the English began to think of the Jews not only as a people who almost three centuries earlier had been banished from English territory but also as a potential threat to the increasingly permeable boundaries of their own social and religious identities. The challenge of preserving these boundaries was

6. Todd M. Endelman, *The Jews of Britain, 1656 to 2000* (Berkeley: University of California Press, 2002), 15. As Endelman notes, some years earlier the Jewish community may well have been more than twice this size, but the mounting persecution had already taken its toll.

7. Anthony Munday, *A view of sundry examples reporting many straunge murthers* (London, 1580), 103. My thanks to Lena Orlin for giving me this reference.

intensified by the difficulties of pointing to physical characteristics that unmistakably distinguished English Christians from Jews."[8] Obviously, for men, one major difference—albeit usually a hidden one—was circumcision. For Jewish women, there was no such obvious sign. In fifteenth-century Italy, there was an attempt to insist that all Jewish women have their ears pierced as a sign of difference, but the movement failed—earrings were a fashion among Gentiles as well.

"Turn Jew" and Actual Jew

The idea that any English person might in sudden nightmare terms "turn Jew" or "become Jew" was a part of early modern English culture. In 1654 Ralph Josselin, a seventeenth-century clergyman, dreamed "that one came to mee and told me that [John] Thurloe was turned Jew."[9] This dream had no connection with reality; Oliver Cromwell's secretary of state never stated he was Jewish or had any interest in converting to Judaism. The dream, however, demonstrated the deep cultural anxiety that anyone might do so. We can see it as well in the proverbial phrases so often heard on the Elizabethan stage. "I am a Jew . . . else"—a suggestion that wrong behavior turns one into a Jew. For example, in *Much Ado About Nothing*, when Benedick is tricked into thinking that Beatrice is in love with him and recognizes his love for her, he says, "If I do not take pity of her, I am a villain; if I do not love her, I am a Jew" (3.1.240).

From 1290 until the mid–sixteenth century, there is no evidence of organized communities of Jews in England. Lucien Wolf's archival research turned up a total of sixty-nine Jewish men, women, and children who had been in England or had relatives there between 1539 and 1555. In the reign of Henry VIII, Jorges Anes, a native of Spain baptized at the time of the expulsion who found the pepper trade profitable, became George Ames, founder of a great Tudor Anglo-Jewish family. His children and grandchildren would be very active in Elizabeth's reign. He ended up in Portugal, but after his death in 1538 his wife Elizabeth returned to London about 1541.[10]

---

8. James Shapiro, *Shakespeare and the Jews* (New York: Columbia University Press, 1996), 7.

9. Alan MacFarlane, ed., *The Diary of Ralph Josselin, 1616–1683* (London: Published for the British Academy by the Oxford University Press, 1976), 337.

10. David S. Katz, *The Jews in the History of England, 1485–1850* (New York: Oxford University Press, 1994), 3.

In 1535 a wealthy widow of a Portuguese Jew, Beatriz de Luna, also known as Gracia Menesia, visited London with her daughter Reyna, her sister-in-law, and her nephew, for an extended visit on the way to Antwerp. She was delighted to find a small community of Spanish and Portuguese Jews of about one hundred with their own secret synagogue. This community had financial support and business connections with Antwerp. We know a bit more about this community from some of the Spanish and Italian inquisition records.[11] In 1540 Alves Lopes held a synagogue in his house and lived in the Hebrew manner, albeit in secret. We learn from the Inquisitor records of Gaspar Lopes that when he was visiting England and stayed with Alves on the Sabbath, there were "other false Christians to the number of about twenty . . . and that it is true that whenever any refugee false Christians come from Portugal to go to England and Flanders and thence to Turkey and elsewhere, in order to lead the lives of Hebrews, they come to the house of the said Alves, who helps them to go whither they want for this purpose."[12] The records also hint at the importance of Jewish women in cooking ritual meals and helping to maintain the religion in secret. But this community was understandably unstable. In 1541 the Spanish pressured Henry VIII's government to arrest all those suspected of being Jewish and to take over their property. Eventually the Jewish merchants were released, but in the meanwhile much of the community dispersed.[13] Though Catholic Spain and Protestant England were often at odds, Henry obviously found it politically useful to join religiously with the Spanish against the Jews.

A number of the musicians who played for the king were also Italians of Jewish origin. Henry VIII employed nineteen of these musicians at court. This group assimilated quickly and intermarried with the English so that their children and grandchildren were practicing Christians, only partially aware of their Jewish origins. One of these was the early-seventeenth-century poet Aemelia Bassano Lanier, daughter of court musician Baptist Bassano. Lanier's interest in Old Testament heroines may suggest her own connection with her roots.

There were also some secretly observant Jews in Bristol and some connections between London and the community in Bristol. In the late 1540s and early 1550s in Bristol, the community held religious services in the house of Henrique Nuñez, and Yom Kippur was observed as well as the Sabbath and

---

11. Lucien Wolf, *Essays in Jewish History,* ed. Cecil Roth (London: Jewish Historical Society of England, 1934), 76.

12. Wolf, *Essays,* 81; and Shapiro, *Shakespeare and the Jews,* 69.

13. Endelman, *Jews of Britain,* 17.

festivals. Nuñez's wife, Beatriz Fernandes, taught new Jewish immigrants prayers and baked the unleavened bread for Passover. Nuñez, as was the case for other members of the community, continued to practice his faith in secret while outwardly remaining a member of the Anglican Church.[14]

We do have a reference to a beautiful young Jewish woman who was briefly in England in the 1590s, though she and her compatriots hid their religion. Jewish-Dutch historian Daniel Levi de Barrios at the end of the seventeenth century related the account of the origins of the community of the Portuguese Jews of Amsterdam. He described the beautiful Marrano Maria Nuñes of Lisbon, who was sailing on a ship with her four relatives when the boat was seized by the English and brought to London. Levi de Barrios claims that an English duke fell in love with Maria Nuñes; Elizabeth invited her to court to see the beautiful woman for herself. According to the story, Elizabeth delighted in her guest, and she and Maria paraded through London in the royal carriage. The duke, meanwhile, could not persuade Maria Nuñes to marry him, and the queen allowed the party to continue on their voyage to Amsterdam; once there, they were able to live openly as Jews. David Katz points out, "There is some evidence that this incident, at least the capture of the ship conveying the five Portuguese among whom was a young lady, took place in April 1597. Yet, even if true, Queen Elizabeth for her part would not necessarily have known of the Jewish origins of her guests."[15]

Some Jews in England in the sixteenth century went through a formal, public conversion. These public conversions were celebrated; in order to break even more with the old self and identity, these new converts also received new names. In 1577 Jehuda Menda, who had lived in London for six years, publicly stated that he utterly forsook his former idolatrous ways and strange worship, leaving behind the false search for a new Messiah. He also forsook his name and asked to be called Nathaniel. Following his conversion, John Foxe preached for four hours. While more of the records document male conversions, there were also conversions by Jewish women. In 1532, in one of her last acts as queen, Catherine of Aragon and her daughter Mary served as godmothers to two Jewish woman from southern Europe, Aysa Pudewya and Omell Faytt Isya, who had converted to Catholicism; Aysa became Katherine Whetely and Omell became Mary Cook.[16] The

14. C. J. Sisson, "A Colony of Jews in Shakespeare's London," *Essays and Studies* 23 (1937): 38. I am also deeply grateful to Charles Meyers, who shared his work on the Nuñez family and more generally on Jews in Renaissance England with me in manuscript.

15. Katz, *The Jews in the History of England,* 101–2.

16. Michael Adler, *Jews in Medieval England* (London: Edward Goldston, 1939), 328–32.

conversion to Catholicism took on an ironic tone, given that only a year later England broke from the Catholic Church, with Henry VIII, now married to Anne Boleyn, becoming head of the Church of England. In the 1530s these women were given some governmental support, then they disappear from the records. We do not know if the new Katherine and Mary converted once again to Henry's Church of England or again felt the chill of persecution.

But still, if someone who had been a Jew became too successful, no matter if there was a conversion, the person could still be targeted, with the anti-Jewish attitudes of the English people coming to the foreground. This became clear in London in 1594 with the case of Roderigo Lopez, a medical doctor. A Portuguese of Jewish background, he came to England in 1559. Around 1563 Lopez married thirteen-year-old Sarah, daughter of Dunstan Anes, born Gonsalvo Anes the son of a Jew in Portugal; the wealthy Anes family had settled in London about 1540, and in 1557 Dunstan had become a freeman of the Grocers' Company. They had at least seven children, three daughters and four sons. The Lopez family publicly attended Christian services but apparently secretly continued to practice as Jews. One way we know this is that Lopez contributed to the upkeep of the secret synagogue in Antwerp.

Hector Nuñez was another distinguished physician who had come from Portugal via Antwerp and lived outwardly as a Christian. He settled in London in 1549 after a decree from the Holy Roman Emperor ordered the New Christians—those who had converted from Judaism—to leave Antwerp. In 1566 Nuñez married Leonora Freire. He was successful both as a physician and as a trader. According to Lucien Wolf, we do not know if Nuñez still practiced Judaism, but "his wife was a devout Jewess." In 1593 she sent, through Lopez, a contribution to the secret synagogue that Lopez was supporting.[17]

Lopez was so successful that he became physician to Elizabeth I. He was convicted, on what may have been quite problematic evidence, of planning to poison the queen and was executed in 1594. Two months after his execution, Sarah Lopez wrote to the queen begging for aid, "in consideration of her afflicted and miserable estate," since all of Lopez's property had been confiscated by the Crown. Sarah described herself as "the sorrowful mother of five comfortless and distressed children born in the realm." Sarah requested that the queen restore the lease of the Lopez house as well as her household, and her other goods, a plea Elizabeth granted, along with money to support

---

17. Lucien Wolf, "Jews in Elizabethan England," *Transactions of the Jewish Historical Society of England* 11 (1928): 8, 9.

the education of Lopez's young son Anthony, suggesting that she may have had doubts about Lopez's guilt. Elizabeth had delayed the execution for some months, but anti-Jewish sentiment in London was so strong that the queen had finally agreed. Lopez was intensely targeted as a demon Jew even though he claimed he was Christian.[18] But many people did not consider even Jews who converted to Christianity "true Christians," and it is little wonder. It is hard to overcome the definition of Jew as smelly, vile, demonic, and more like a dog than a human simply because of baptism.

Monstrous Jewish Woman

One might also wonder if the Jewish woman who did not convert was even more monstrous than her male counterpart, since as Jew she was negating any positive female characteristics. We will see this in the actions of Eve Cohan's mother later in the chapter. In a popular ballad, well known in the Elizabethan period, that was roughly based on a murder that occurred in Lincoln in 1255 there is a particularly monstrous Jewish woman. An illegitimate eight-year-old boy named Hugh disappeared at the end of July. His body was discovered a month later in a well on the property of a Jewish man. On threat of torture and promise of pardon if he only confessed, the Jew told the authorities that the most prominent Jews of England, in Lincoln for a wedding, had participated in the murder since, he confirmed, they crucified a Christian boy every year as a ritual. Henry III had the Jew's pardon revoked, and the man was brutally executed; close to a hundred Jews were taken to London and imprisoned. Eighteen or nineteen were executed, and Henry III confiscated their goods and wealth. This event was eventually portrayed in the popular ballad *Sir Hugh, or the Jew's Daughter,* in which the Jew's daughter lures young Sir Hugh into her house, slaughters him, and hides his body in a gutted pig carcass. Many versions of the ballad developed during the centuries, over the course of which the Jew's daughter became more and more of a monster.

---

18. There is an enormous debate on whether in fact Lopez was guilty. David Katz argues that he was. See Katz, *The Jews in the History of England,* 100. Very recently, Edgar Samuel argues that Lopez was most likely not guilty but that Lopez had acted "stupidly and dishonestly" (ODNB 2005), which made him an easy target. Edgar Samuel, "Lopez, Roderigo (c. 1517–1594)," in *Oxford Dictionary of National Biography,* ed. H. C. G. Matthew and Brian Harrison (Oxford: Oxford University Press, 2004); online ed., ed. Lawrence Goldman, January 2008, http://0-www.oxforddnb.com.library.unl.edu:80/view/article/17011 (accessed September 16, 2008).

> She laid him on a dressing-board,
> Where she did sometimes dine;
> She put a penknife in his heart,
> And dressed him like a swine.[19]

In the original event, the boy is at the bottom of the social ladder; he is a bastard child, and his body is found on the property of a Jewish man. Centuries later, the child has become noble, the Jewish murderer female, and the well a gutted pig, which is especially ironic given that the eating of pork is forbidden to Jews. In the ballad, the Jew's daughter is even more horrific in her actions than the depiction of the potential queen-murderer Lopez. During the Lopez trial, Christopher Marlowe's play *The Jew of Malta,* written a few years earlier, was put on to standing-room crowds. The title character, of course, is the Jewish villain Barabas.

Abigail, The Jew's Daughter

Barabas takes great pride in the artistry of his crimes, and he eventually becomes a monster and a bogeyman-figure. He brags to his Turkish slave Ithamore:

> As for myself, I walk abroad at nights
> And kill sick people groaning under walls;
> Sometimes I go about and poison wells;
> ... And [with] tricks belonging unto brokery,
> I filled the jails with bankrupts in a year,
> And with young orphans planted hospitals,
> And every moon made some or other mad. (2.3.176–78, 194–97)

Barabas is the embodiment of all of the monstrous beliefs about Jews in Elizabethan England. Similar characters appear in nondramatic forms of entertainment. For example, Thomas Nashe's 1594 novel, *The Unfortunate Traveler,* features two Jewish villains—one conducts sadistic medical experiments, and the other enjoys flogging Christian women.[20] Barabas eventually commits the most heinous of all crimes: he murders his only daughter.

---

19. Francis James Child, ed., *The English and Scottish Popular Ballads* (1888, repr. New York: Dover Publications, 1965), 3:245.

20. Gerard Glassman, *Anti-Semitic Stereotypes without Jews: Images of Jews in England, 1290–1700* (Detroit: Wayne State University Press, 1975), 72.

At key moments, such as when Abigail rescues his hidden wealth, Barabas proclaims how much he loves his daughter, but even then Abigail is merely a cherished possession, an object, intertwined with his wealth. "O my girl, oh gold, oh beauty, oh my bliss!" (II.i.55). In *The Merchant of Venice,* Salanio claims that Shylock has made a similar statement after his daughter Jessica runs off to her Christian lover with as much of her father's wealth as she could carry: "As the dog Jew did utter in streets: / 'My daughter! O, my ducats! O, my daughter!'" (2.8.14–15). The Christians of Venice are suggesting that Shylock does not know which disturbs him more, as he cries out for "my daughter, my ducats"; indeed, perhaps the two have coalesced in his mind.

In the first act of *The Jew of Malta,* Barabas discusses his love for his daughter through this parallel:

I have no charge, nor many children,
But one sole daughter, whom I hold as dear
As Agamemnon did his Iphigen:
And all I have is hers. (1.1.135–38)

But such a comparison would make the alert theatergoer uneasy, to say the least. At the bay of Aulis, the Greek fleet did not have the wind to sail to Troy because Agamemnon, the military leader, had insulted the goddess Artemis. Agamemnon sends word to his wife, Clytemnestra, to have Iphigenia brought to Aulis so that he can have her married; instead, he sacrifices his daughter Iphigenia to appease the goddess and begin his war to retrieve Helen and restore the Greeks' sense of self-honor.

For Barabas, rather than "honor" it is wealth and individualism, and he too will use his daughter to achieve his ends. Instead of lying himself, as Agamemnon did to his wife, Barabas convinces Abigail to lie instead. She promises him, "Thus father shall I much dissemble" (1.1.289). Pretending to become a Christian nun, Abigail moves back into their home, which had been confiscated by the Christian governor and turned into a nunnery. When night comes, she throws the wealth Barabas had hidden out of a window to her waiting father and then returns to him.

The reference to Agamemnon is not the only hint of Abigail's fate at her father's hands. For Barabas, revenge on the Christian governor is far more important than the happiness, or even life, of his obedient daughter. When the governor's son Don Lodowick comes to court Abigail, Barabas viciously mutters to himself, "But ere he shall have her, / I'll sacrifice her on a pile of wood" (3.3.52–53). Ruth Hanusa persuasively argues that this is a reference to the Old Testament story of Jephthah, who promised God that if he were to win the impending battle, he would sacrifice as a burnt offering whatever emerged from his house to greet him upon his return. Although distraught that it was his daughter, and not some animal, who ran out of the house, Jephthah kept his vow.

Abigail becomes completely alienated from Barabas, who is even more of a monster than Shylock. Abigail fakes a conversion to join a nunnery to help her father, but she later becomes so horrified with her father's schemes to have Don Lodowick and Don Mathias (whom Abigail loves) kill each other that she really does convert and begs the nunnery to take her back as a postulate. Even then, Abigail maintains some loyalty to her "hard-hearted father," as she calls him (3.3.38). She says as an aside, "Oh, Barabas, though thou deservest hardly at my hands, yet never shall these lips bewray thy life" (3.3.75–77). Though the nuns do take her in, Abigail finds that everyone doubts the sincerity of her conversion. Barabas, on the other hand, does not, calling her "False, credulous, inconstant Abigail!" (3.4.27). Barabas kills Abigail by poisoning the entire nunnery of two hundred. Jephthah's daughter was allowed to be with her female companions for two months before her death; Abigail dies in the company of other women, but with no warning, and these women, the nuns, do not really trust her.

Jessica, The Jew's Daughter

Like Abigail in *The Jew of Malta,* in *The Merchant of Venice* Jessica is the only Jewish woman in the play. She has no like person with whom to share her fears or joys. Though Venice is filled with Christians, even Shylock has his friend Tubal with whom he can commiserate. Jessica's mother Leah is dead, and although later in the play Shylock will speak movingly of Leah, he never does so to Jessica. Though he is distraught that she has left, which could certainly suggest his strong feelings for her, he never expresses them to her. From the very first time we see Jessica, we sense her feelings of isolation and despair. She tells Launcelot the clown, who is leaving her father's service: "I am sorry thou wilt leave my father so; / Our house is hell, and thou a merry devil / Didst rob it of some taste of tediousness" (2.3.1–3). But though Jessica considers her house hell, she is already contemplating her own escape. She asks Launcelot to give Lorenzo a letter—a letter that will help arrange her elopement. Jessica's description of her home may well not be reliable, especially as she is attempting to justify to herself why it is acceptable not only to leave her father but also to steal as much of his wealth as she can carry. We have no evidence that Shylock is cruel to his daughter, but it seems that through her relationship with Lorenzo, Jessica has begun to accept the dominant culture's perception of Shylock, the Jewish moneylender, as a monster.[21]

Jessica feels torn and conflicted over her feelings and her planned actions. She says to herself:

> Alack, what Heinous sin is it in me
> To be ashamed to be my father's child!
> But though I am a daughter to his blood,
> I am not to his manners. O Lorenzo,
> If thou keep promise, I shall end this strife,
> Become a Christian and thy loving wife! (2.3.16–21)

Right from the beginning, Jessica may be expressing some doubts about Lorenzo. "If" he keeps his promise, then she will end her sense of conflict and marry him. If—not when.

Perhaps one reason for Jessica's doubts is that she is not only planning to elope with Lorenzo. She is planning to take a great deal of her father's wealth with her when she does. Lorenzo does send Jessica reassuring messages through Launcelot—"Tell gentle Jessica I will not fail her" (2.4.20–22)—but he is also very concerned about the money. He tells his friend Gratiano "how I shall take her from her father's house, / What gold and jewels she is furnished with" (2.4.30–31). Lorenzo continues in his speech to Gratiano to praise Jessica, but with some doubts on his side as well. He asks that misfortune never dare to "cross her foot" unless fortune "do it under this excuse, That she is issue to a faithless Jew" (2.4.35–37). The suggestion that being Shylock's daughter may justify any ill fortune that may befall Jessica makes her Jewishness her defining characteristic, indeed a negative one that she may not be able to overcome. After Shylock leaves Jessica in the house—continually warning her to keep the house locked up—Jessica knows that she may have seen her father for the last time. "Farewell; and if my fortune be not crost, / I have a father, you a daughter, lost" (2.4.56–57). And by her decision to marry a Christian and convert, she ensures that she is completely lost to Shylock.

When Jessica elopes with Lorenzo, she asks, betraying her insecurity, "Who are you? Tell me for more certainty." Lorenzo answers reassuringly that it is "Lorenzo, and thy love." Jessica: "Lorenzo certain, and my love indeed, / For who love I so much? And now who knows / But you, Lorenzo,

---

21. Robert Wilson's 1584 play *Three Ladies of London,* written a few years earlier than *The Merchant of Venice,* plays against stereotypes because of its positive depiction of a Jewish moneylender, but he does not have a daughter so it is not relevant to this discussion.

whether I am yours?" (2.6.27–32) When Lorenzo again reassures Jessica, she tosses him a casket filled with gold. One wonders—at least I wonder—if at the back of Jessica's mind is the belief that for Lorenzo, Jessica with the gold is one thing, and Jessica without the gold would be quite something else. Jessica did not only take her father's gold. She also stole her father's ring. Would Lorenzo be so quick to elope with his "Jewess" if she had come to him emptyhanded? And if I question this as I read the text or see it acted on stage, I argue, Shakespeare is implying that his character Jessica may have wondered about this as well.

The scene with Jessica at the window tossing down the gold to Lorenzo echoes the scene from *The Jew of Malta* in which Abigail, at the window of the convent that had once been their house, tosses the gold to Barabas. When we remember what Barabas later does to Abigail, it certainly casts a pall over this scene between Jessica and Lorenzo. As Jeremy Tambling points out, not only are Jessica and Lorenzo ambiguous in this context, but so is Abigail in *The Jew of Malta:* "Abigail is innocent, yet finds herself, thanks to her codification within male discourse, engaged in doubtful actions throughout."[22]

We can hardly be surprised that Shylock is outraged and distraught when he returns to find that Jessica has fled. But our first introduction to it is not done directly—rather we learn of it from some of Antonio's friends who are utterly contemptuous of Shylock. Solanio tells Salerio that "the dog Jew did utter in the streets: / 'My daughter! O my ducats! O my daughter!'" (2.8.14–15) Salerio responds that all the boys of Venice follow Shylock and mock him. But though other characters mock Shylock for linking Jessica and wealth, isn't this exactly what Lorenzo does during the elopement? Wealth certainly seems to spark male attraction in this play; however much Bassanio might claim to be in love with Portia, his first mention of her refers directly to her fortune: "In Belmont is a lady richly left" (1.1.161). In this world, wealth is signified by rings. We learn of three rings in this play: the ones Portia and Nerissa give to Bassanio and Graziano, which are not valued properly, and one deeply valued by Shylock, given to him by his late wife.

Shylock's friend Tubal had gone to Genoa to seek Jessica and returns with bad news. He cannot find her but has heard many stories of her extravagance with Shylock's money. Shylock's anguish and anger over the loss of Jessica and her betrayal of him are heartwrenching. "I would my daughter were dead at my foot, and the jewels in her ear! Would she were hearsed at

---

22. Tambling, "Abigail's Party," 106. For a further discussion of the connections between Jessica and Abigail, especially this gesture, see the discussion in Christopher Spencer, *The Genesis of Shakespeare's* The Merchant of Venice (Lewiston, NY: Edwin Mellen Press, 1988), 36–38.

my foot, and the ducats in her coffin!" (3.1.83–85). That statement strongly suggests that Jessica's loss is more devastating to Shylock than the loss of the money—he wishes the ducats were in her coffin, rather than in his pocket. The depth of the anger reflects how deeply Shylock is hurt by Jessica's actions. The money is in some ways symbolic of the entire sense of loss for Shylock, a concrete symbol of a complex emotion. But the worst betrayal is when Tubal tells Shylock that Jessica traded a ring for a monkey. "It was my turquoise; I had it of Leah when I was a bachelor. I would not have given it for a wilderness of monkeys" (3.1.113–16). This statement pulls together a number of themes: the importance of family ties, the sense of loss, and the importance of having a tangible reminder of a departed loved one. It is one of the rare allusions to Jessica's mother. Jessica is motherless with a difficult, complex relationship to Shylock, and she feels isolated from the Christians of Venice. Though she believes that she has found love with Lorenzo, she seals her love with the theft from her father, indeed, with the very ring that has such meaning to him. The rings in the play signify not only wealth but also marriage. During the famous trial scene, Bassanio, who later gives away his wife's ring, says that even though he is married to a woman infinitely dear to him, he would sacrifice her to save Antonio. Shylock's response is a telling one: "These be the Christian husbands!" (4.1.293).

While Portia has been most welcoming to Bassanio's friends, including Lorenzo, she shows little concern for Jessica. From the start it is clear to those in Belmont that Jessica is still a Jew, conversion or no conversion. Lorenzo's friend clearly marks Jessica as "other" when they arrive by stating, "Who comes here? Lorenzo and his infidel!" (3.2.217). Adelman notes that neither Bassanio nor Portia register Jessica's presence, in Belmont or anywhere else: "Bassanio's welcome, reiterated by Portia, extends only to Lorenzo and Salerio; neither Bassanio nor Portia speak directly to her either at her entrance or anywhere else in this scene."[23] Jessica's discomfort would have been intensified once news from Belmont arrives that her father Shylock is threatening Antonio's life with his demand for his "bond." Ralph Berry suggests that, throughout her dealings with Jessica, Portia treats her with "an icy courtesy that projects a very strong sense of distance and distaste."[24] As Adelman suggests, Belmont is not "as distant from England as one might suppose: though they were few in number, the conversos in London may have posed their own

23. Adelman, "Her Father's Blood," 6.
24. Ralph Berry, *Shakespeare's Comedies: Explorations in Form* (Princeton: Princeton University Press, 1972), 14.

kind of blood-conundrum and their own challenge not only to Christian universalism but also to the idea of nationhood."[25]

Portia places the management of her household in Lorenzo's hands when she leaves to go rescue Antonio. The subsequent Belmont scenes are about Jessica, her husband Lorenzo, and the clown Launcelot. Launcelot teases Jessica about being a Jew. This can be played in a more or less comic or tragic manner, depending on the production. It is quite laughable when Launcelot jokes about how conversion can hurt Christians economically by raising "the price of hogs" (3.5.19), since more people will now desire rashers of bacon, another reminder that pork, the use of the pig carcass by the Jew's evil daughter notwithstanding, is taboo for Jews. But jokes can also hide bitter feelings, and Launcelot's statement to Jessica that "truly I think you are damned" (3.5.4) is hardly funny. As Lisa Lampert points out, Launcelot is stating that "despite her conversion and marriage to a Christian...whatever her intentions, there is something essentially Jewish about her."[26] Jessica cannot escape her ill fortune—her eventual damnation—because she is the daughter of Jews and thus by blood a Jew—no conversion can truly erase it. Richard A. Levin argues that by the end of Act III, scene 5, Launcelot is not the only one making Jessica feel isolated: "Even her husband is regarding her as alien."[27]

While the trial is going on in Venice, we have another scene between Lorenzo and Jessica in Belmont. They sit outside romantically in the moonlit garden and talk and tease about classic lovers. But, as has often been pointed out, the lovers they discuss are faithless or tragic: Troilus and Cressida, Pyramus and Thisbe, Dido and Aeneas, Medea and Jason. They are, in Paul Gaudet's description, "paradigmatic figures of romantic tragedy, legendary exemplars that associate love with disruption, grief, suicide, and sorcery."[28] Austin C. Dobbins and Roy Battenhouse depict this scene as a "harmonizing of jest and deeper truth.... The jest depends on the fact that the love story of Lorenzo and Jessica has only a surface likeness.... Their own venture in love has not been one of tragic miscarriage."[29] But I still argue that these examples are perilous parallels. Cressida betrayed Troilus, who was later killed by Achilles. Pyramus assumed that a lion had killed his love Thisbe, so he committed suicide, as Thisbe did when she found Pyramus's dead body. Suicide was common among these couples: abandoned Dido threw herself

---

25. Adelman, "Her Father's Blood," 4.
26. Lampet, *Gender and Jewish Difference,* 161.
27. Richard A. Levin, *Love and Society in Shakespearean Comedy: A Study of Dramatic Form and Content* (Newark: University of Delaware Press, 1985), 80.
28. Paul Gaudet, "A Little Night Music," *Essays in Theatre* 13 (1994): 3.
29. Dobbins and Battenhouse, "Jessica's Morals," 117.

on a burning pyre. As for murderous Medea, her husband's new bride was merely the prologue; the main action was the slaughter of her sons.

Catherine Belsey argues that these allusions are romantic transformation that make what was once dangerous safe and domestic, while Linda Woodbridge suggests that naming Medea as a mythic daughter who renews her father-in-law is Shakespeare's way of making the audience feel less troubled about Jessica's treatment of her father Shylock; given Medea's later behavior toward her husband Jason and their children, however, I find such interpretations problematic.[30] Jessica and Lorenzo, as well as the audience, surely know that these are not positive models for the newly married couple, and Jessica's allusion to Medea may well suggest her resistance, just as Lorenzo's reference to Cressida could be an indirect means to question Jessica's sexual virtue. Jessica says in what may be a joking manner to Lorenzo:

> In such a night did young Lorenzo swear he loved her well
> Stealing her soul with many vows of faith,
> And ne'er a true one. (5.1.12–14)

As Mary Janell Metzger points out, "playful or bitter," Jessica's description of her elopement "hints at the difficulty of establishing trust between persons of different religions, colors, classes."[31] It is possible that Jessica's reference to "soul," "faith," and lack of fidelity in these lines may suggest that living as an outsider in Belmont has made her already ambivalent and regretful about her conversion as well as her marriage. Lorenzo's teasing response shows little understanding: "In such a night did pretty Jessica, like a little shrew, / Slander her love, and he forgave it her" (5.1.20–22). For Lorenzo, Jessica needs forgiveness. Jessica tells Lorenzo that she could "out-night" him, but they hear a messenger coming, who tells them Portia is returning home. The conversation is bantering, but it is undercut by the examples used, which may signal the future of Jessica and Lorenzo's relationship to be problematic. We see this even more in the following discussion, when Lorenzo calls for music.

Those Who Were "Others" Cannot Appreciate Music

One area in which the English perceived those who were different, such as Jews, as inferior was their purported response to music. To the English, music

---

30. Catherine Belsey, "Love in Venice," *Shakespeare Survey* 44 (1992): 43; and Linda Woodbridge, *The Scythe of Saturn: Shakespeare and Magical Thinking* (Urbana: University of Illinois, 1994), 318.

31. Metzger, "Now by My Hood, a Gentle and No Jew," 60.

was a way to connect the human on earth to God, and there was frequent talk
of "the celestial music of the spheres." Many English believed that listening
to, or participating in, holy music was another way for humans to understand
the divine, however briefly. For the English, the belief that they could truly
compose, understand, appreciate, and make beautiful music was part of their
sense of superiority. These attitudes were coupled with a belief that those
who were "other," those who were different, could not appreciate or create
beautiful music and thus were that much less truly human or able to reach
toward heaven. For example, many of the English believed that the music of
Africans was nothing more than dreadful sounding confusion. In 1555 William Towerson returned from traveling in Africa, and told how the singing of
African women "falls ill to our ears." In 1555 William Waterman translated
Johannes Boemus's *The Fardle of Facions conteining the auncient maners, customes
and lawes of the peoples enhabiting the two parts of the earth called Affrike and Asie.*
The book described the Icthiophagi tribe as a sexually promiscuous group
who enjoyed singing but it is "full untuned."[32]

Even though the Jews who came to Henry VIII's court from Italy in the
1530s were brought to England to make music, we see the same belief system
about Jews in the drama of Elizabethan England. In *The Jew of Malta*, Barabas
shows his contempt for the music that meant the most to the English audience when he proclaims, "There is no music to a Christian's knell: / How
sweet the bells ring, now the nuns are dead, / That sound at other times like
tinkers' pans!" (4.1.1–3). Later, he disguises himself as a French musician
to eavesdrop on the traitorous Ithamore more effectively. Barabas, however,
unable to play his lute properly, excuses his poor performance by saying the
instrument is out of tune.

In *The Merchant of Venice* Shylock is portrayed as someone who not only
cannot appreciate music, it actually appears to pain him. In the last scene that
Shylock has with his daughter Jessica, he leaves her at home to go to a feast
at the home of Bassanio. As he is departing, he urges his daughter to close
the windows against the music of the masquers in the street.

What, are there masques? Hear you me, Jessica
Lock up my doors, and when you hear the drum
And the vile squealing of the wry-necked fife,

---

32. Anthony Gerard Barthelemy, *Black Face, Maligned Race: The Representation of Blacks in English
Drama from Shakespeare to Southerne* (Baton Rouge: Louisiana State University Press, 1987), 59–60;
and Joannes Boemus, *The Fardle of Facions,* trans. William Waterson (1555) (Edinburgh: E. and
G. Goldsmid, 1888), II, 39–40.

Clamber not you up to the casements then,
To gaze on Christian fools with varnished faces;
But stop my house's ears—I mean my casements;
Let not the sound of shallow foppery enter
My sober house. (2.5.29–37)

For Shylock, this music is not only something that could pollute his house,
which has come to represent his own identity to such an extent that he mis-
takes its windows for his ears, it could as well dangerously distract and seduce
his daughter. But even more than that, however, hearing music, at least the
"vile squealing of the wry-necked fife" the Christians perform, actually appears to cause him pain.

This is the final time that Shylock gets to see his daughter, since Jessica
takes advantage of his absence to elope with the Christian Lorenzo. Though
Jessica converts to Christianity, some of the characters continue to mock her
as a "Jewess." Once Jessica is in Portia's Belmont as Lorenzo's newly converted wife, she herself appears ambivalent about music. While Lorenzo and
Jessica are out in the gardens in the moonlight, Lorenzo calls for musicians
to come and entertain them.

When the music starts, Jessica tells him, "I am never merry when I hear
sweet music" (5.1.69). If Christians argue that Jews cannot appreciate music,
Jessica in this statement is, by her own designation, still an alien, still an outsider. The sadness the music calls forth from her may also be a reference to
her conflicted relationship with her father, a suggestion of how torn she may
be that she has abandoned him for Lorenzo. If Jessica's wistful statement to
Lorenzo, "I am never merry," is a reference to her past, Lorenzo's response
will only serve to alienate her further from her father and make her more
isolated from Lorenzo himself:

The man that hath no music in himself
Nor is not moved with concord of sweet sounds,
Is fit for treasons, stratagems, and spoils;
The motions of his spirit are dull as night,
And his affections dark as Erebus.
Let no such man be trusted. (5.1.83–88)

Since Erebus is a dark place near Hell, Lorenzo seems to be telling his wife,
and the audience, how the untrustworthy Shylock is so dark and dull that
he is damned, an echo of Salerio, who has earlier called Shylock "the devil."
And one wonders how this would make Jessica feel, to be considered by her

husband as the daughter of an untrustworthy, devilish Jew, an echo of her earlier conversation with Launcelot.

Those on the margins of Elizabethan England, including Jews, were often feared and despised. The characterizations of members of this group on stage both reflected and reinforced these attitudes. In a play such as *The Jew of Malta,* the Jew is the unmitigated villain. In *The Merchant of Venice* there are more glimpses of humanity in Shylock. One way those in Elizabethan England demonstrated their sense of superiority over others in a frightening and changing society was their belief that they could appreciate music, that *they* had music in themselves. But clearly this internal music did little to make the dominant English treat those who were different, "other," in more humane, and human, terms. Jessica's comment about music and sadness are her last lines in the play. Though the play continues for another three hundred lines, she never speaks again.

She never asks Portia or Bassanio how her father is; she never responds to the news of the trial. Lorenzo, on the other hand, is elated with the news Portia brings him, that he will receive yet more of Shylock's wealth, which he describes as "manna for starved people" (5.1.294). This terminology is an ironic twist, given that the word *manna* refers to the food miraculously provided for the Israelites during their flight from Egypt. It can also mean, as Lorenzo no doubt intends it, as something valuable that one receives unexpectedly. Does Jessica share her husband's joy at this further wealth? While silent, the character is a physical presence on stage, and must react in some way—even by doing nothing—in the action of the play as it closes.

The Isolation of the Jewish Woman in Drama

There can be great variation over how Jessica and her relations with the other · characters are portrayed on stage. As Paul Gaudet points out, while Jessica might be able to be passed over in critical readings of the play, "she must be accommodated in performance."[33] In the 1974 Jonathan Miller production of *The Merchant of Venice* starring Laurence Olivier and Joan Plowright as Portia, Portia can never quite remember Jessica's name—she is always stumbling over it while the names of Bassanio's other friends roll easily off her tongue. Richard A. Levin observes that "the National Theatre Company's 1970 production of *The Merchant* rightly takes her remark [about sweet music]

---

33. See Paul Gaudet, "Lorenzo's 'Infidel': The Staging of Difference in *The Merchant of Venice*," in *The Merchant of Venice: Critical Essays,* ed. Thomas Wheeler (New York: Garland, 1991), 351–75.

as evidence of Jessica's alienation from Belmont and her husband."[34] In the 1995 production in New York at the Public Theater with Ron Leibman as Shylock, Lorenzo and Jessica stand away from each other as they look at the moon and talk of potentially false lovers.[35] In a production in the summer of 1995 at the Folger Shakespeare Library with Michael Tolydo as Shylock, Jessica once at Belmont is completely isolated from the other characters, and especially from Lorenzo; she shrinks from his touch. In this production, we see her at the end of the play on a balcony, alone, alienated both from her father Shylock and from her husband Lorenzo.

Another production, again in Washington, D.C., this time at the Shakespeare Theatre Company in the summer of 1999 with Hal Holbrook as Shylock, showed a Lorenzo who, once Jessica threw the casket down, was so entranced by the wealth he almost forgot Jessica. Once in Belmont, the other characters—including Lorenzo—treat Jessica with contempt. The garden scene is not one of lovers teasing each other romantically in the moonlight but rather a scene of scathing bitterness, as Jessica realizes that Lorenzo has married her only for her money. Jessica converts out of love for Lorenzo, only to find that she is still "the Jew."

Both Marlowe and Shakespeare had a Jewish woman character in the plays under discussion, but each author was a non-Jewish man writing in at least certain ways from the point of view of the dominant culture of the late Elizabethan age. We cannot read or watch these plays to know the lives of Jewish women of the time with any accuracy. But their function in the plays is interesting. Though both Shylock and Barabas have other male Jewish compatriots, Abigail and Jessica are alone. Both Jessica and Abigail have strained relationships with their fathers, and the mother of neither character is alive at the time of the action of the play. There is deep poignancy in the turquoise ring—and that that is almost all we know about Leah, Jessica's mother. We know even less about Abigail's mother. There is perhaps a haunting reference to Abigail's mother when Barabas jokes to the friars about confession, claiming his one sin is fornication, adding "But that was in another country, and besides the wench is dead." We do not know to whom Barabas is referring, but if this is his dead wife, Abigail's mother, how dismissive and contemptuous.

Neither Jessica nor Abigail has a mother, neither has any Jewish woman friend, and neither is really accepted into Christian society, even though both

---

34. Levin, *Love and Society*, 82.
35. I am grateful to Ju Yin Ko for describing to me this scene from the 1995 production at the Public Theater in New York.

convert. Perhaps the reason that in each case the daughter deserts the Jewish father is that it lessens the fear of the power of the Jewish man of the English Renaissance by diminishing him. Neither Barabas nor Shylock commands the daughter's love or loyalty. For the Elizabethan audience, this defection may well be a relief. It makes the Jewish male less powerful and less threatening, because the daughter has abandoned him. The Jew is so powerless he cannot control his own household. From what little we know of hidden Jewish culture in the Elizabethan age, women participated fully and were involved with each other in the community. Though they outwardly practiced Anglicanism with their families, they also continued their own rituals. How different for Jessica and Abigail, how vulnerable each one is. Abigail dies by her father's hand, but even Jessica is silenced and potentially isolated. As earlier discussed, many staged versions of *The Merchant of Venice* end with Jessica on stage apart from the other characters—the 2004 film of *The Merchant of Venice* has her standing by the water looking at her turquoise ring—but it was the supposed contempt for this ring that was the final straw for Shylock. Is a Jessica who has kept the ring, though she has still deserted her father, so much better? And even though the film's depiction of Lorenzo is of a loving husband and not a fortune hunter, does the image of Jessica contemplating her mother's ring suggest that this is still an isolated woman whose identity is not accepted in any culture? The drama that surrounds Shakespeare's Jessica, however, pales in comparison to the described travails of *converso* Eve Cohan, who immigrated to England in the late seventeenth century.

The Jews in Seventeenth-Century England

We know there was a Jewish community in London at the time both *The Jew of Malta* and *The Merchant of Venice* were first staged. This fragile Jewish community ended in 1609 with internal battles that led one group to denounce the others as secret Jews; the authorities resolved the situation by expelling all Portuguese merchants in London on the grounds that even if some were not Jewish, this would rid England of those who were.[36] In the 1630s, because of the economic rise of Britain, *converso* Jewish merchants came back to London. While their Jewishness was not open, it was known, but in the 1640s and early 1650s the government and religious authorities did little to harass this community, probably, as Todd Endelman reasons, because there

---

36. Endelman, *Jews in Britain,* 17.

was too much else occupying everyone. Still, some were appalled. Royalist James Howell wrote to a friend in Amsterdam, "Touching Judaism, some corners of our city smell as rank of it as yours doth there."[37]

While the Jews were readmitted to England in 1656 under Oliver Cromwell, it had more to do with the millenarian belief that the end of the world was coming, a worldview that demands the restoration of the Jews, rather than any positive feeling toward the Jewish people. In the mid–seventeenth century, the commercial and religious opposition to Jews was very strong.[38] And we can see how these attitudes continued as the century progressed. A 1680 pamphlet written by William Lloyd, the bishop of St. Asaph, about the conversion of Eve Cohan to Christianity clearly demonstrates this. The bishop's purpose in writing the tract was not merely to tell Eve's story:

> This Recital was thought necessary, to let the Nation see what sort of People these Jews are, whom we harbour so kindly among us; who, as they yet lie under the guilt of that Innocent Blood, which their Fathers wished might rest on them and their Children: so continue not only in their obstinate Infidelity, but do still thirst after the Blood of such of their Nation as believe in Him whom their Fathers Crucified.[39]

The text, while highly critical of the Jews, also reproaches Christians who do not treat the sincerely converting Jewish woman well.

In some interesting ways the life of Eve Cohan as depicted by the bishop echoes certain views of the converted daughter in Renaissance drama, who is also not treated sympathetically by many Christians, who consider such a convert a "counterfeit." While Eve was fatherless, rather than motherless, her mother is depicted as deeply cruel when Eve wishes to convert. She locked Eve in the house, as Shylock in some senses attempts to shut in Jessica; she threatened to poison Eve, as Barabas poisons Abigail.

Eve, who grew up in Holland, was the daughter of the wealthy Abraham Cohan, who died when Eve was a small child. Her mother Elizabeth was the daughter of a professor at the University of Leyden, who, though "a Jew in his heart," presented himself as a Christian, and Elizabeth did the same with

---

37. James Howell to R. Lewis, January 3, 1655, *Epistolaie Ho-Elianae: The Familiar Letters of James Howell*, ed. Joseph Jacobs (London, 1892), 2: 617, cited in Endelman, *Jews in Britain*, 19.

38. Endelman, *Jews of Britain*, 27.

39. *The Conversion & Persecutions of Eve Cohan, Now called Elizabeth Verboon, A Person of Quality of the Jewish Religion, Who was Baptized the 10th of October, 1680, At St. Martins in the Fields, By the Right Reverent Father in God, William, Lord Bishop of St. Asaph* (London, 1680), 25. See also Wolf, *Essays in Jewish History*, 124–25.

her children. Eve, however, was very musical, which suggests her true Christian ties, and the music teacher Elizabeth hired also discussed Christianity with Eve and gave her a New Testament that she secretly read. He took her to Church, supposedly so that she could listen to the music, but secretly allowed her to stay and listen to the sermons as well. Eve desired not to be a counterfeit Christian but to be a true one.

Eve's mother, however, sensed what was going on and fired the music master. She then began to treat Eve with great severity. She kept her as a prisoner at home for six months and then threatened to poison her if she converted. At one point, "for eight days together, she durst eat nothing that they gave her, till she saw others taste of it before her" (3). Her mother often beat her, reminding us of the "Jewishly" behaving Amy Harrison, who beat her god-daughter to death. She would not allow her to come to the front door or look out the windows. Despite this treatment, Eve decided she must dedicate her life to Christ, even though she was afraid her mother would have her killed.

At the same time, Michael Verboon, a servant of her eldest brother Jacob Cohan and thus a resident of the Cohan house, was in love with Eve and asked her to marry him. Eve hoped that with Michael's help she could be brought to a place of safety and truly convert. The two escaped to Brussels, but disliking the practice of Catholicism, they then went on to England. They had not yet married, as Eve was not sure if she wished to do so, and Michael agreed that they would live as brother and sister. Though Eve's mother was wealthy, according to the bishop, she took nothing of her mother's with her when she fled—unlike Jessica. She then started calling herself Elizabeth to break from her old life and to begin her new Christian one. In certain ways the name was an odd choice; since Elizabeth was her mother's name, it was not such a break at all.

Michael got rooms for them in a house in London, and they attended the Dutch Church, still living chastely. But the mother of Eve, or Elizabeth as she was now called, was not content to allow her child this freedom and sent her son Moses Cohen, along with their cousin Samuel, whom her mother hoped her daughter would marry, to go to London and bring the wayward convert home. Verboon feared greatly that her family might persuade Elizabeth, as I will now call her, of this course or even do it by force, so he convinced Elizabeth to marry him. The Jews later claimed, in order to slander this new convert's character, that Elizabeth married Verboon because she was about to give birth to his child, but the bishop proclaimed that Elizabeth did not become pregnant until after the wedding and then miscarried the child due to the fear caused by her evil relations. Moses and Samuel tried to convince Elizabeth to return with them; they wanted her to deny her husband and her Christianity. When that did not work, they consulted Michael Levi, a "Sollicitor for the Jews" living in London (7). Levi visited Elizabeth and "made her many promises of Large Rewards, both of Gold and Silver, if [it] would perswade her to go back to her Mother" (7). But Elizabeth rejected all the offers.

Levi suggested having Verboon arrested and bribed bailiffs to carry this out. But when they came to the house, the sympathetic landlady, Mistress Lavigne, different from most Christians because of her willingness to aid a converted Jew and her family, helped Verboon escape out the window. Hoping to get her back to Holland by force, Michael Levi then employed a man named Hammond to arrest Elizabeth Verboon, under the name Eve Cohan, because her mother had claimed that her daughter had stolen money from her. Eve was taken to prison; to break her will, she was told that if she was pregnant, they would take the baby away after the delivery and she would never see it again.

In the meanwhile, Mistress Lavigne, unlike many of the Christians in London who had no concern for a converted Jew, watched the prison carefully, fearing that "Jews should have brought some to have bailed her out, that so they might get her into their Power" (11). Hammond's attempts at both bribery and threats did not deter Mistress Lavigne; he began to call her "witch" and "bawd" and tried to drag her by the hair. When this still did not scare her off, he told a mob she was a "papist bitch, a harbourer of Jesuits," though in fact she was a good Protestant; only the friends with her saved her from the anti-Catholic mob (13). What helped the new convert most was that while Elizabeth was at Mistress Lavigne's house, the landlady had brought the theologian Dr. Du Veil to talk with Elizabeth. When she was imprisoned, he went to the bishop of St. Asaph, who visited her. He then wrote to counterparts in Holland and found that "every thing that Mistris Verboon had told him, proved to be true" (17).

Elizabeth was put on trial for being a thief. But just like Antonio, she was saved. The judge dismissed all charges since it was clear "that the whole Business was a Conspiracy of the Jews, of which Levi was the Chief Contriver" (19). Yet Elizabeth suffered even more; the dreadful treatment by the Jews caused her to miscarry. When she recovered, the bishop baptized her and formally gave Eve her new name, Elizabeth, at a ceremony in the Church of St. Martin-in-the-Fields. "She has since said, that she felt an unusual Joy in her Mind, when she was initiated to Christianity, having now performed what she had long purposed and wished to do, and though she saw a Jew in the Church, looking and laughing at her in the very time, this did not a whit disorder her" (24). In this story the mother is the Jewish monster and the daughter is the heroine because she completely denounces her Jewish self. Eve/Elizabeth is never really developed as a full human being beyond victim, however, and she is never shown with any other Jewish women, echoing the isolation of Jessica and Abigail. Yet even though this pamphlet is supposedly all about how Jewish woman Eve Cohan becomes Christian woman Elizabeth Verboon, its real point is to use her to show the horrors of Jewish people. And it also demonstrates the impossibility of a Jewish woman completely becoming a "true Christian."

❧ CHAPTER 4

Shakespeare and the Decline
of the Venetian Republic

Sometime in the final months of Elizabeth I's reign, a depressed Venetian took a long walk along the Thames. Giovanni Carlo Scaramelli had come to England as an envoy of the Senate to negotiate a case of piracy involving a Venetian ship and, more generally, to get Elizabeth to do something about the increasing number of English pirates in the Mediterranean. According to his commission, Scaramelli was to inform the queen that "great damage is being done and large booty made by the English who infest these seas. The English ill treat and plunder all alike. . . . [These] acts of piracy committed on the high seas, tend to destroy the ancient trade between our respective countries."[1] Like all Venetian envoys and ambassadors, Scaramelli was a skilled observer not just of the court but also of the whole country where he served.[2] As he roamed London and conversed with merchants, burghers, and courtiers, he discovered a change in the European economy that ultimately threatened Venice even more than piracy: "A large

---

1. *Calendar of State Papers and Manuscripts Relating to English Affairs, Existing in the Archives and collections of Venice and in Other Libraries of Northern Italy,* ed. Rawdon Brown et al., 38 vols. (London: Longman, Roberts, and Green, 1864–1947), 9:530. Hereafter cited as *CSP.*

2. For general discussion of the Venetian diplomatic correspondence, see Garrett Mattingly, "The First Resident Embassies: Medieval Italian Origins of Modern Diplomacy," *Speculum* 12 (1937): 423–39; and Donald Queller, "The Development of Ambassadorial Relazioni," in *Renaissance Venice,* ed. J. R. Hale (London: Faber, 1973), 174–96.

English ship called 'The Royal Exchange,' arrived here three days ago from Syria. Her cargo is worth, they say, three hundred thousand ducats, between indigo, silk, spices, drugs, bombazine, and other goods. All this in other days would have been discharged at Venice." A few days later, Scaramelli noted that "an English ship called the 'Phoenix,' laden with currants in Venice has reached England, a distance of four thousand miles, in less than two months."[3]

What Scaramelli observed firsthand were the effects of mercantile, technological, demographic, and political developments that modern historians have grouped together as factors contributing to the sixteenth-century decline of Venice.[4] Scaramelli's letters—as well as similar ones written by bailos, or the officers who oversaw Venetian diplomatic and commercial affairs in Constantinople, factors, governors, and other diplomats throughout the now waning sphere of Venetian influence—are useful and provocative because they resist what can appear retrospectively as historical inevitability. They bring home the individual and emotional costs that get lost when we narrate historical transitions in terms of comparative rates of import and export, accounts of technological change, or political developments that closed access to some markets and opened it to others. They also sometimes insist in surprising ways on the intimacy with which sweeping changes— the rise of some nations and the decline of others—are interconnected and on the extent to which their parallel occurrence is predicated, precipitated, impeded, and sometimes even forestalled through individual instances of micro-negotiation.

In Scaramelli's letters, nothing is more striking than the contrast between his nostalgia for lost Venetian preeminence and the late Elizabethan patriotism and mercantile confidence voiced in the names of the offending ships. For an English observer, the ships' names—"The Royal Exchange," "The Phoenix"—underscored the nation's pride in its new commercial expansion. The phoenix was a favorite emblem of their queen, and the Royal Exchange was the celebrated mart founded by Thomas Gresham, the man commemorated in Heywood's popular play *If You Know Not Me, You Know Nobody* as

---

3. *CSP* 9:549.

4. Like so many other aspects of Venetian historiography, the notion of a *cinquecento* decline is open to debate. As long ago as 1973, Frederic Lane concluded that "comparing all the signs of wealth and poverty, well-being and misery among the various class of Venetians in 1600 with what we know of them in 1400 or 1500 gives on balance little basis for speaking of a general economic decline." *Venice: A Maritime Republic* (Baltimore: Johns Hopkins University Press, 1973), 334. But Lane also conceded that "it was on the seas that Venice's response to [changing commercial conditions] was least adequate." To the extent that other Europeans identified Venice's economic welfare with its maritime preeminence, its failure to keep up with the Portuguese and later the Dutch and the English signaled to them a general systemic decline.

a "royal merchant."[5] Taken together, the names present an idealized bond between the ancient monarchy and the rising merchant class as the heart of the new economy. But Scaramelli was not an Englishman. He was a Venetian who recognized that English expansion depended on his own nation's contraction. The names revealed a new economic order in which Venice would not be able to compete. While the English merchants, captains, courtiers, and the queen herself looked forward to a glorious future, one in which their Mediterranean triumphs would be schools for their further expansion into Atlantic and Indian oceans, Scaramelli looked back to a receding past. If England was a phoenix, it was rising on Venice's ashes.

Scaramelli's remarks echoed those of other Venetian envoys and consular officers throughout the Mediterranean world. As Maffio Michiel, the governor of the Venetian trading colony of Zante on the west coast of the Peloponnesus, complained to the Doge and Senate,

> The English are becoming absolute masters of these waters. . . . They are utterly supplanting your subjects in the carrying trade, weakening your customs and ruining the merchant service, as your Excellencies must be well aware. The English are not satisfied with having absorbed Venetian trade in the West entirely, but are devoting themselves to a similar object in the Levant. They trade in their own ships to the ports of Alexandria, Alexandretta, and Smyrna and other Turkish cities in Asia Minor, and in the Archipelago, where our ships only used to trade, to the great benefit of the State and of private individuals.[6]

In Constantinople, where the Republic once enjoyed exclusive trading privileges, Venetians dreaded the arrival of English ships bearing broadcloths to the Turk and carrying away luxury goods to England. As Girolamo Capello, the Venetian ambassador to the Sultan, wrote in a ciphered letter to his masters in Venice,

> After waiting a long time for the Queen of England's present to the Sultan, they say that the ship which is bringing it has at last passed the Dardanelles. It brings a cargo of woolen cloth and other high-class goods. . . . The Turks are much pleased at the arrival of this ship as they consider it a confirmation of their alliance with England which they

5. On Elizabeth's use of the phoenix, see Helen Hackett, *Virgin Mother, Maiden Queen: Elizabeth I and the Cult of the Virgin Mary* (Houndmills, U.K.: Macmillan, 1995), 220.

6. *CSP* 9:536.

think is highly important for holding the king of Spain in check. . . . If the trade in woolen cloth especially makes way here, as is expected, on account of its excellence and its appearance, in which the Turks delight, the Venetian trade will receive a great blow.[7]

The English now enjoyed all the advantages once monopolized by the Republic: access to lucrative markets, state-of-the-art seamanship, a reputation for quality merchandise, and, best of all, a favorable political position with the Mediterranean world. Ironically, the neutrality that had kept Venice from colliding with Spain on the Italian peninsula now cost it its former standing with the Sultan, who preferred doing business with a power that openly shared his hostilities.

As passionately as these Venetian voices sounded from the eastern end of the Mediterranean, it was perhaps in London itself that the consequences of England's encroachment on the Venetian economy were most evident. G. D. Ramsey has noted that the third quarter of the sixteenth century witnessed the virtual undoing of the ancient Italian mercantile colony in London.[8] Venetians, and Italians in general, had become conspicuous by their relative absence, and the ones to be found in London were increasingly likely to be intellectuals, artists, and religious refugees rather than merchants engaged in trade. Their presence marked a brain drain that was itself another symptom of Italian social, political, and cultural disruption.

Paradoxically, the disappearance of actual Italians from the wharfs and custom houses of London coincided with a proliferation of Italians on the English stage, often in plays based on Italian sources. We don't know if Scaramelli saw any plays during his stay in London, but if he did, he may well have seen English actors aping the manners of his countrymen. Shakespeare had set one romantic comedy after another in northern Italy, and Marston had used the rivalry between Italy's greatest maritime states as the backdrop for two plays recounting the tragic love between the Venetian Mellida and the Genoese Antonio. Shakespeare's *Othello,* with its warnings about "supersubtle" Venetian women, would open about a year after Scaramelli's visit, soon to be followed by yet another Venetian play, Jonson's *Volpone.* The next several years witnessed many more plays with Italian settings and with plots derived from Italian sources.

---

7. *CSP* 9:371–72.

8. G. D. Ramsey, "The Undoing of the Italian Mercantile Colony in Sixteenth-Century London," in *Textile History and Economic History: Essays in Honour of Miss Julia de Lacy Mann,* ed. N. B. Harte and K. G. Ponting (Manchester: University of Manchester Press, 1973), 22–49.

Scholars have long explained this interest in Italy on moral, political, and religious grounds, such as fascination with the region's Catholicism, the allegedly looser sexual mores of its major cities, the republicanism of Venice, and the despotism of Milan and Naples.[9] But these Italian plays, particularly when read in the context of contemporary diplomatic and mercantile correspondence, also suggest that the stage was responding to shifting mercantile relations between England and its Italian trading partners. England was no longer the solid exporter of wools that purchased currants, wines, and other Mediterranean goods transported predominantly on Italian ships. As Scaramelli recognized, England itself had become a major importer of Mediterranean produce and luxury goods, all carried on its own ships.

As a declining competitor for new markets and trade routes, Venice provided both inspiration and admonition for the English. London was poised to become the new Venice, and England was about to assume the intimate alliance with the sea that had long characterized the waning Mediterranean republic. Plays by Dekker, Heywood, and other writers of citizen comedy captured the excitement that attended the expansion of English merchants into new, and newly discovered, markets. The sea no longer served England primarily, in the words of Shakespeare's John of Gaunt, "in office of a wall." It had become the country's primary route to wealth and power, a medium bringing it into advantageous contact with other nations rather than shielding it from them.

But other writers looked more guardedly at England's transition into an import-based economy as a threat to the country's moral and social integrity. Preachers and satirists condemned maritime adventure as a godless, foolhardy pursuit of vanities. Sir John Davies decried the folly of people who "trust a *Merchant,* that may *breake; /* More than that *King,* of whom all *Kings* do

---

9. I am indebted throughout to the voluminous scholarship on Anglo-Italian cultural relationships in the early modern period. See especially Robert C. Jones, "Italian Settings and the 'World' of Elizabethan Tragedy," *Studies in English Literature* 10 (1970): 251–68; G. K. Hunter, *Dramatic Identities and Cultural Traditions: Studies in Shakespeare and His Contemporaries* (Liverpool: University of Liverpool Press, 1978), 103–21; John Lievsay, *The Elizabethan Image of Italy* (Ithaca: Cornell University Press, 1964); Murray Levith, *Shakespeare's Italian Settings and Plays* (New York: St. Martin's Press, 1989); Louise George Clubb, *Italian Drama in Shakespeare's Time* (New Haven: Yale University Press, 1989); and Jack D'Amico, *Shakespeare and Italy: The City and the Stage* (Gainesville: University Press of Florida, 2001). I have found especially useful the essays in Michele Marrapodi et al., eds., *Shakespeare's Italy: Functions of Italian Locations in Renaissance Drama* (Manchester: Manchester University Press, 1997). Two books deal especially well with the impact of the Venetian republican legacy: David C. McPherson, *Shakespeare, Jonson, and the Myth of Venice* (Newark: University of Delaware Press, 1990); and Andrew Hadfield, *Literature, Travel, and Colonial Writing in the English Renaissance, 1545–1625* (Oxford: Oxford University Press, 1999), 226–42. See also J. R. Mulryne, "History and Myth in *The Merchant of Venice,"* in Marrapodi et al., eds., *Shakespeare's Italy,* 87–99.

seeke?"[10] In *The Spiritual Navigator,* Thomas Adams argued that merchants epitomized a self-destructive pride in earthly prosperity:

> How many Ships haue bene thus cast away! How many Merchants hopes thus split? They call their vessels by many prosperous names: as the Successe, the Good speed, the Triumph, the Safeguard; How vaine doth one Rocke proue all these titles!... The world, as the Sea, is a swallowing Gulfe. It deuoures more then the Sea of Rome: yea, and will deuoure that to at last. It swallowes those that swallow it: and will triumph one day with insultation ouer the hugest Cormorants, whose gorges haue bene long ingurgitated with the world; In visceribus meis sunt: They are all in my bowels. The Gentleman hath swallowed many a poore man: the Merchant swallowes the Gentleman: & at last this Sea swallowes the Merchant.[11]

Adams's sermon, like Scaramelli's dispatches, registered the national pride signified by the names of the ships in the English merchant fleet. But unlike many of his English compatriots, Adams repudiated it as an arrogance that blinded people to the consequences of their quest for gain. The sea poised to swallow the unsuspecting merchant offered the perfect metaphor for a commercial world distracting people from the true security they could find only in God.

If England was about to follow the Venetians in forging a mythic bond to the sea, moralists like Davies reminded them just how unreliable that relationship might be. Any celebration of England's rising place in the European economy carried a melancholy countertext: assuming Venice's mantle as a great trading power could also mean assuming its vulnerability to fiscal and moral decay. One of the most poignant reminders of that possibility was a popular treatise on Venice often credited with inaugurating an English interest in Venetian republicanism, Gasparo Contarini's *De magistratibus et republica Venetorum.* Although Contarini celebrated the Venetian constitution as a model of rationality, order, and the rule of law, he concluded his argument by noting that the Republic was as subject to mutability as anything else in Nature:

> For nature so works that nothing can be permanent among men, but all things, no matter how perfectly they seem to have been established

---

10. John Davies, *The Muse's Sacrifice* (London, 1612), 133.

11. Thomas Adams, *The blacke devil or the apostate. Together with the wolfe worrying the lambes. And the spiritual navigator, bound for the Holy Land. In three sermons* (London, 1615), 25, 15.

at the beginning, require restoration after some years, since nature in-
clines toward the worse; just as the body, though sated with its midday
meal, cannot long remain sound unless dinner follows some hours later.
Thus in everything it is necessary to assist and renew declining nature.
May God help us to follow reason in this too, and devise such a remedy
that everything needful may be provided in our Republic.[12]

Contarini's appeal to natural analogies almost sets the matter of Venice's
decline—both the determination of its causes and the discovery of a remedy—
beyond political analysis. Throughout the treatise, confidence in the stability
of the nation's constitution rests uneasily alongside a darker suspicion that
catastrophe is inevitable, even for the savvy Venetians: "For nature so works
that *nothing* can be permanent among men." Perhaps no single work so inspired Englishmen to recreate their country on Venetian lines. But the more
carefully Englishmen read Contarini, the more his treatise suggested that
England's displacement of Venice might herald England's own eventual displacement by some future commercial power.

Shortly before Contarini's tract—which had already circulated in Latin,
French, and Italian—appeared in English translation, yet another "Venetian"
voiced a similar melancholy on the English stage. Antonio, the titular hero
of Shakespeare's *The Merchant of Venice,* begins the play with the observation,
"I know not why I am so sad," and, as Shakespeareans have long noticed,
never really gets over his sadness. Nor do we ever find out what is causing
it. Recent critics have tried to account for it on the grounds that Antonio is
a prototype of the alienated homosexual or the anxious English merchant.
More recently, Phyllis Rackin has treated his sadness as a projection of a pervasive ambivalence about the expansion of the English economy in the late
sixteenth century, an ambivalence that anticipates "our own predicament in a
world where expanding global trade is promoted as a universal, humanitarian
benefit, [while] ethnic warfare and racist hate crimes seem to be escalating in
every corner of the globe."[13]

While I welcome Rackin's efforts to situate the play's representations of
affect in the history of public commerce, her reading, like most accounts of

---

12. Quoted and translated in William J. Bouwsma, *Venice and the Defense of Republican Liberty*
(Berkeley: University of California Press, 1968), 153. For discussion of Contarini's impact on En-
glish, and more generally European, political thought, see Elizabeth G. Gleason, *Gasparo Contarini:
Venice, Rome, and Reform* (Berkeley: University of California Press, 1993); McPherson, *Shakespeare,
Jonson,* 20, 22–23; and Hadfield, *Literature, Travel,* 46–58.

13. Phyllis Rackin, "The Impact of Global Trade in *The Merchant of Venice,*" *Shakespeare Jahrbuch*
138 (2002): 72–88, quotation 88.

Shakespeare's place in the European expansion, historicizes his plays more from the perspective of the troubled *ends* of that transition than of its equally troubled *beginnings*. After all, Antonio describes himself as "sad," and I am reluctant to equate melancholia with anxiety. Within either a pre- or post-Freudian analysis, the two states have different psychogenic origins; as responses to the history of sixteenth-century commerce, they suggest divergent geographies and events. If Antonio is merely a surrogate for English merchants contemplating untapped markets in the Levant, the East Indies, and ultimately the Atlantic, his primary emotions may be the anxiety and ambivalence of someone on the brink of a new national identity. But that reading discounts the play's Italian setting as a mere cover for contemporary English experience.[14] It also ignores the play's vestiges of a fundamentally medieval Mediterranean economic order represented in Shakespeare's source, a fourteenth-century story of a gentile merchant's dependence on a Jewish moneylender. Most importantly, an Atlanticist/Indian-Oceanist telos suppresses the experience of historical contingency that *The Merchant of Venice*, like the documents in the Venetian Archivio di Stato, so effectively captures. By the time Shakespeare wrote the play in the late 1590s, merchants, diplomats, and observant travelers knew that Venice was in trouble. But no one necessarily knew what was going to happen to the Republic, what its fate might mean for the Atlantic powers poised to inherit its mantle. In all its ambiguities, Shakespeare's play captures that uncertainty as observers around Europe contemplated Venice's illustrious past, its troubled present, its uncertain future, and the implications of its history for other nations increasingly invested in maritime commerce.

The Merchant of Venice offers one of Elizabethan England's most eloquent testaments to the place of melancholia in the drama of early modern imperial expansion. The anxiety that attended England's emergence as a major mercantile power in the Atlantic intersected not just with a heightened awareness of the Italian city-states in the Mediterranean that it was displacing, but also, arguably, with an impeded mourning for them. Shakespeare's play commemorates, castigates, and imaginatively revitalizes decaying Venice with all the conflicting attitudes that might attend any heir's response to the

---

14. Only one critic, David McPherson, has suggested that Antonio's sadness might have something to do with Venice's commercial difficulties in the late sixteenth century. Even he draws back from too close an association between the predicaments of the character and the city in which he lives: "I certainly do not mean to construct an historical allegory here in which Antonio somehow stands for the entire Venetian merchant trade, and its decline is symbolized by his sadness." McPherson, *Shakespeare, Jonson,* 54. In McPherson's reading, the city's decline primarily provides a background that renders Antonio's bankruptcy plausible.

decline of a parent whose death underwrites his or her own prosperity. In recreating the maritime republic in a London theater, the play exaggerates, denies, foregrounds, excuses, and covers up those aspects of the city's political, social, and economic life to which Venetians like Contarini and foreign visitors alike attributed its difficulties: its failure to break into the Atlantic trade, its embattled position within a Mediterranean world now dominated by Ottomans in the east and the Spanish Habsburgs in the west, its celebrated openness to foreigners, and its ambivalence toward the creation of a greater Venetia on the Italian mainland that might offset its dependence on the sea.

The Florentine Connection: Ser Giovanni Fiorentino and a Pound of Venetian Flesh

In engaging England's conflicted response to Venice and the specter of waning maritime preeminence, Shakespeare transformed a text that was itself a monument to a prior moment of mercantile rivalry, the Florentine Ser Giovanni's story of a Venetian merchant who secures a loan from a malicious Jew by offering a pound of his own flesh as collateral. Ser Giovanni included the story in *Il Pecorone,* a Decameron-like collection of tales. Shakespeare's dramaturgy may lure his audiences into believing that they are glimpsing something of Venice in its sixteenth-century social complexity, but what Shakespeare primarily imitates is not Venice per se but a Florentine fantasy about the city during the fourteenth century. The all-but-anonymous Ser Giovanni anticipated and in great part scripted Shakespeare's ambivalence toward Venice as the model of a rich but potentially unstable mercantile society.[15] By recovering the original Italian context of Ser Giovanni's story and then analyzing Shakespeare's departures from it, I hope to situate *The Merchant of Venice* more precisely in the history of Anglo-Venetian and, more generally, Atlantic and Mediterranean rivalry.

When Ser Giovanni wrote, Venice and Florence had reached critical moments in their own respective developments and in their interaction with each other. In Venice, the post-plague years witnessed a massive increase in the public debt, currency instability, and escalating tensions with Genoa, the Republic's chief trading rival. The conflict with Genoa embroiled Venice in four wars, the last of which, the scarring War of Chioggia (1378–81), opened the year Ser Giovanni seems to have begun *Il Pecorone.* The fourteenth

---

15. For a comprehensive discussion of the work's authorship and dating, see Enzo Esposito's introduction to his edition of *Il Pecorone* (Ravenna: Longo Editore, 1974), vii–xxxiii.

century's final decades were also difficult for Florence, where factional conflict finally erupted in the Ciompi uprising of 1378 by wool workers and other craftsmen against the dominant guilds. Although the rebellion ushered in the most democratic government Florence had ever known, within five years the reforms were overturned. In general, the late fourteenth century witnessed a serious economic depression triggered by a Europe-wide collapse in the demand for Florentine wool. Florentines experienced rising prices, strikes, hunger riots, and mob violence against prominent members of the city's regime. The Commune resorted to drastic tax measures to support a controversial war against the papacy, and numerous bankruptcies followed. The famous Guardi firm failed in 1371 with a loss of one hundred thousand florins.[16]

Throughout these turbulent decades, Venetian-Florentine relations were relatively stable. Venice hosted a large Florentine merchant community, and the cities regularly traded with each other. They shared a common commitment to republican government in the face of rising despotism. Both cities, for example, worried about the Visconti seizure of power in Milan. When Genoa, Naples, and Rome succumbed to ecclesiastical pressure during the War of the Eight Saints (1375–78) and expelled all Florentine merchants residing within their cities, Venice continued to do business with its fellow republic in defiance of papal orders.[17] Florence similarly refused a 1372–73 invitation from the King of Hungary to assist him in his war against Venice.

But despite the appearance of mutual good republican will, there were also underlying tensions. Economic self-interest sometimes interfered with ideological loyalties. In the early fifteenth century, Doge Tommaso Mocenigo cautioned against too strong a commitment to Florence in the face of Visconti expansion. Milan was a major trading partner who supplied the Venetians with most of their imported agricultural produce. Mocenigo even argued that Florence's demise might be a good thing, since talented Florentine merchants—used to living in a republic—would relocate to Venice and bring their wealth and entrepreneurial talents with them. Venice was a more closed society than Florence, which had a measure of genuine social mobility. Venice, in contrast, did not; by the late thirteenth century, membership in the *gran consiglio* was already closed on the strict basis of heredity.[18] If the

16. Gene A. Brucker, *Florentine Politics and Society, 1343–1378* (Princeton: Princeton University Press, 1962), 244–96.

17. Brucker, *Florentine Politics,* 311.

18. See Hans Baron, "A Struggle for Liberty in the Renaissance: Florence, Venice, and Milan in the Early Quattrocento," *American Historical Review* 58 (1953): 544–70. See also Baron, "The

aristocratic Venetians looked on the Florentines as parvenus, the Florentines saw the Venetians as snobs, cheats, and lechers. In *The Decameron,* Boccaccio condemned the city as the receptacle of all filthiness (*d'ogni bruttura ricevitrice*) and used it for his story about a friar who seduces an arrogant and none-too-chaste matron by convincing her that he is the angel Gabriel.[19]

Because of the generally friendly relationship between the two cities, Venice was one of the cities where young Florentine merchants typically completed their training by serving in the foreign branch of a Florentine firm. But Florentines hardly saw Venice as a place free from dangers. In 1387, for example, factors and employees of several Florentine companies resident in Venice were embroiled in a scandal that attested to the city's corrupting influence. When several young Florentines lost all their cash in high-stakes gambling, they stayed in the game by issuing letters of credit drawing on their home offices. Their eventual losses had a devastating impact on the Florentine business community. Goro Abizzi complained from Venice to a Florentine colleague that "all honest men and merchants everywhere should act together to drive from the [business] world these men who have been responsible for the destruction of the [Pecora] company, which has always been one of the best in this city."[20]

This bankruptcy in Venice has several analogies with the story on which Shakespeare based *The Merchant of Venice.* In Ser Giovanni's original version, the Bassanio character, Gianetto, is Florentine rather than Venetian, and the third son of a rich merchant who made his fortune in the Black Sea and Mediterranean trade. When the father realizes he is dying, he bequeaths his wealth to his two elder sons and gives Gianetto only letters of introduction to his Venetian friend Ansaldo, *"il più ricco mercatante che sia oggi tra' Cristiani"* (88).[21] Ansaldo lavishes presents on Gianetto, sets him up in Venetian society, and even outfits a ship for him to begin his career as a merchant. When the ship is lost, Ansaldo outfits another one for him and, when that one is also lost, a third. Pressed to his financial limits, Ansaldo raises money for the third ship by borrowing from a Jew of Mestre, a mainland suburb, and the story continues much as in Shakespeare.

By turning the Florentine Gianetto into the Venetian Bassanio, Shakespeare deleted what may have been the most important feature of Ser Giovanni's

Anti-Florentine Discourses of the Doge Tommaso Mocenigo (1414–23): Their Date and Partial Forgery," *Speculum* 27 (1952): 323–42.

19. Boccaccio, *Decameron,* ed. Vittore Branca (Turin: Einaudi, 1991), 490.

20. Gene A. Brucker, *Renaissance Florence* (Berkeley: University of California Press, 1969), 75.

21. All references are to the 1974 Esposito edition and are cited by page number in the text. I have provided my own English translation of the quoted passages.

story for its original Italian audience, its reflections on Venice as a place where young Florentines served their mercantile apprenticeships. As the story unfolds, Ser Giovanni characterizes Venice as a place of great wealth and opportunity but also as a place of exotic danger. Gianetto spends an enormous amount of Ansaldo's money in efforts to keep up with Venetian fashions:

> Di che Gianetto cominciò a usare cogli uomini di Vinegia, cominciò a fare cene e disinari, cominciò a donare, vestire famigli, comperare di buoni corsieri, giostrare, bigordare, come quello ch'era sperto e pratico e magnanimo e cortese in ogni cosa. (90–91)
>
> [So Gianetto began to associate with the gentlemen of Venice, began to host dinners, and began to make gifts, livery servants, purchase fine horses, joust, tilt, as one who was experienced and practiced and magnanimous and courteous in everything.]

His makeover works beautifully. Before long, he is embraced by the notoriously closed and xenophobic upper echelons of Venetian society. But like the actual Florentine factors and mercantile employees who ruined themselves and their companies in the 1387 gambling scam, Gianetto ventures everything and loses it on a grand, ultimately disgraceful scale. According to the story that he later tells Ansaldo and everyone else in Venice, his ship went down and he alone escaped by clinging to a piece of wood. In fact, he loses his ship to a woman. In the course of his voyage, he lands at the estate of the infamous lady of Belmonte, a rich widow who promises herself and her wealth to any guest who is able to bed her without falling asleep. There is, of course, the usual romance trick: she drugs her would-be lovers with a sleeping potion before they come to her chamber, and the next day they must suffer the consequence of having all their worldly possessions confiscated. Gianetto succumbs twice to her trick and only succeeds at last because a servant who likes him reveals her mistress's secret.

In the story, the lady's wager epitomizes the risk inherent in Venice's economic dependence on the sea. Whereas Shakespeare, as I will later argue, associates Belmont with the Venetian mainland, Ser Giovanni presents it as a distant coastal estate, several days' voyage from Venice, and casts its mistress as a latterday Circe. Since the Adriatic coast of Italy is relatively flat, the name "Belmonte" may suggest that she lives somewhere along the Dalmatian coast. This area was notorious throughout the Middle Ages and early modern period for its pirates, and there is certainly a hint of piracy in the lady's conduct toward her visitors. But regardless of her precise ethnic or national identity, Ser Giovanni's view of the maritime basis of the Venetian economy could not be clearer: the Republic's relationship to the sea—so touted in its mythic self-understanding—balances enormous, sometimes even exotic, opportunities against enormous risks.

Gianetto's journey from Florence to Venice and beyond the sea to Belmonte transforms the typical story of a Florentine youth who gambles away a fortune in Venice into a more general critique of Venetian society. In leaving Florence, Gianetto abandons the security of a diversified economy, where the wealth of foreign trade is bolstered by the wealth of domestic manufacture, the celebrated wool industry that greedy Venetians like Mocenigo imagined relocating to Venice. What he discovers is a society where gambling is not only an avocation but a practice on which the economy rests. All Venetians are essentially gamblers in their dependence on the sea. The young merchants who invite him to sail with them in a convoy to Alexandria speak of their risk-laden undertaking as a kind of diversion:

> Or avenne che due suoi cari compagni volsono andare in Allessandra co lloro mercantanzie e co lloro due navi, com'eglino soleano fare ogni anno. Di che eglino el dissono con Gianetto s'egli volea dilettarsi d'andare co lloro per vedere del mondo, e massimamente quel Domasco e quel paese di là. (91)
>
> [Then it happened that his two dear companions wanted to go to Alexandria with their merchandise and their two ships, as they were accustomed to do each year. Discussing this with Gianetto, they asked if he would like to amuse himself by going with them to see the world, and especially Damascus and its surroundings.]

The sangfroid with which Ansaldo accepts Gianetto's losses suggests the indifference of a whole society inured to the possibility of financial catastrophe: "Figliuol mio, e' non ti bisogna vergognare da me, che usanza è che delle nave rompino in mare." [My son, you don't need to be ashamed around me, since it is usual for some ships to break up at sea.] (96) Not surprisingly, Gianetto himself considers running back to the greater security of Florence after disaster strikes him a second time. But with Ansaldo's encouragement, he commits himself to *la vita veneziana,* allows his friend to borrow money from a Jew of neighboring Mestre, and ventures their common fortune yet again. By this point in the narrative, he has so internalized the Venetian addiction to adventure, figured symbolically as his obsession with the elusive lady of Belmonte, that return to Florence has become impossible.

The deal with the Jew of Mestre on which the plot turns underscores one of the most crucial points of divergence between Florentine and Venetian society in the late *trecento*: the role of Jewish moneylenders in the respective republican economies. Venice was one of the first major Italian cities to allow Christian residents to borrow money from Jews; Florence was one of the last. Despite Church condemnations of usury, Christian moneylenders operated clandestinely in Florence throughout the fourteenth century. These money-lenders included men of the highest social rank, and they adamantly opposed admitting Jews into the city proper, although Jewish pawnbrokers had oper-ated in the city's territories for decades. In 1396, the commune authorized Jews to lend money in Florence itself at 15 percent interest, a figure so low that the city fathers probably meant it more as a threat to Christian lend-ers than as a serious offer to Jews. Despite such tepid overtures, Christians retained their monopoly until 1437, shortly after Cosimo de' Medici's return from exile. In general, Jewish moneylending in Florence followed a typical pattern: its appearance tended to coincide with the decline of the republican communes and the rise of despots.[22]

Venice was one of the few places that did not conform to that pattern. When the Republic acquired the mainland suburb of Mestre in 1338–39, it allowed Jewish lenders to operate there. In trying to resolve the economic crisis created by the Fourth Genoese War (1378–81), it permitted them to operate within the city itself. Historians have sometimes exaggerated the extent to which fourteenth-century Venice accepted the presence of Jewish moneylenders and the overall quality of Jewish life before the establishment of the first Ghetto in 1516, when Jews were finally granted permanent residence within the city.[23] Throughout the Late Middle Ages, Jews were subjected to perpetual threats of expulsion, forced to wear identifying badges, and threatened with fines and imprisonment if they dared to have sex with a Christian. But even if they were granted nothing approximating the rights of Venetians, they were nevertheless a feature of Venetian life in the late fourteenth century and, in further contrast to Florence, a significant element in the city's lending economy.

Ansaldo's decision to borrow money from a Jew of Mestre thus fore-grounds a principal factor distinguishing Venetian from Florentine eco-nomic practice: the city's dependence on a Jewish moneylending community

22. Léon Poliakov, *Jewish Bankers and the Holy See From the Thirteenth to the Seventeenth Century*, trans. Miriam Kochan (London: Routledge and Kegan Paul, 1977), 56–57.

23. See Benjamin Ravid's correction of the traditional view that Jews had been an integral part of Venetian life as early as the twelfth century in "The Venetian Government and the Jews," in *The Jews of Early Modern Venice*, ed. Robert C. Davis and Ravid (Baltimore: Johns Hopkins University Press, 2001), 3–30. See also Ravid, "The Jewish Mercantile Settlement of Twelfth and Thirteenth-Century Venice: Reality or Conjecture?" *Association for Jewish Studies Review* 2 (1977): 201–26.

living just across the lagoon on the Venetian mainland. If the story had been set in late medieval Florence, Ansaldo would have borrowed money from a Christian, possibly one from the highest social ranks. But in Venice, the likeliest candidate would be a Jew. The grotesqueness of the unnamed Jew's bargain quickly became a trope for the Jewish community's perceived parasitic, even cannibalistic, relationship to the Venetian economy. Venice was no more dependent on moneylending than any other Italian commercial center, including Florence. But its precocity in borrowing money from Jews—a practice that Florence would not generally adopt until the middle of the fifteenth century—underscored the dependence. Jewish moneylending, unlike its Christian counterpart, could not be disguised as an act of Christian charity. It was a business deal, one that reminded everyone of Venice's commercial bonds to foreign communities both abroad and even living within its own territory. As Ser Giovanni recognized, the Venetians' pride in their city and its wealth entailed repressing a potentially humbling awareness that the city never fully controlled its own destiny.

In contrast to Shakespeare's later adaptation of the story, nothing in Ser Giovanni's denouement diminishes this impression of a city dependent not just on the wealth but ultimately on the good will of foreigners. While Shakespeare domesticates Portia by situating her Belmont only a short *traghetto* ride across the lagoon from Venice, Giovanni's unnamed lady of Belmonte retains her foreign aura throughout the novella. She has no Paduan uncle, introduces no Christian rhetoric into the proceedings, and never mentions the laws of Venice. She simply tells the Jew that he will be beheaded if he sheds one drop of Ansaldo's blood in the process of extracting the pound of flesh. Recognizing that he has been trapped, the Jew tears up his bond and leaves without hearing any anything about the state's determination to defend its citizens against foreigners. As in *The Merchant of Venice,* a foreigner has placed a Venetian life in jeopardy. But in Giovanni's version, another foreigner—not a woman with Venetian ties—redeems it. The Venetian citizen, and by extension the Republic itself, plays a passive role in this contest between foreign wits.

Although Ser Giovanni's story has a happy ending for Gianetto and his Venetian patron, it does not necessarily have a happy ending for Venice. Venetian laws and Venetian wealth prove incapable of protecting Venetian citizens from the malevolence of foreigners. What finally saves the day is the cleverness of the lady of Belmonte, a woman who herself first appeared as a kind of exotic threat with her potions and conspicuous symbolic castrations. Giovanni never lets us quite forget her mysterious, almost sinister associations with magic and even violence. Just before the trial scene, she smears her face with a secret herb to make sure that Gianetto cannot recognize her. When she later accuses him of giving her ring to a former Venetian lover, Giovanni tells us that "he looked as if he had been cut through the heart with a knife" (*parve che le fusse dato d'un coltello nel cuore*), a phrase that both recalls her earlier adversarial relationship to him and links her directly to the Jew in a kind of foreign blood thirst for natural and adoptive Venetian blood (118). She finally yields both herself and her property to Gianetto not as a Venetian lady but as a descendant of Circe, a figure of romance who removes the hero and his old friend alike forever from Venetian society and places them in the magical security of Belmonte.

In the end, Venice has served as a step on Gianetto's ultimate journey from Florence to Belmonte, an example of what Fredric Jameson has called a "vanishing mediator," something that catalyzes social change but whose presence in the final social synthesis is negligible.[24] When Gianetto and even Ansaldo—a lifelong resident—leave the city once and for all, their departure exposes a question at the heart of Venetian society: what finally defines the city as a sovereign entity if its wealth derives from foreigners; if its young men are constantly en route to Alexandria or Damascus; and if its noblest and richest citizens eventually relocate themselves in the more recognizably feudal, land-based economies of places like Belmonte? A fourteenth-century Venetian would have had eloquent answers to such questions that emphasized the stability of the Republic's constitution, the perfection of its laws, and the venerable duration of its marriage to the sea.[25] But Ser Giovanni never mentions the city's laws and treats the sea as an expression of everything opposed to a stable sovereign identity. The Florentine fiction foregrounds the anxieties about identity that haunted Venice itself in the Late Middle Ages, with its ever more stringent articulations of the *serrata,* the laws that restricted membership in the city's governing counsels to those who could prove a longstanding hereditary residence.

Venice, that disturbingly open society located just at the point where land yields to the open sea, became for both Ser Giovanni and later writers an

24. See Fredric Jameson, "The Vanishing Mediator; or, Max Weber as Storyteller," in Jameson, *The Ideologies of Theory: Essays 1971–1986,* vol. 2, *Syntax of History* (Minneapolis: University of Minnesota Press, 1988), 3–34.

25. On the closed character of Venetian society, see Dennis Romano, *Patricians and Popolani: The Social Foundations of the Venetian Renaissance State* (Baltimore: Johns Hopkins University Press, 1987); Gerhard Rösch, "The *Serrata* of the Grand Council and Venetian Society, 1286–1323," and Stanley Chojnacki, "Identity and Ideology in Renaissance Venice: The Third *Serrata,*" in *Venice Reconsidered: The History and Civilization of an Italian City-State, 1297–1797,* ed. John Martin and Dennis Romano (Baltimore: Johns Hopkins University Press, 2000), 67–88, 263–94.

image of the threat maritime commerce posed to stable personal and national identity alike. In the years between *Il Pecorone* and *The Merchant of Venice,* the factors that contributed to Ser Giovanni's unsettling depiction of the city became even more prominent. Foreign residents played an even greater role in the city's economic life. In 1573, the city irritated the papacy by allowing its Greek community to establish an Orthodox Church only a short walk from the Piazza San Marco. By the end of the sixteenth century, Venice's Jewish community epitomized the city's cosmopolitanism, with eight synagogues serving German Ashkenazim, Spanish and Portuguese Sephardim, and Levantines from Turkey and the Middle East. Although Jews were restricted to residence in the Ghetto, forced to wear distinctive clothing, and openly resented by much of the city's Christian population, they enjoyed enough freedom to develop one of early modern Europe's most dynamic centers of Jewish cultural and intellectual life. Sophisticated Christians visited the Ghetto, formed friendships with its residents, and even attended synagogue services to hear celebrated rabbis deliver their sermons in Italian. One prominent Venetian cleric, the friar Paolo Sarpi, enjoyed such close personal and intellectual ties with Jews like the celebrated rabbi Leone di Modena that Rome refused him a bishopric.[26]

Visitors found Venice's comparative openness to foreigners both fascinating and repulsive. A Parisian visitor during the regency of Catherine de' Medici was horrified that the Venetians entrusted moneylending to Jews:

I have great reason to fear that I will first impart a righteous disgust for this memorandum by explaining a strange feature which cannot, however, be concealed. The Republic of Venice, like the other sovereign states of Italy, has understood that it would be very useful to the

---

26. Throughout the period, the Republic's highest governing bodies strengthened the Jews' economic position. In 1523, for example, the Senate voted to establish a *monte di pietà,* a kind of Christian loan house that would break the city's dependence on the Jews and ultimately encourage their expulsion. Only a year later, the more powerful Council of Ten not only rejected the controversial measure but ordered its proponents to drop the scheme immediately and never mention it again, on pain of death. To this day, no one knows what prompted the Council to protect the city's Jewish interests even to the point of threatening to shed the blood of its Christian citizens. Their decision probably reflects the perennial Venetian fear of despotism, in this case the specific fear that the administrators of a *monte di pietà* might become so rich and powerful that they could undermine the city's republican constitution. But the Council's patronage of the Jews also may suggest its sense of how important Jewish merchants would soon become in maintaining the city's international commerce even during periods of open war. Venetian Jews, for example, could continue to trade with places like Antioch, Damascus, and Constantinople when Venetian citizens could not.

poor to find a place where they can receive on their personal belongings the wherewithal to relieve their pressing poverty, but it has made strange use of this reflection and I believe it is only at Venice that the Monte di Pietà is run by Jews.[27]

Both Sir Henry Wotton, James I's ambassador to the Republic, and his chaplain, William Bedell, discussed theology with Venetian Jews; like many other visiting Christians, Bedell attended and admired Jewish sermons. When the famous traveler Thomas Coryat visited Venice in 1611, he commented on the Jews' scrupulousness in observing the Sabbath and attended synagogue services. But Coryat also had many negative things to say about the Ghetto, and his ambivalence reinforces his general sense of Venice itself as a city overrun by prostitutes, non-Christians, and other undesirables. Coryat complained that men entered the sanctuary without doffing their hats or kneeling to show their respect for God. He noted that the service itself was characterized "not by a sober, distinct, and orderly reading, but by an exceeding loud yaling undecent roaring, and as it were a beastly bellowing of it forth."[28] If his account of a theological discussion that he enjoyed with a learned rabbi attests to an open intellectual commerce between Jews and gentiles, it also underscores a persistent anti-Semitism: according to Coryat, their conversation had hardly begun when they were waylaid by forty or fifty Jews determined to thrash him for criticizing their religion.[29] He claimed that he escaped without serious injury only because a fellow Englishman, the ambassador Henry Wotton, happened to be passing by in a gondola and rescued him. Like Gianetto and Ansaldo in Fiorentino's anti-Semitic story, Coryat learns that even the Venetian authorities cannot protect anyone against the wrath of the Venetian Jewry. He also noted that Jews rarely converted to Christianity, because they would have to give up all that they had previously acquired from poor Christians "by their griping extorcion" (1:374).

Although Coryat wrote over two centuries after Fiorentino, they share, at bottom, a similar view of Venice as a dangerously open, fundamentally unstable society. The persistence of this representation ignores the significant changes in Venetian, and more broadly Italian, society that took place during the fifteenth and sixteenth centuries. Jews, for example, were more than

27. Bibliothèque nationale, Paris, MSS. fr. 11366–67, translated and quoted in Poliakov, *Jewish Bankers*, 203.

28. Coryat, *Coyrat's Curdities Hastily gobled up in five Moneths travells . . . and now dispersed to the nourishment of the travelling Members of this Kingdome* (Glasgow: James MacLehose and Sons, 1905), 1:371.

29. Coryat, *Coyrat's Curdities,* 1:371.

ever a central part of Venetian economic life; since the beginning of the sixteenth century, they were just as likely to be merchants in their own right as moneylenders. Their unique commercial ties to the Ottoman Empire had in fact helped the economy to function during periods of war, when Venetian Christians were unable to trade in Constantinople and other Turkish ports. Several factors contributed to the contraction of Venetian commerce in the sixteenth century, but the presence of a large and thriving Jewish community was not one of them. But by the end of Elizabeth's reign, the old suspicions about Venice's openness to strangers combined with the realization that the Republic no longer ranked among Europe's preeminent commercial powers. From the vantage of twenty-first-century hindsight, Venetian cosmopolitanism was not only a symptom of the country's longstanding mercantile success. It had contributed directly to that success by making the city an attractive market for diverse trading partners. But in the late sixteenth century, perceptions of cosmopolitanism were bound up with perceptions of moral decadence and economic decline. The time was ripe for a powerful early modern appropriation of Ser Giovanni's story of a Venetian merchant and a Jew determined to have his pound of flesh.

Shakespeare's Fantasy of Venice Triumphant

As scholars have noted, Shakespeare created his image of Venice using an almost infinite array of possible influences: travel books; general histories of Italy and more specific histories of Venice; literary evocations of the city by Boccaccio, Cinthio, and other writers; plays by continental and English contemporaries; pictures of the city and its landmarks; and the most elusive probable source of all: conversations with Venetian visitors to London and with English men and women who had spent time in Venice. These oral, written, and pictorial sources stood between his vision of the city and the one that Ser Giovanni crafted in the late fourteenth century, and they undoubtedly influenced his appropriation of the tale. Previous scholars have tried to pinpoint exactly what Shakespeare did and did not know about contemporary Venice, and what sources allowed him to imagine the city as accurately as he did.[30] I want to focus more specifically on the intertextual drift between *Il Pecorone* and *The Merchant of Venice* as the best evidence we have for trying

---

30. See especially Levith, *Shakespeare's Italian Settings,* 12–39; and McPherson, *Shakespeare, Jonson,* 17–26.

to gauge something even more elusive: the significance of his imaginative project of recreating the Mediterranean city on the English stage.

By the late sixteenth century, Ser Giovanni's tale could easily have served as an etiological myth for Venice's sixteenth-century decline. Outside observers and even some self-critical Venetians felt that the city's openness to strangers, its subjection to the vagaries of the sea trade, and its failure to balance commercial risks with the cultivation of an allegedly more stable agricultural and manufacturing economy on the mainland were leading to disaster.[31] Ser Giovanni's story potentially reinforced another stereotype about the city, its vulnerability to powerful, independent women. Visitors worried as much about the nuns and abbesses who flouted conventual discipline as about courtesans like the celebrated writer Veronica Franco, whose literary activities and connections with important public figures placed them at the center of the city's cultural and civic life.[32] Ser Giovanni's donna di Belmonte was not Venetian, but her predatory relationship to her would-be lovers could have been easily assimilated to a sixteenth-century discourse of complaint against the city's ten thousand or so courtesans and the fiscal, moral, and physical threat they posed to unsuspecting Venetian gentlemen.

Shakespeare develops some aspects of Ser Giovanni's story along these predictable lines. Unlike the Jew of Mestre in his source, for example, Shylock lives in Venice itself, a change that suggests some awareness that the Venetians had embraced the Jewish community more fully since the trecento and had Jews living in their midst. As I will argue, this development makes Shylock a greater threat to Venice than Ser Giovanni's nameless Jew. But in general, instead of exacerbating Ser Giovanni's presentation of Venice as a city susceptible to foreign domination, Shakespeare counters it by portraying a city whose laws and customs ultimately resist the threat posed by figures like Shylock. Shakespeare's Venice, in contrast to Ser Giovanni's, is a more cohesive community, with customs and legal traditions that encourage trade and bolster the city's distinctive national identity. Far from developing the Florentine subtext into an etiology for Venice's sixteenth-century difficulties, Shakespeare transforms it into a fantasy about their successful resolution.

As a revision of its source story in *Il Pecorone*, *The Merchant of Venice* works as a defense against the subtext's darker vision of a state on the brink of cultural and political disintegration. It exchanges the vision of Venice in

---

31. See Lane, *Venice*, 306–7.

32. See Margaret F. Rosenthal, *The Honest Courtesan: Veronica Franco, Citizen and Writer in Sixteenth-Century Venice* (Chicago: University of Chicago Press, 1992); and Jutta Gisela Sperling, *Convents and the Body Politic in Late Renaissance Venice* (Chicago: University of Chicago Press, 1999).

decline for the myth of Venice preserved. This rewriting of Ser Giovanni signals more than Shakespeare's private literary agon with a precursor. His fantasy of a mercantile empire that survives the threat of foreign domination removes Venice from the narrative of international rivalry in which one country's rise depends on another's eclipse. In the process, it absolves London theatergoers of their role in Venice's economic contraction. Despite rumors that one of Antonio's ships has miscarried on the Narrow Seas, England has nothing to do with Venice's catastrophe, and that catastrophe itself turns out to be mere rumor anyway. The denouement ultimately allays fears that any country that emulates Venice at its mercantile height will eventually follow it into decline.

In transforming Ser Giovanni's story of Gianetto's personal triumph over the Jew of Mestre into a larger myth of civic preservation, Shakespeare alters his protagonists' national identities. In the story, the merchant Ansaldo is the only named Venetian. Gianetto is a Florentine and the lady rules a feudal state located somewhere far from Venice. Shakespeare constricts this geographic range by recasting Gianetto as Bassanio, a native Venetian, and by domesticating the lady. Portia lives just across the lagoon on the Venetian mainland and has an uncle who lives in Padua, the nearby university town under Venetian auspices,[33] Whereas Ser Giovanni's lady pretends to be a lawyer from Bologna, a papal possession in Shakespeare's day, Portia proves loyally Venetian in taking on the persona of a Paduan lawyer and basing her judgments on specific Venetian laws. Nor does she ever resort to anything as exotic as sleeping-potions and face-altering drugs in bringing about the play's comic denouement. In contrast to Ser Giovanni's story of multinational relationships among a Florentine, a Venetian, and a Belmontese, *The Merchant of Venice* focuses on Venetians. By adding minor characters like Lorenzo, Gratiano, Solerio, Solanio, and the Gobbos, Shakespeare conveys a much broader sense of Venice as a civil society. Whereas Ser Giovanni looked at Venice primarily as a Florentine outsider through the perspective of his callow Florentine protagonist, Shakespeare draws his audience into a closer imaginative identification with the city by making all his central players Venetian.

To the extent that we see all the Christian protagonists as Venetians, their individual conflicts coalesce in a national project of preserving Venice's independence and legal integrity against foreign challenges. Like Ser Giovanni,

---

33. Portia indicates the distance when she tells Balthazar to meet her at the "traject...the common ferry" that "trades" between Belmont and Venice (3.4.53, 54). A *traghetto* is simply a ferry that sails among the islands within the Venetian lagoon. Unlike Gianetto's ship in Ser Giovanni's story, it is not a seagoing vessel.

Shakespeare recognizes the threat that the city's dependence on international trade poses to its identity as a discrete country with its own customs, laws, and bloodlines. In mirroring Venice's predicament across the play's several interlocking plots, he amplifies both its scope and its significance. As the Venetians ward off attacks and overtures from Jews, Moroccans, Aragonese, and even Englishmen, Ser Giovanni's anti-Semitism broadens into a more general xenophobia. The more self-conscious and pointed this xenophobia becomes, the more the Venetians manage to have it both ways, to remain a discretely bounded national entity while maintaining their mercantile pre-eminence within an expanding European economy. Xenophobia turns out to be a crucial factor stanching the drift toward cultural, racial, and potentially political fragmentation and revealing a surprising coherence of laws and values on which the plot, and the preservation of the Venetian oligarchy, ultimately turn.

The "preservationist" directions of Shakespeare's revision appear most conspicuously in his transformation of the sinister lady of Belmonte into the resourceful Portia. Ser Giovanni's lady has no history beyond her reputation for tricking her would-be lovers into forfeiting their property. We know nothing about her father, her ancestors, or even her true feelings for Gianetto or anyone else in the story. Perhaps building on Ser Giovanni's hint about the father's capricious will that first sends Gianetto to Venice, Shakespeare introduces the story of the three caskets, which differentiates Portia from her quatrocento model. At first, her father's posthumous control over Portia's marriage seems to epitomize common stereotypes about the tyranny of Venetian fathers over their household, stereotypes to which Shakespeare returned in *Othello*. Portia herself laments her father's posthumous authority but is powerless to resist it, "so is the will of a living daughter curb'd by the will of a dead father" (1.2.24–25). Bassanio may find something seductively classical in the spectacle of Belmont as "Colchis' strond" and Portia's suitors as so many Jasons, but the reality of her reduction to a golden fleece could not be more contemporarily Venetian. The city had become notorious as one of the most competitive marriage markets in Europe. Aristocratic daughters came to their husbands with such rich dowries that nothing was left for their younger sisters, who were then sent to convents in scandalously high numbers by their sharp-dealing fathers.[34]

---

34. See Stanley Chojnacki, *Women and Men in Renaissance Venice: Twelve Essays on Patrician Society* (Baltimore: Johns Hopkins University Press, 2000), 9, 76–94. On forced conventualization, see also Jutta Gisela Sperling, *Convents and the Body Politic*.

In Shakespeare's play, the Venetians' notorious openness to foreigners exacerbates the father's posthumous tyranny. Actual Venetians were notoriously endogamous, primarily out of fears of diluting aristocratic bloodlines. But Portia's father markets his daughter as widely as possible, in what first appears to be almost a parody of Venice's willingness to trade with Catholics, Protestants, Orthodox, and even non-Christians. Portia's body threatens to become a metonym for Venice itself, conceived as a commercial center where all the nations of Europe do business. In her resentment of this fate, Portia voices some of the play's most racist and xenophobic sentiments. The miscegenation to which her father's will threatens to subject her carries the threat of de facto disintegration as a recognizable Venetian, a fate that she comically displaces onto the grotesque Englishman, Lord Falconbridge, who seems to have "bought his doublet in Italy, his round hose in France, his bonnet in Germany, and his behavior every where" (1.2.74–76). In a world where national identities are purchased and blended on the open market, being a nubile Venetian lady becomes more a liability than a privilege.

The two suitors who eventually appear on stage, the Princes of Morocco and Aragon, point even more specifically to Venice's predicament as a late-sixteenth-century trading power. The princes that threaten Portia with a foreign marriage come from the two countries, Spain and Morocco, that guarded the Straits of Gibraltar and closed off Venetian access to the Atlantic trade routes that lay beyond. Since the 1559 Treaty of Cateau-Cambrésis, the king of Spain enjoyed virtual dominion over Italy—except for Venice—by virtue of his Aragonese bloodlines. The master narrative of Venetian foreign policy in the late sixteenth century was a balancing act between the two empires—the Spanish and the Ottoman—that dominated the eastern and western ends of the Mediterranean where Venice once reigned supreme. Although the Moroccans and the Ottomans were often enemies, their shared Islamic heritage invited popular confusion. Courted first by Morocco and then by Spain, Portia stands almost as an allegory of Venice's sixteenth-century predicament as a waning mercantile empire witnessing the Mediterranean basin fall under Spanish and Islamic domination.

By refiguring contemporary Mediterranean politics as a romance, the story of the three caskets achieves on the level of fantasy the objective that Scaramelli and his compatriots failed to achieve in the real world: a reversal of Venice's declining fortunes and a reassertion of its independence and vitality as an economic power. In the end, the Venetian Bassanio wins Portia in an act that dispels the threats of miscegenation to which her father's will seemed to subject her. Bassanio's remarks at the moment of the choice, moreover, point to a re-formation of Venice's image as a decadent, crassly commercial city in the worst sense of the word. His love for Portia not only replenishes his squandered fortunes but apparently transforms him from a spendthrift playboy into a spokesperson for values that distinguish him as a prudent Venetian from the materialism of his rivals:

> The world is still deceiv'd with ornament....
>   Therefore then, thou gaudy gold,
> Hard food for Midas, I will none of thee;
> Nor none of thee, thou pale and common drudge
> 'Tween man and man; but thou, thou meagre lead,
> Which rather threaten'st than dost promise aught. (3.2.74, 101–5)

Such lines locate in Bassanio, and more generally in the Venetians as a nation, a suspicion of ornament, a preference for worth that passes show, and a trust in earnest labor—however threatening—over easy, empty promises.[35]

Miscegenation and an imperialist lust for precious metals are not the only threats to Venetian society that Bassanio wards off in marrying Portia. He also overcomes what Ser Giovanni had presented as the dangers of Venice's dependence on the sea. As numerous scholars have noted, the union between Portia and Bassanio integrates, at least as fantasy, commercial and landed interests.[36] Portia's inherited wealth offsets the risks of future investment, and Bassanio's entrepreneurialism offsets the risks of stagnating land values in an increasingly commercialized economy.[37] The neatness of this resolution was not possible in *Il Pecorone,* where the lady of Belmonte was not Venetian and her marriage to the Florentine Gianetto suggested a reconciliation of

---

35. Although the choice of "meager lead" over "gaudy gold" and drudge-like silver might suggest a contempt for material interests altogether, several recent critics have demonstrated how it locates the play at a telling moment in the history of late European mercantilism. See Mark Netzloff, *England's Internal Colonies: Class, Capital, and the Literature of Early Modern English Colonialism* (Houndmills, U.K.: Palgrave-Macmillan, 2003), 20–26.

For further discussion of the play's place in the emergence of capitalism, see Walter Cohen, *The Drama of a Nation: Public Theater in Renaissance England and Spain* (Ithaca: Cornell University Press, 1985), 195–211; Lars Engle, "'Thrift is Blessing': Exchange and Explanation in *The Merchant of Venice,*" *Shakespeare Quarterly* 37 (1986): 20–37; Thomas Moison, "'Which is the Merchant Here? And Which the Jew': Subversion and Recuperation in *The Merchant of Venice,*" in *Shakespeare Reproduced: The Text in History and Ideology,* ed. Jean E. Howard and Marion F. O'Connor (New York: Methuen, 1987), 188–206; and Michael Ferber, "The Ideology of *The Merchant of Venice,*" *English Literary Renaissance* 20 (1990): 431–64.

36. See Lawrence Danson, *The Harmonies of* The Merchant of Venice (New Haven: Yale University Press, 1978); and Cohen, *Drama of a Nation,* 208–11.

37. As Mark Netzloff observes, "Portia serves to domesticate the threats of capital formation to the national economy, translating economic innovation into the residual categories and hierarchies of landed property and the patriarchal household." Netzloff, *England's Internal Colonies,* 29.

mercantile and feudal interests that was denied the Venetians. There were, at least in Ser Giovanni's fourteenth-century fantasy, no landed Venetian heiresses to marry. Shakespeare solves the problem by relocating Belmont, the "beautiful mountain," to the notoriously flat Venetian "terra firma," the Republic's territories on the Italian mainland just across the lagoon.

Finally, Portia strikes a cathartic balance between two common stereotypes of Venetian women either as closely penned wards of overly protective fathers or as courtesans whose sexual and social freedoms unsettled the patriarchal basis of Venetian, and more broadly European, society. Portia is chaste, and her obedience to the terms of her father's seemingly capricious will marks her as the ideal Venetian daughter surrendering herself to an arranged marriage. But once she marries Bassanio, Portia hardly conforms to the image of the sequestered wife characterized by Coryat and other foreign visitors: "For the Gentlemen do even coope up their wives alwaies within the walles of their houses.... So that you shall very seldome see a Venetian gentleman's wife but either at the solemnization of a great marriage or at the Christning of a Jew, or late in the evening rowing in a Gondola" (1:403). The ingenuity, rhetorical skill, and willingness to participate in the conventionally all-male domain of a public court associate Portia more with famous courtesans like Franco, the paradoxical "honest courtesan," whose literary talents won them public ac-clamation, sometimes even as artistic representatives of the Venetian republic. Franco, for example, published impassioned lyrics praising Venice as an "ex-traordinary marvel that astonishes nature" ("*singolare / meraviglia e stupor de la natura,*" Capitolo 12, 20–21).[38] She later participated in Henri III's state visit to Venice and presented a copy of her recently published *Lettere familiari a diversi* to Montaigne.[39] While Portia inherits the chastity and filial obedience characteristic of the well-guarded Venetian daughter, she combines it with something of the courtesan's intellectual vitality and civic commitment.

In the trial scene that marks the climax of her public career, Portia appears as a woman defender of the republic in ways that distinguish her from her model in *Il Pecorone* and make her look more than a little like Franco, Gas-para Stampa, and other learned Venetians. Portia reconciles within herself and in her marriage to Bassanio longstanding disjunctions that cinquecento

38. "Capitolo 12" ("*Oh quanto per voi meglio si faría*"), in Franco, *Poems and Selected Letters,* ed. Ann Rosalind Jones and Margaret F. Rosenthal (Chicago: University of Chicago Press, 1998), 126. Translation mine. For further discussion of controversies surrounding women's education in Italian Renaissance society, see Pamela J. Benson, *The Invention of the Renaissance Woman: The Challenge of Female Independence in the Literature and Thought of Italy and England* (University Park: Pennsylvania State University Press, 1999).

39. See Rosenthal, *Honest Courtesan,* 116, 155.

observers associated with Venetian decadence: commitment to Venice's sea-based commerce *and* the greater stability of a land-based fortune on terra firma, the chastity of the sequestered daughter *and* the civic performativity of the *cortigiana onesta*. The moment Bassanio's choice of the leaden casket seals their marriage and dispels the threat to her own pure Venetian bloodlines, she steps into her destiny as the supreme defender of the city's mercantile aristocracy against foreign malevolence.

In Shakespeare, the pound-of-flesh plot recapitulates the basic pattern of the choice of the caskets. Just as Portia found herself helpless to resist the miscegenating implications of her father's will, Antonio finds himself helpless before a legal culture that seems to protect foreigners more than Venice's own citizens:

> The Duke cannot deny the course of law;
> For the commodity that strangers have
> With us in Venice, if it be denied,
> Will much impeach the justice of the state,
> Since that the trade and profit of the city
> Consisteth of all nations. (3.3.26–31)

Shakespeare borrows this sense of legal paralysis directly from Giovanni, where the Venetians similarly regret their powerlessness to forestall tragedy:

> Ma pure considerato Vinegia esser terra di ragione—e il giudeo avea le sue ragioni piene e in publica forma—non si li usava di dire il contradio per nessuno.
> [But considering that Venice was a land of rights, and the Jew had his rights full and in public form, no one dared to deny them] (109).

Ser Giovanni attributes these reflections to Venetians gossiping before the trial begins. In Shakespeare, they factor into the trial itself, when Bassanio begs the Duke to "wrest once the law to [his] authority" and spare his friend's life (4.1.215). When Portia insists, even before the Duke can reply, that "there is no power in Venice / Can alter a decree established," her words suggest the incapacity not only of the Venetian legal system but even of its highest elected official to defend the lives of its citizens against the rights of foreigners (218–19). As an ironic innkeeper puts it in Ser Giovanni, the Venetians "have made too much of rights" ("*faccisi troppa ragione,*" 110).

But just when Shakespeare seems to have followed Ser Giovanni in an indictment of Venice as a place whose laws favor foreigners even when they are conspiring against its citizens, he alters the Italian plot to vindicate the

Venetian legal system. Like Portia, the lady of Belmonte saves Ansaldo's life by introducing the technical distinction between cutting flesh and shedding blood. But in Ser Giovanni, that is the end of the story: the Jew surrenders his principal and the Christians take his money and run back to Belmonte. Portia not only subjects Shylock to a harsher penalty but also transforms the occasion into a ringing reassertion of Venetian values.[40] That she has to cross-dress and take things into her own hands still reminds us that the men of Venice may be inept in getting themselves out of trouble. But in Shakespeare, they are inept simply because they are men—not because they are Venetians. In terms of national identity, Portia is one of them. When she dons the costume of a lawyer educated in nearby Padua rather than Fiorentino's more distant Bologna, she casts her judgments specifically in terms of Venetian laws enacted to safeguard the interests of Venetians against foreigners:

> Take then thy bond, take thou thy pound of flesh,
> But in the cutting it, if thou dost shed
> One drop of Christian blood, thy lands and goods
> Are by the laws of Venice confiscate
> Unto the state of Venice. . . .
> It is enacted in the laws of Venice,
> If it be proved against an alien,
> That by direct of indirect attempts
> He seek the life of any citizen,
> The party 'gainst the which he doth contrive
> Shall seize one half his goods. (4.1.308–12, 348–53)

As the trial scene unfolds, the word *Venice* resounds like a charm disabling Shylock's malice and reestablishing the city's threatened integrity. Portia alone uses it seven times in presenting herself as the staunchest defender of the city, its laws, its citizens, and its values. In redeeming Antonio from Shylock, she redeems the city itself from its excesses and dispels the associated threats of death, foreign subservience, and national disintegration.

In yet another departure from Ser Giovanni, the court does not simply deny Shylock his bond. Antonio, Portia, and the Duke also come together in a much more conspicuous assertion of the inferior position of foreigners in Venetian society by ordering the confiscation and entailment of Shylock's

---

40. For an alternative account of these Shakespearean additions as an attempt to satisfy the *audience's* desire for revenge against Shylock, see Stephen Orgel, *Imagining Shakespeare: A History of Texts and Visions* (Houndmills, U.K.: Palgrave Macmillan, 2003), 162.

property. The outsider who plotted against the citizen must owe his wealth solely to the condescending benevolence of the Venetian people. In a final, perverse *contrapasso,* his forced conversion makes him, in an almost parodic way, a member of the Christian society that he attempted to traduce. Critics have long cited the harshness of this sentence as a factor that blurs the moral lines between Shylock and the Venetians and exposes the superficiality of the latter's Christian commitment to mercy. But as a revision of Ser Giovanni, who treated the equity accorded Venice's resident foreigners as a sign of the republic's weakness, Shakespeare's denouement suggests that Venice finally asserts the social boundaries that will protect its citizens' lives and fortunes.

This recuperative denouement, in which a noblewoman from the Veneto saves a Venetian merchant from disaster, was not available to Ser Giovanni, who wrote significantly before the expansion of the late fifteenth and sixteenth centuries. His story ended happily enough for Gianetto and Ansaldo, but not at all for Venice. Nor is there any textual evidence that Ser Giovanni, a good Guelphish Florentine, was interested in redeeming the image of Venice that his fiction so powerfully criticized by associating it with reckless investments and subjection to foreign moneylenders. Shakespeare's relationship to Venice was more complex. His play creates an unforgettable image of the city whose decline contributed to the rise of England itself as a commercial power. As we have seen, he outstrips Ser Giovanni in exposing the allegedly decadent aspects of Venetian culture that his contemporaries associated with the city's waning significance. But in the turn toward a comic ending centered on Portia's judicial genius in the courtroom, he also creates a fantasy of a new Venice, one that imposes strict limits on foreign influences and ultimately regains its prestige as a commercial giant. In the final moments, three of Antonio's ships return safely with their cargoes from Mexico, India, and presumably other ports where no Venetian ever sailed. Nerissa and Portia are safely united with their husbands, the tensions between the city's identities as an old trading power and the master of new expansion on terra firma are resolved, and Venice emerges as the uncontested master not only of the Mediterranean but of the Indian and Atlantic Oceans that lie beyond the Pillars of Hercules.

The movement from Venice threatened to Venice preserved came to dominate later narratives about the city, but perhaps what most defines the *peripeteia* in its original Shakespearean formulation is its implausibility. Some of the play's fantasy elements derive directly from its Italian source, including the last-minute distinction between cutting flesh and shedding blood that staves off disaster. But Shakespeare's greater realism paradoxically makes some things harder to believe than they were in the original. By first introducing the lady of Belmonte as a magician who works wonders with magic potions, for example, Ser Giovanni dispelled the suspicion that someone might recognize her during the trial: the ointments that altered her appearance were foolproof. Portia, on the other hand, is not a witch armed with potions. She relies on nothing more magical than costumes, intelligence, and the ability to act. Her success attests to her brilliance and, on a metadramatic level, to the magic of Shakespeare's theater. But the scene's effect depends partly on the sense that someone might recognize her at any moment. Like other moments of metadramatic self-consciousness in Shakespeare, it foregrounds its own implausibility.

In much the same way, Shakespeare underscores the fantasy of his own final evocation of Belmont as a golden world insulated from legal, financial, and physical risk. When Portia gives Antonio the letter relating the good news about his ships, for example, she insists that he "shall not know by what strange accident / I chanced on this letter" (5.1.278–79). By withholding the details, she heightens the aura of magic and romance that she inherits from her Italian prototype. But her lines also makes the denouement seem too good to be true, an effect that Shakespeare heightens by isolating Antonio in the play's final moments. As scholars have often noted, he remains alone after his coupled friends pair off for their wedding nights.

Antonio's melancholy, as well as the suspicions attending Jessica and Lorenzo's mixed-race marriage that Levin discussed in the last chapter, are symptomatic of a more general consciousness that Venice's redemption is a wishful fantasy more akin to romance than to comedy per se. Like the turn toward consolation at the end of a pastoral elegy, its effect depends a half-suppressed awareness that the happy ending—in which all shipwrecks prove illusory—is a projection of longings rather than an experience of history. *The Merchant of Venice* has long attracted critics interested in the psychology of fantasy formation in great part because the play feels so much like a fantasy embedded in an overarching representation of leaden reality. Such readings often center on the distinction between Belmont and Venice, the former imagined as a place of generosity and benevolence protectively distanced from the hard dealings of the Rialto. By reading the play more closely against its Italian source and showing how far Shakespeare goes in domesticating Portia as a Venetian lady dwelling in the nearby Venetian terra firma, I have challenged the geographical basis for these distinctions. But I have also kept intact the sense of the play as a metacommentary on the production of fantasy, albeit more in communal or even national terms than individual ones.

The opposition that matters most to the play's historical fantasy is not so much that between Venice and Belmont as that between Venice and London.

Shakespeare's Venice is not simply a cover for London. It is instead a monument to the city whose decline predicated London's rise. This is the troubling historical fact that the fantasy of Venice's redemption never fully dispels. In the fantasy, a clever Venetian lady thwarts the Jewish outsider's efforts to destroy one of the city's leading citizens. At least on the surface, her triumph is a vindication of the city's laws and institutions. But, as Stephen Orgel has noted, Shylock's name is neither Hebrew nor Italian.[41] It is instead the one incontestably English name in the play, since even "Jessica" seems to be a female form of the Hebrew Jesse. Orgel has argued that the Englishness of Shylock's name dissolves the distance between Venice and London by reminding us that he is no better or worse than a lot of money-grubbing Elizabethan Puritans. But on another level, Shylock's English name underscores the distance between the two cities. Every time his name is spoken, it potentially disrupts the conventions through which the play aligns its English audience with its Italian heroes in a common opposition to a Jewish usurer. His English name points to the dominant historical narrative that was unfolding throughout the Mediterranean during the 1580s and 1590s. In this narrative, voiced so powerfully by Scaramelli and other Venetians envoys and factors, English merchants rather than Jewish moneylenders were responsible for the city's fiscal straits.

Shakespeare prioritizes Ser Giovanni's fantasy of an evil Jewish moneylender over the more immediate threat of English merchants encroaching on the Venetian trade. But he hints at this darker, contemporary history through such details as Shylock's English name and the loss of Antonio's first ship in the English Channel, at Goodwin Sands (3.1.2–5). One again, Shakespeare complicates his fantasy to keep us from fully embracing it. By the end of Act V, we can almost believe that London's rise was not contingent on Venice's decline, that both countries could have prevailed against pernicious foreign threats, and even that mercantile success did not depend on someone's loss. But in the final moments, Antonio's melancholy, like that of the Venetian envoy Scaramelli, reminds us of the illusion of such happy conclusions. By the late 1590s, Venice's decline had become a patent precondition of the rise of England and the other Atlantic powers, a fact that provides Shakespeare's comic fantasy its persistently elegiac undersong.

---

41. Orgel, *Imagining Shakespeare*, 152–55.

❧ PART III

Dangerous Reading
in The Taming
of the Shrew

The ships that returned to England from increasingly distant ports of call carried not only foreign passengers and foreign merchandise but also foreign ideas about religion, property, law, and the management of public and domestic space. Above all, they carried books. Whether written in Latin or the modern continental languages, these books introduced new ways of thinking that might be domesticated as fundamentally English, repudiated as alien and subversive, or occupy a controversial position somewhere in between. While only members of the elite could read these books in their original languages, many of them soon circulated in English translations and redactions. The moment people began to discuss what they had read, the new ideas entered an oral culture that was accessible to literate and illiterate alike. Before long, the ideas began to change behavior.

The assimilation of Protestant beliefs that developed in Germany and Switzerland showed how quickly a body of thought might lose its foreign aura and become part of the English national imaginary. By the 1590s, those who persisted in their ancestors' Catholicism appeared to be the outsiders. Propagandists convinced their Protestant neighbors to think of them as a dangerous fifth column allied with England's Spanish enemies.

Religion was only one aspect of English society affected by foreign books. Romances, plays, and books of poetry changed the way people thought about love, marriage, and family life. Roger Ascham, who happily embraced the new religion, famously denounced romances "made in Italie, and translated in England" for corrupting the manners of English men and women: "They open, not fond and common wayes to vice, but such subtle, cunnyng, new, and diuerse shiftes, to cary yong willes to vanitie, and yong wittes to mischief, to teach old bawdes new schole poyntes, as the simple head of an English man is not hable to inuent, nor neuer was hard of in England before, yea when Papistrie ouerflowed all."[1] Despite Ascham's denunciations, Italian romances and other foreign genres transformed texts written, read, and performed in England. As Ascham feared, such literature probably did change the way people felt and acted. Sylvius's mock-Petrarchan courtship of Phoebe in *As You Like It* may well be Shakespeare's joke on the way his own Italianate comedies, as well as those written by his contemporaries, taught the apprentices and shopkeepers of London "subtle, cunnyng, new, and diuerse" ways of experiencing and describing love.

Like other late Elizabethan authors, Shakespeare was indebted to two powerful, arguably foreign, intellectual movements: Renaissance humanism and the Reformation. He was also a primary channel for their ultimate English assimilation. Our final section examines *The Taming of the Shrew* as his earliest and most sustained exploration of the impact of both on the English household. As the debate between Erasmus and Luther over freedom of the will suggested, the two movements were not fully compatible. But Shakespeare seems to have been less interested in theological and philosophical differences than in the effect that humanist and Protestant pedagogical traditions might have on the place of women within the home and, by implication, on English society at large.

The first generation of feminist scholars blamed the Reformation for diminishing the power that women sometimes enjoyed under the old ecclesiastical order. A renewed emphasis on Scripture, for example, gave new force to St. Paul's dicta against women speaking in churches. The Reformation disbanded religious orders in which women like St. Hilda of Whitby rose to high office. But, as Levin argues in her chapter on *The Taming of the Shrew*, Pauline strictures were not the final word. Protestant writers like Foxe created a new cultural role for women as passionate defenders of the Gospel, one that tempered New Testament emphasis on wifely obedience. Levin finds an analogue for Katherine's struggles with Petruchio in Foxe's account

---

1. Roger Ascham, *The scholemaster, or plaine and perfite way of teachyng children, to vnderstand, write, and speake, the Latin tong but specially purposed for the priuate brynging vp of youth in ientlemen and noble mens houses, and commodious also for all such, as haue forgot the Latin tonge* (London, 1570), 27r.

of Katherine Parr's struggles with Henry VIII in the final years of his reign. Henry embraced a series of theological and ecclesio-political positions anathematized by forward-looking Protestants like Anne Askew, Katherine Parr, and other women honored by Foxe. According to Levin, Foxe's heroines and Shakespeare's Katherine alike represent a new kind of Englishwoman empowered by Reformation teaching to play a leading role in the country's evangelization.

Reading the play against Ludovico Ariosto's *I suppositi,* Watkins comes to a darker, alternative interpretation of Katherine's story as a reaction against the financial and intellectual freedoms that women potentially enjoyed in Renaissance Italy. The sixteenth century witnessed a flowering of women's scholarly and creative activity, especially in the Veneto, the most common setting for Shakespeare's Italian plays. While it is unlikely that Shakespeare knew the works of women writers like Gaspara Stampa and Veronica Franco directly, plays like *I suppositi* would have given him insight into one of the material factors that distinguished Italian women from their English counterparts: their title to their own dowries. In responding to this possibility as an Italian threat to the English household, *The Taming of the Shrew* reinforces the English doctrine of coverture, which merged a woman's legal and property rights with those of her husband. As the old adage put it, husband and wife were one person in the eyes of the law—and that person was the husband. Watkins sees Petruchio's taming as an English counter to the humanist, conspicuously Italianate, education that Katherine and her sister Bianca have received from their father, an education that has heightened their sense of freedom from male authority.

CHAPTER 5

Many Different Kates

Taming Shrews and Queens

Henry VIII's sixth and last wife, Katherine Parr, was a woman of intelligence and courage who was also a committed evangelical Christian. Katherine's father, Sir Thomas, died when she was only five, and her mother Maud, during her widowhood, made sure that her children, both male and female, were well educated. As Susan E. James notes, Maud provided Katherine with an example of skill and independence that would have a life long effect on her daughter. Katherine became proficient in French, Italian, and Latin.[1] When Katherine caught Henry's eye after his disastrous fifth marriage to Katherine Howard, she was twice widowed and had had no children. Katherine was then living in the household of Henry's older daughter Mary as one of her ladies. Mary and her household visited court, and Henry took note of Katherine. Though Katherine was far from eager to marry the king, she must have felt that she had little choice. And who could blame her reluctance? Two of her predecessors had had their

---

This is a much expanded and revised version of an essay first published in the volume I coedited with Debra Barrett-Graves and Jo Eldridge Carney, *"High and Mighty Queens" of Early Modern England: Representations and Realities* (New York: Palgrave, 2003), 171–86.

1. Susan E. James, "Katherine [Katherine Parr] (1512–1548)," in *Oxford Dictionary of National Biography*, ed. H. C. G. Matthew and Brian Harrison (Oxford: Oxford University Press, 2004). There is considerable debate over just how proficient Katherine's Latin was and when she learned it. She did apparently study and improve her Latin while she was queen.

marriages annulled, one had died in complications caused by childbirth, and two were beheaded. Katherine must have felt at risk as queen.

Katherine Parr's dangers as queen were dramatically presented in the *Acts and Monuments,* as John Foxe presented the lives of many other women, both of high and low status. The stories of a number of powerful women in peril that Foxe related later made their way into early modern drama: Lady Jane Grey in Thomas Dekker and John Webster's *The Famous History of Sir Thomas Wyatt* (1607), the Princess Elizabeth in Thomas Heywood's *If You Know Not Me, You Know Nobody, Part I* (1605), and Catherine Willoughby in Thomas Drue's *The Duchess of Suffolk* (1631). In at least some of these plays, Foxe's influence in the depictions was pronounced. Katherine Parr has also been characterized in a number of early modern plays. John King argues that in Nicholas Udal's *Ralph Roister Doister,* written in the reign of Edward VI and published early in the reign of Elizabeth, the character Dame Christian Custance reflected "the Protestant piety" of Katherine Parr.[2]

More directly based on Foxe is Samuel Rowley's early Jacobean Henry VIII play, *When You See Me, You Know Me* (1605), which narrates the dangers that Katherine's Protestant views exposed her to. Another intriguing parallel that may be drawn with Katherine Parr is her namesake in one of Shakespeare's comedies performed in late Elizabethan London, the one where Kate is known as a "curst shrew." We know that Shakespeare used Foxe as a source for a number of his dramas, such as *King John.* A telling connection between Foxe and Shakespeare more relevant to this argument is in his late play *The Famous History of the Life of King Henry the Eighth,* or *All is True,* possibly co-authored with John Fletcher. In *Acts and Monuments,* Foxe not only tells the story of the near escape of Katherine Parr but also works in a very similar one about Thomas Cranmer, Archbishop of Canterbury, whom villainous Stephen Gardiner attempts to destroy and, as in the Queen Katherine story, King Henry appears to agree with Gardiner, again the villain, to the arrest but then at the last moment saves the champion of the true faith—much to the discomfort of Gardiner and his allies.

Foxe describes how Gardiner worked "to bring the Archbishop out of credit with the king" by having the Bishop of Winchester tell Henry how, because of Cranmer, "the realme was so infected with heresies and hereticks, that it was daungerous for his hyghnes." Henry agreed to the "sute against the Archbishop (but yet meaning not to have hym wronged and utterly geven over unto their handes) graunted to them, that they should the next

---

2. John N. King, *English Reformation Literature: The Tudor Origins of the Protestant Tradition* (Princeton: Princeton University Press, 1982), 306.

day commit hym to the Tower for his tryall." But the night after he gave this order to Gardiner, Henry had Cranmer brought to him at court, and the two walked in the gallery so that they could speak privately. Henry told Cranmer that the next morning he would be arrested for heresy and taken to the Tower. Cranmer knelt before his king and replied, "I am content if it please your grace, and with all my hart, to go thether at your hyghnes commaundement, and I most humbly thanke your majesty, that I may come to my triall." Cranmer's response assured Henry of his integrity but also his naivete:

> Oh Lord, what maner a man be you? What simplicity is in you?...Do not you know what state you be in with the whole world, & how many great enemies you have? Do you not consider what an easye thing it is to procure three or foure false knaves to wytnes against you? Thinke you to have better lucke that way then your master CHRIST had? I see by it, you wyll runne headlong to your undoing, if I would suffer you?

Henry then assured Cranmer he would keep Cranmer out of his enemies' hands and gave him a ring, telling him when arrested to ask to be brought before the king; if refused, "if no intreaty or reasonable request will serve, then deliver unto them this my ryng." All worked beautifully, and Henry was able to proclaim before the Council how Cranmer was above "all other a most faythfull subject unto us."[3]

This story is exactly reproduced in Shakespeare's play. Cranmer is sent for, and he and the king talk privately in the gallery. Henry tells Cranmer of the "grievous complaints" against him (1.1.99). Henry is impressed by Cranmer's response to this most terrible of news and wonders that Cranmer does not realize "at what ease / Might corrupt minds procure knaves as corrupt / To swear against you?" (1.1.131–33). Shakespeare's Henry, like Foxe's, then asks Cranmer to consider the fate of Christ. Henry gives Cranmer his ring and assures the archbishop:

> If entreaties
> Will render you no remedy, this ring
> Deliver them, and your appeal to us
> There make before them. (1.1.149–52)

---

3. John Foxe, *Acts and Monuments [...]* (1570 edition), 2042. All Foxe citations from the Human Rights Initiative website hriOnline, Sheffield, U.K. Available at www.hrionline.shef.ac.uk/foxe/, accessed September 29, 2006.

As in Foxe, in the great confrontation scene Henry protects Cranmer and lambastes those who try to move against him. There are clear parallels between Foxe's Henry/Cranmer/Gardiner story and his Henry/Katherine/Gardiner story. If Shakespeare knew one, he was certainly familiar with the other.

I suggest that in *The Taming of the Shrew,* we hear echoes of the confrontation between Katherine and Henry, the threats to Katherine, and the concerns about an educated or strong-willed wife. Though Rowley's story follows Foxe more closely, it is *The Taming of the Shrew* that examines thoroughly the ways a husband can tame a woman who moves beyond accepted gender expectations and what the woman must do to survive within the situation. But in *The Taming of the Shrew,* these concerns are embodied not only in Kate but even, eerily enough, in Bianca as well, though Bianca is traditionally seen as a brainless beauty who fools her father by her quiet and ladylike demeanor and then, once married, turns out to be spoiled and disobedient. I suggest instead that Bianca also reflects Katherine Parr's interest in education and ability to use traditional feminine behavior to survive.

We cannot know that Shakespeare intended his Kate in *The Taming of the Shrew* in any way to parallel Foxe's Katherine, but certainly the issues raised in Foxe in some ways reverberate in Shakespeare. And questions of what it meant for women to be literate, to use their education to develop their sense of identity, are critical to the religious as well as lay cultural ethos of early modern England. For the historical Katherine Parr, her study of evangelical religion—especially its role in developing an English Protestant nation-state—was vitally important, which is also clearly demonstrated in the depictions of Katherine in Foxe and Rowley. But while Protestants also urged that the husband was the head of the household in all matters, including religion, Katherine Parr had to be coerced into saying that she accepted this model. In Shakespeare's play, the questions of female education and male control are secular, and thus less ominous, but here also we have male power and female submission, even if presented in a comic frame.

Yet we might also question how much lessons of obedience really had an impact on sixteenth-century marriages. The 1563 homily on marriage was very frequently read in the churches, not only whenever someone married but also whenever the minister felt that a married couple in his congregation needed to hear it. The perspective on women expressed in the homily is frequently found in a range of texts of the period. It states that "woman is a weak creature, not endued with the strength and constancie of mynd, therefore they be the sooner disquieted, and they bee one more prone to all weake affections and dispositions of mynde, more than men do." The homily also reminded the husband that because of these qualities, he "oughte to wynke at some thinges" his wife does, and that when he does need to reprove her, women are more easily convinced "rather by gentle wordes then by strypes." But the advice for the wives is far more explicit: "Wyves, be ye in subjection to obey your owne husbande. . . . As for theyr husbandes, them must they obey, and cease from commaundyng, and perfourme subjection." There will be concord in the marriage "when the wyfe is readye at hande at her husbandes commaundemente: when she wyll apply her selfe to his wyll . . . when she wyll eschewe all thynges that might offende hym." The homily also warns explicitly about wives who do not act appropriately: "When the wyves be stubborne, frowarde, and malapert, theyr husbandes are compelled thereby to abhorre and flee from their owne houses, even as they should have batayle with theyr enemyes." But the homily also has clear advice for women if they do behave this way, and this is clearly the advice aimed at Katherine Parr as her story is narrated in *Acts and Monuments*. It parallels explicitly what she has to do to survive in her marriage to Henry VIII. Unruly women are told:

Therefore let them beware, that they stand not in their faultes and wilfulnes: but rather, let them acknowledge theyr folyes and saye: my husband, so it is, that by my anger I was compelled to do this or that, forgeve it to me, & herafter I will take better hede. . . . And they shall not do this onely to avoyde stryfe and debate: but rather in the respect of the commaundement of God.[4]

With Katherine, as we will see, avoiding strife, rather than respecting God's commandments, seems to be her motive, though Foxe praises her for her behavior nevertheless.

That the homily on marriage telling wives of the importance of obeying their husbands was read aloud so frequently at church could mean that women heard this so often that they inculcated the message. It could also, however, mean it had to be read so often because wives refused to be submissive. Also, while many marriages caused both husband and wife great unhappiness and led to serious ill-treatment of women, there were also many marriages in Elizabethan England that clearly were based on mutuality and brought joy to both partners. Sir John Harington's advice as to what to do

---

4. *The second tome of homelyes of such matters as were promised and ... set out by the aucthoritie of the Quenes Majestie: and to be read in every paryshe churche agreablye* (2nd edn., London: In Powles Churche-yarde, 1563) STC 13663, available at Early English Books website, http://O-eebo.chawyck.com, images 254–64, accessed September 29, 2006.

about "the shrew wife" is telling in that way. He remarks that the "booke of taming a shrew, which hath made a number of us so perfect, that now every one can rule a shrew in our contrey, save he that hath her." Harington then gives two possible ways of dealing with a wifely shrew. "One is, let them never have their willes; the other differs but a letter, let them ever have their willes." While Harington admits "the first is the wiser," it is the second that he personally "make choice of." D. H. Craig describes Harington's marriage to Mary Rogers, whom Harington nicknamed "Mall," as "lively but resilient"; the two clearly loved each other deeply.[5]

The dangers and pleasures for women who were scholars and readers in the sixteenth century and then spoke out about what this might mean for them as wives flows in part from two international intellectual movements, humanism and Protestantism. In a number of ways, these movements conflicted with the developing sense of the patriarchal household, both in the individual sense of the husband as head of the household and the collective sense, of king as head of the household of his people in England. A number of those who spoke out as brave and articulate advocates of the English Reformation were educated women: Anne Askew, Lady Jane Grey, Catherine Willoughby, Lady Anne Bacon, Elizabeth I, and, of course, Katherine Parr. In both this chapter and the next, an English play, again set in Italy, allows for this conflict to be acted out.

Henry VIII's Last Wife Katherine

Foxe's presentation of Katherine Parr and Henry is powerful, but its accuracy is a matter of much scholarly debate. According to Foxe, Bishop Stephen Gardiner and other conservatives plotted against Queen Katherine and manipulated Henry into signing an arrest warrant. Katherine only saved herself by her thorough submission to the king. Several scholars have accepted the presentation of Henry's threat to Katherine's well-being in Foxe as being historically accurate, and a number of them quote the dialogue between Henry and Katherine as supplied by Foxe.[6] Susan James asserts that Foxe's account

5. Sir John Harington, *A New Discourse of a Stale Subject, called the Metamorphosis of Ajax,* ed. Elizabeth Story Donno (New York: Columbia University Press, 1962), 153–54; and D. H. Craig, *Sir John Harington* (Boston: Twayne Publishers, 1985), 10.

6. J. J. Scarisbrick, *Henry VIII* (London: Eyre and Spottiswoode, 1968), 479–81; David Starkey, *The Reign of Henry VIII: Personalities and Politics* (New York: Franklin Watts, 1986), 144 and idem, *Six Wives: The Queens of Henry VIII* (New York: HarperCollins, 2003), 764; Derek Wilson, *In the Lion's Court: Power, Ambition, and Sudden Death in the Reign of Henry VIII* (New York: St. Martin's Press,

"is considered generally convincing by most scholars," adding that Foxe did refer to his source as a woman in the queen's household.[7] Moreover, Diarmaid MacCulloch suggests that one of Henry VIII's motives for his swing toward reform at the end of the reign "may have been Henry's anger at the conservative attempts to threaten his wife," mentioning not only Foxe but also Matthew Parker as a source for this theory.[8] Foxe experts such as Tom Freeman, Megan Hickerson, and John King argue that the story is apocryphal.[9] They point out that Foxe is the only source for this specific event and that he did not mention it in the 1563 edition of *Acts and Monuments;* it appeared for the first time in the revised and expanded 1570 edition. Susan Wabuda cogently argues, however, that there is much that appears for the first time in the 1570 edition that can be verified, so this is not a reason to discount the Katherine Parr story, which she accepts as accurate.[10]

The danger for Katherine Parr in 1546 was real, however, even if Foxe's presentation of it cannot be established to be the actual story. The atmosphere at court in 1546 was treacherous, especially for Queen Katherine, and much of this was due to the king. Chronically beset by ill health, Henry was in pain and frustrated by his lack of military success in northern France. As Glyn Redworth points out, he also was irritated with Katherine, and these combined events "only served to make the king more vicious and unpredictable than he had been since the time of his marriage to Anne of Cleves. The rift between the royal couple was widely talked about." Katherine's turn toward the reformist religion, which by January 1546 was marked, and her intercessions on behalf of religious radicals certainly did not make her situation easier. Nor did the fact that the women of her privy chamber were outspoken in their evangelical beliefs.

In February 1546, Spanish Ambassador François van der Delft wrote to Charles V letting him know "that there are rumours of a new queen." The

2001), 492; Maria Dowling, *Humanism in the Age of Henry VIII* (London: Croom Helm, 1986), 66–68; and Robert Hutchinson, *The Last Days of Henry VIII: Conspiracies, Treason, and Heresy at the Court of the Dying Tyrant* (New York: William Morrow, 2005), 165–74.

7. Susan E. James, *Kateryn Parr: The Making of a Queen* (Burlington, VT: Ashgate, 1999), 259–60.

8. Diarmaid MacCulloch, *Thomas Cranmer: A Life* (New Haven: Yale University Press, 1996), 356.

9. For a discussion of why this story may well be apocryphal, see Megan L. Hickerson, *Making Women Martyrs in Tudor England* (New York: Palgrave Macmillan, 2005), 185n47; John King, "Fiction and Fact in Foxe's Book of Martyrs," in *John Foxe and the English Reformation,* ed. David Loades (Aldershot, U.K.: Scolar Press, 1997), 32.

10. Susan Wabuda, "The Woman with the Rock: The Controversy on Women and Bible Reading," in *Belief and Practice in Reformation England: A Tribute to Patrick Collinson from his Students,* ed. Susan Wabuda and Caroline Litzenberger (Aldershot, U.K.: Ashgate, 1998), 56. I very much appreciate Professor Wabuda's thorough discussion of this issue with me at the Folger Shakespeare Library, October 2006.

next month Stephen Vaughan, the king's financial agent in Antwerp, wrote to Lord Chancellor Thomas Wriothesley, "This day came to my lodging a High Dutch, a merchant of this town, saying he had dined with certain friends, one of whom offered to lay a wager with him that the king's majesty would have another wife." Cornelus Sceppurus, a member of Charles V's Council, was in London in early April and wrote, referring to the king, that "some change is suspected to be pending."[11] Diane Watt argues that when two members of Henry's Privy Council, Wriothesley and Solicitor-General Sir Richard Rich, themselves racked Anne Askew in the Tower in June 1546, "they were probably motivated by the hope that she would incriminate the queen." Thomas Betteridge suggests that Gardiner and Wriothesley "hoped to use Askewe to link Parr with evangelical and heretical groups in London. Their ultimate aim was to persuade Henry that he was married to a heretic." About the heresy prosecutions of the summer of 1546 aimed at a number of prominent persons, Alec Ryrie also argues that "even Henry's last queen, Katherine Parr, only narrowly escaped arrest."[12]

In terms of Foxe's narrative, Redworth suggests that the story is largely Foxe's invention, although Foxe also knew that when Anne Askew was racked it was in an attempt to cause her to provide links with Katherine's household and that Foxe appeared to have access to the records of the Privy Council: "Once we accept that in the Council's register Foxe saw the essential ingredients of another plot against the queen, it is easy to see how he was tempted to compose a fuller script." And, as Megan Hickerson suggests, "The Catherine Parr story is set against a background which, to Foxe, was not open to question: the torture of the Henrician martyr Anne Askew. . . . It is probably fiction, but fiction dramatizing events believed, rightly or wrongly, to be true."[13]

Taming Queen Katherine in *Acts and Monuments*

But within this discussion, historical accuracy is not really the most significant question. What is most important is the power and influence of the

---

11. *Letters and Papers, Foreign and Domestic, of the Reign of Henry VIII,* ed. James Gairdner, vol. 21, pt. 1 (London: Her Majesty's Stationery Office, 1980), items 289, 364, 552.

12. Diane Watt, "Askew, Anne (c.1521–1546)," in *Oxford Dictionary of National Biography,* ed. H. C. G. Matthew and Brian Harrison (Oxford: Oxford University Press, 2004); Thomas Betteridge, *Tudor Histories of the English Reformations, 1530–83* (Aldershot, U.K.: Ashgate, 1999), 201; and Alec Ryrie, *The Gospel and Henry VIII: Evangelicals in the Early English Reformation* (Cambridge: Cambridge University Press, 2003), 2.

13. Glyn Redworth, *In Defence of the Church Catholic: The Life of Stephen Gardiner* (Oxford: Basil Blackwell, 1990), 233, 234; and Hickerson, *Making Women Martyrs,* 14.

story's highly dramatic confrontation between Henry VIII and Katherine Parr in the early modern period. In Foxe this confrontation leads to Henry planning to have Katherine arrested and examined for heresy because she has been too willing to speak back to him about what she has learned in her readings. The lessons Queen Katherine learns from the event about the dangers of speaking out and what to do to survive echo not only in Samuel Rowley's play about the event but also in *The Taming of the Shrew*, Shakespeare's play about gender roles in marriage, written in the last years of Elizabeth's reign. There are certainly traits that separate Katherine Parr, Rowley's Queen Kate, and Shakespeare's Kate in *The Taming of the Shrew*. And there are also real differences between what we know of the historical Katherine Parr and Foxe's representation of her; for one thing, the real Katherine Parr was a more complex figure. While Shakespeare shows a Kate who stoutly resists being married and doing anything that would please her husband, Foxe describes a Katherine trying very hard to be a good wife to Henry. Writes Foxe: "For never handmayd sought with more carefull diligence to please her mistres, then she did with all paynfull endeavour, to apply her selfe by all vertuous meanes, in all thynges to please his humour."[14]

Though Katherine Parr did indeed attempt to be a good wife to Henry, she had not gone into the marriage willingly. After surviving two arranged marriages, both of which had their difficulties, the thirty-year-old Katherine was in love with the man courting her, Thomas Seymour, and looking forward to what she hoped would be a very different marriage. But Seymour diplomatically drifted from view once Henry began to demonstrate interest in Katherine. Given Henry's track record by this time, it is hardly surprising that she expressed the opinion she would rather be Henry's mistress than his wife and saw her marriage as being more valuable to her family relations than agreeable to herself. In a letter to her brother William, she pointed out that he was "the person who has most cause to rejoice" about her upcoming wedding.[15] She was not the happiest bride when Bishop Stephen Gardiner married her to the king at Hampton Court on July 12, 1543. But Katherine had as little choice about marrying Henry as Kate does about her nuptials with Petruchio. But Katherine, "an impressive and agreeable woman," in the words of J. J. Scarisbrick, did as Foxe argues all she could to please her difficult husband with her patience and good humor.[16]

Despite these qualities, Katherine Parr had problems with her lord and husband, problems that seemed to come from her studies of the Bible and

---

14. John Foxe. *Acts and Monuments [...]* (1570 edition), 1422.

15. James, *Kateryn Parr,* 114, 115.

16. Scarisbrick, *Henry VIII,* 456.

interest in religious reform. Foxe describes how Henry, upon returning from France in 1546, learned that Katherine "was very much given to the readyng and study of the holy Scriptures," spending at least one hour a day in study. She also asked a number of theologians to talk frequently with her. Since Henry did not seem to mind Katherine doing this, it made her "more bold" so that she would "franckly to debate with the kyng touchyng Religion, and therein flatlye to discover her selfe." According to the Oxford English Dictionary, in the sixteenth century *discover* could mean to "To disclose or expose to view (anything covered up, hidden, or previously unseen), to reveal, show." With her study and her convictions Katherine began to "discover" to Henry more of who she really was, to her great peril; for Henry, according to Foxe, "myslyked to be contended withal in any kinde of argument."[17]

For Katherine, this "myslyke" could potentially cost her her life, especially because of "the malicious practise of certain enemyes professed agaynst the truth,...Gardiner B. of Winchester, Wrysley then Lord Chauncelour, and others more as wel," whose conspiracies led "almost to the extreme ruine of the Queene...if God had not marvelously succoured her in that distress." Gardiner and Wriothesley were very worried about Katherine's "free conference with the King in matters of Religion." Katherine usually spoke to the king with "reverent termes & humble talke." But she also took her study of scriptures very seriously, and she seriously discussed the scriptural matters with Henry. Katherine's reverence and humility were not enough when her monarch was in an ill humor. At first their discussions were amicable enough "until at the last, by reason of his sore legge (the anguish wherof began more & more to encrease) he waxed sickly, & therwithal forward, & difficult to be pleased."[18]

When Katherine left the room after one such discourse with Henry, the king then turned to Stephen Gardiner—who had been waiting for just such a moment—and muttered: "A good hearyng...it is, when women become such Clerkes; & a thing much to my comfort, to come in myne old dayes to be taught by my wife." Gardiner was delighted with Henry's disenchantment with Katherine, doing all he could to encourage it more strongly, telling Henry "how daungerous and perilous a matter it is and ever hath bene for a Prince, to suffer such insolent woordes." He also argued that "speaking those wordes that she did speake, and defending those arguments that she dyd defend...by law deserved death....These and such other kindes of Winchesters flattering phrases, marvelously whetted the kyng, both to anger and

17. John Foxe. *Acts and Monuments [...]* (1570 edition), 1422.
18. John Foxe. *Acts and Monuments [...]* (1570 edition), 1422.

displeasure towardes the Queene." Henry allowed Gardiner to write up articles against Katherine that might contribute to her execution, and the bishop secretly began to gather information against Katherine's religious practices. Gardiner planned to have Katherine arrested and "caryed by Barge by night unto the Tower." What happened next in Foxe is an extravagant coincidence that makes great drama despite its improbability. The bill of articles signed by Henry was mislaid and found by "some godly person" who immediately warned Katherine. Not surprisingly, given the track record of her predecessors, she "fell incontinent into a great melancholy and agony."[19]

Katherine's weeping and wailing disturbed Henry, so he sent his physician Dr. Thomas Wendy to see what the matter was, first confiding in him that "he intended not any longer to be troubled with such a Doctresse as she was...but yet charging hym withall upon peril of his lyfe, not to utter it to any creature livyng." Despite his oath, Wendy, who thought highly of Katherine, "in secret manner" warned her. Foxe suggests that this was Henry's plan—that the doctor would break his word and tell Katherine how she ought to behave to save herself. Indeed, argues Foxe, Henry only gave his word to Gardiner "dissemblyngly," never intending to harm Katherine but rather concocting an elaborate charade as a way to teach Gardiner a lesson. It was also clearly a way to teach Katherine submission, with Wendy acting in proxy for Henry. Wendy told Katherine of the "sayde Articles devised agaynst her" but assured Katherine that if she were "to frame and conforme her self unto the kings mynde...and shewe her humble submission unto hym, shee shoulde finde hym gracious and favourable unto her."[20] Here was a clear recipe of what was acceptable behavior for a woman and one no doubt often taught. In *The Taming of the Shrew*, Petruchio's servant says to Kate: "Say as he says, or we shall never go" (4.5.11).

Katherine had the presence of mind to tell her ladies to dispose of all of their illegal religious books. Then she went to Henry, in his bedchamber, who immediately began to argue with her over religion. Katherine "myldly, and with a reverent countenaunce" responded to Henry with a long speech that Foxe provides:

Your Majestie (quoth she) doth right well know...what great imperfection & weakenes by our first creation, is alotted unto us women, to be ordeyned and appoynted as inferiour and subject unto man as our head, from whiche head all our direction ought to procede: and that,

---

19. John Foxe. *Acts and Monuments [...]* (1570 edition), 1423–24.
20. John Foxe. *Acts and Monuments [...]* (1570 edition), 1424.

as God made man to his owne shape and lykenes, wherby he beyng endued with more speciall giftes of perfection, might rather bee stirred to the contemplation of heauenly... euen so also made hee woman of man, of whom and by whom shee is to bee gouerned, commaunded and directed. Whose womanly weakenes and naturall imperfection, ought to be tolerated, ayded and borne withall, so that by his wisedome such thinges as be lackyng in her, ought to be supplyed.

Sithence therfore that God hath appointed such a naturall difference betwene man and woman, and your Majestie beyng so excellent in giftes and ornamentes of wisedome, and I a seely poore woman so much inferiour in all respectes of nature unto you: how then commeth it now to passe that your Majestie in such diffuse causes of Religion, will seme to require my Judgement? Whiche when I haue uttered and sayd what I can, yet must I and will I referre my Judgement in this and all other cases to your Majesties wisedome, as my onely anker, supreme head, and gouerner here in earth next under God, to leane unto.

One would certainly expect such a submission to be enough, but Henry was still not placated. He accused Katherine of trying to teach him, rather than be taught by him. "You are become a Doctor, Kate, to instruct us (as we take it) and not to be instructed, or directed by us." Katherine protested that this was not so, that indeed she "have ever bene of the opinion, to thinke it verye unseemely and preprosterous for the woman to take upon her the office of an instructer or teacher to her Lorde, and husband, but rather to learne of her husbande, and to bee taught by him." Katherine protested that she was simply trying to learn and that her other motive was to take Henry's mind off his painful leg. Finally, Katherine humbled herself enough and Henry expressed himself delighted with her submission: "And is it even so sweete hart.... Then perfect friendes we are nowe againe." Henry kissed and embraced Katherine and told her that those words out of her mouth had done him more good than a present of £100,000.[21]

The taming of Katherine—and also of Gardiner—was not over, however. Henry did not cancel the arrest order. Gardiner and his colleagues, especially Wriothesley, unaware of the reconciliation, continued with their plans, with Henry doing nothing to stop them. Instead, the next day, Henry sat with Katherine in the garden and allowed the guards led by Wriothesley—to his good fortune, Gardiner was not there—to come forward to arrest her. Only

---

21. John Foxe. *Acts and Monuments [...]* (1570 edition), 1424–25.

then did he berate Wriothesley, calling him an "arrant knave, beast, and foole." Though Henry had agreed to drawing up the articles against Katherine, Foxe argues that he never intended to use them, implying that Henry's scheme was a lesson for Gardiner and his crew. Certainly this ploy worked to keep the conservatives at Henry's court, Gardiner and Wriothesley, in line. We do not know if this was the king's intention, just as we do not know if Gardiner's attack on Katherine actually took place. But even if controlling Gardiner and the other conservatives was what Henry planned, it was also a most effective way for Henry to teach Katherine not to behave in a manner he deemed inappropriate in a woman—to tame her. As Scarisbrick suggests, though we cannot know Henry's motives, cannot know whether or not he ever intended to go through with Katherine's arrest, the whole elaborate charade might well have been a way "to frighten Catherine, or to break her evident independence of mind." J. K. McConica concurs, pointing out that even if it was all a lesson concocted by Henry against Gardiner, what also comes through is "the King's real anger at the Queen's independence of opinion, or his great jubilation at his victory.... Once [Katherine] submitted, he apparently lost interest in her views, and her establishment... was unthreatened."[22]

In his discussion of Katherine, Foxe clearly approves of her as one who survives by posing as a "silly poor woman" despite her considerable intelligence. Before we argue that Foxe himself was demeaning Katherine, however, we must remember, as pointed out in chapter 1 in connection with Foxe's discussion of Perotine Massey, *silly* in the sixteenth century also meant "deserving of pity, compassion, or sympathy" or "helpless or defenceless." Certainly Katherine in this situation is deserving of compassion because of how defenseless—how in danger—she is.

Taming Queen Kate in *When You See Me, You Know Me*

Samuel Rowley's *When You See Me, You Know Me* is a play that has received little scholarly attention, but that is beginning to change.[23] Margot Heinemann

---

22. Scarisbrick, *Henry VIII,* 481; and James McConica, *English Humanists and Reformation Politics under Henry VIII and Edward VI* (Oxford: Clarendon Press, 1965), 226.

23. All quotations from this play come from Samuel Rowley, *When You See Me, You Know Me* (Oxford: The Malone Society Reprints, 1952). For scholarship on this play, see Faith M. Nostbakken, "Rowley's *When You See Me You Know Me:* Political Drama in Transition," *Cahiers Elisabéthains: Late Medieval and Renaissance Studies* 47 (1995): 71–78; Jo Eldridge Carney, "Queenship in Shakespeare's Henry VIII: The Issue of Issue," in *Political Rhetoric, Power, and Renaissance Women,* ed. Carole Levin

argues that of the plays on Reformation history mostly based on *Acts and Monuments* performed in late Elizabethan and early Jacobean London, *When You See Me* is "a particularly lively and subversive example," and while based on Foxe, there are "imaginative alterations." The chronology of the play bends history and in some way turns it on its head. Henry's fool Will Sommers is a character throughout, and he shows not only wit but courage; he is also a strong Protestant. Will is in opposition to the villainous Catholic churchmen Cardinal Wolsey, Bishop Bonner, and Bishop Gardiner. The first part of the play deals with Henry and his third wife, Jane Seymour, and her death when his son was born. In the later section, scenes 8–10, Charles Brandon is sent off to France to bring Henry's sister Mary, the newly widowed Queen of France, home to England; Henry's son Prince Edward is old enough to be tutored by Thomas Cranmer; and Henry has decided on a new wife:

> Commend me to the Ladie Catherine Parry,
> Give her this Ring, tell her on Sunday next
> She shall be Queene, and crowned at Westminster:
> And Anne of Cleave shall be sent home againe. (1420–23)

Before Katherine even appears on the stage, the audience is told both about her views and the dangers they represent to her. When Cardinal Wolsey learns she is to be the next queen, he is appalled and tells Bishop Bonner and Bishop Gardiner:

> Holy Saint Peter sheeld his Majestie,
> She is the hope of Luthers heresie:
> If she be Queene, the Protestants will swell
> …
>
> But Bishops weele to Court immediately,
> And plot the downfall of these Lutherans:
> …
>
> I doe suspect that Latimer and Ridly,

and Patricia A. Sullivan (Albany: State University of New York Press, 1995), 189–202; Joseph Candido, "Fashioning Henry VIII: What Shakespeare Saw in *When You See Me, You Know Me*," *Cahiers Elisabéthains: Late Medieval and Renaissance Studies* 23 (1983): 47–59; Marsha S. Robinson, *Writing the Reformation: Actes and Monuments and the Jacobean History Play* (Burlington, VT: Ashgate, 2002); Kim H. Noling, "Woman's Wit and Woman's Will in *When You See Me, You Know Me*," *SEL* 33 (1993): 327–42; and Margot Heinemann, "'God Help the Poor: The Rich Can Shift': The World Upside-Down and the Popular Tradition in the Theatre," in *The Politics of Tragicomedy: Shakespeare and After,* ed. Gordon McMullan and Jonathan Hope (London: Routledge, 1992), 151–65.

Chiefe teachers of the faire Elizabeth,
Are not sound Catholickes, nor friendes to Rome,
If it be so, weele soone remove them all:
Tis better they should dye, then thousands fall.
    (1489–91, 1494–95, 1500–03)

Kate, as she is known in the play, demonstrates her intelligence, courage, and commitment to Protestantism as a religion of the people from her first moment on stage. When Kate as the new queen meets Will Sommers, the king's fool, she immediately lets him know that she is delighted by his loyalty to the king. Will responds that he does love his master. But that is not all:

KING: I had rather hee should have the poores prayers then the Popes.
QUEENE: Faith I am of thy mind Will, I thinke so too.
KING: Take heed what yee say Kate, what a Lutheran?
WOLSEY: Tis Heresie faire Queene, to thinke such thoughts.
QUEENE: And much uncharity to wrong the poore. (1609–13)

These first lines set up the situation for the rest of the play. Kate is a brave woman who is willing to challenge the greed of the Catholic Church, which frightens Henry and causes Wolsey to brand her ideas as heretical in the presence of the King; yet neither King nor Cardinal can silence the Queen.

The next crisis of the reign happens soon after this exchange. Lord Dudley appears on stage to announce to the King that Duke Brandon, as he is called here, has returned from France with a royal wife. When Henry inquires as to the wife's identity and is told it is his sister, "the late Queen of France," Henry appears furious: "Dares any Subject mixe his blood with ours, without our leave?" (1716, 1719) When Brandon and Mary enter, Henry commands "Off with his head" and orders that Brandon be taken to the Tower (1724). When Mary begins to beg for her husband's life, Henry adds, "And beare our carelesse sister to the Fleete" (1735). Appalled, Kate immediately begs for mercy for the couple: "Oh my Lord, let me intreat for them" (1740). But Henry then reveals that this is only being done to scare the couple:

Tut, Kate, though thus I seeme
A while to threaten them,
I meane not to disgrace my sister so. (1742–45)

Henry has them brought back to court and tells them:

> Deare Brandon, I imbrace thee in mines armes:
> Kind sister, I love you both so well.
> I cannot dart another angry frowne
> To gaine a kingdom. (1752–55)

Henry's supposed anger and then forgiveness of Mary and Brandon, which allows him to control, manipulate, and pull the other characters' strings like a puppet master, works as a foreshadowing of the more dangerous anger and then forgiveness of Kate, though in that case Henry himself is being manipulated by the Bishops Gardiner and Bonner.

Soon after the King's forgiveness of his sister and her new husband, there is a meeting between the two bishops in which they express their fear and outrage over Cranmer's teachings to Prince Edward and the great growth of Luther's ideas in England. Gardiner informs Bonner, "We must prevent this ranckor that now swells so big. . . . They have a dangerous head, and much I feare" (2120–22). Bonner worries that the King will lean toward these heresies but Gardiner reassures him:

> GARD: Tis doubtfull he will bend, but sure
> Queene Katherens a strong Lutheran, hard yee not
> How in presence of the King and Cardinall,
> She exsterp against his Holinesse.
> . . .
> BON: . . . 'tis a perilous thing,
> Queene Katherin can do much with Englands King.
> GARD: I Bonner, that's the summe of all.
> There must be no Queene, or the Abbies fall. (2124–28, 2131–34)

Bonner suggests that he and Gardiner go "and incense the King," which will bring Kate to ruin (2149). The bishops soon have their opportunity. We see them walking with King Henry and the Queen, who is very concerned with all the bloodshed the different religious perspectives have brought about. She suggests that Henry call a council with other rulers and

> peruse the bookes,
> That Luther writ against the Catholickes,
> And superstitions of the Church of Rome
> And if they teach a truer way to heaven,
> . . .
> Why should they not be red and followed? (2208–11, 2213)

Henry is impressed with the idea; he may especially like it as Kate has suggested that he call a council and make a ruling with other monarchs. But when he asks Bishop Gardiner what he thinks of the plan, Gardiner assures him that it is "Most unlawfull my deare Soveraigne, Unlesse permitted by his Holynesse" (2216–17). But this does not silence Kate, who asks for the reason behind this ruling. Her question suggests to Henry that he should "heare the Bishops and my Queene dispute" (2220). Kate is certainly "content to hold them Argument" as long as Henry understands that she is "a weake Scholler" and that he takes "no exceptions at my womans wit" (2221–24). But despite these disclaimers, she is ready to make a most articulate case for her position:

> Pray tell the King then, what Scripture have yee,
> To teach religion in an unknowne language?
> Instruct the ignorant to kneele to Saints,
> By bare-foote pilgrimage to visite shrines,
> For money to release from Purgatorie,
> The vildest villaine, theefe, or murderer,
> All this the people must believe you can,
> Such is the dregs of Romes religion. (2252–60)

Gardiner's only response is to brand this "the speeches of . . . hereticks" (2261). Soon after, Kate asks for permission to go fetch for the king some religious writings that support her position. But once she is gone, Henry shows, with a speech almost straight from Foxe, that he is not so pleased to have such an articulate, independent thinking wife:

> a sirra, we have women doctors,
> Now I see Mother a God, here's a fine world the whilste,
> That twixt so many mens opinions
> The holy Scriptures must be banded thus. (2271–75)

Gardiner is quick to follow up on this, suggesting that such behavior causes "detriment" to Henry's "crowne and sacred dignitie" (2276–77). But then he goes further:

> They that would alter thus Religion,
> I feare they scarcely love your royall person. (2277–78)

While at first Henry warns Gardiner to take heed, Gardiner assures the king that he is only speaking out because of his love and duty to the king, that his conscience tells him he must. Immediately Henry becomes worried and begs Gardiner to inform him "Whose the ring-leader of this lusty crew?" (2295–96). Gardiner, once he has assured himself from the king that he will be pardoned for anything he has to say, is quick to spring the trap on the Queen:

> Then if our royall person will be safe,
> Your life preferude and this faire Realme in peace.
> And all these troubles smoothly pacifide,
> The Queene deare Lord must be removed from you. (2300–2303)

To convince Henry further, he relates that Kate, unbeknownst to the King, is having secret meetings with a sect of Lutherans who are not only against God but, perhaps more important to Henry, also against the king: "Seeking by tumults to subvert the state... is treason capitall against the Crowne" (2310–12). Henry is easily persuaded:

> Mother a god these proofes are probabell,
> And strong presumptions doe confirme your words. (2318–19)

Henry then calls for his Council to meet, promising to root out Luther's followers from England no matter who they are. Gardiner is elated and says in an aside to Bonner:

> Now Bonner stir, the game is set a foot,
> The king is now incenst, lets follow close
> To have Queen Katherne shorter by a head,
> These heresies will cease when she is dead. (2336–39)

Henry is already so enraged about the Queen that when he meets with his Council, he orders that a warrant be drawn up for Kate's arrest, commanding that she be taken to the Tower under strong guard. He informs the Council:

> If she of treason be convict, I sweare,
> Her head goes off, were she my kingdoms aire. (2366–67)

The scene then shifts to young Prince Edward, working with his tutor, Thomas Cranmer, described in the list of characters as "afterward Archbishop of Canterbury." There is clearly great affection and respect between Edward and Cranmer. We see how strongly Protestant Prince Edward is when he receives letters from each of his sisters. He is so upset with Mary's letter telling him that she is praying to the Virgin Mother and all the angels and saints that he be preserved from idolatry that he stops reading it before he is finished. But he is delighted by Elizabeth's letter, which begs him to be stead-fast in his faith. Edward says of this sister, "Loving thou art, and of me best beloved" (2420). He promises to meditate on her virtues and pray to Christ for both of them. But Edward does not have time to meditate long; soon a messenger comes from his father expelling Cranmer from Court. Edward is deeply concerned: "My tutor thrust from court so sodainly, this is strange" (2464). But things soon become stranger yet. Kate begs permission to con-verse with Edward and then tells him that one of her Gentlemen found an article dropped on the floor that has terrified her:

I am accusde of treason, and the king
Is now in cousell to dispose of me,
I know his frowne is death, and I shall dye. (2473–75)

This theme continues to be emphasized for the audience. Kate later says again: "The King is angry and the Queene must dye" (2541). Edward com-forts Kate and tells her not to worry. He promises to go to the king himself and work out a peace between his father and Kate.

In this section of the play, Rowley portrays an elderly king who has been tricked into believing that he should be in fear of his life. He is not the power-ful manipulator of Foxe but rather a pathetic, if still dangerous, old man. When Prince Edward comes to speak with him, Henry insists that guards accompany them:

Must English Harry walke with armed Gards,
Now in his old age, must I feare my life,
By hatefull treason of my Queene and wife. (2575–77)

Even when Edward pleads with his father, Henry tells him that he does not even want to hear about Kate and expresses panic when a messenger tells him that she is at the door and entreats Henry that she may she speak with him:

So nere our presence, keepe her out I charge ye.
Bend all your Holbeards point against the dore,
If she presume to enter strike her through.
. . .

Mother a god, stand close and gard it sure,
If she come in, ile hange ye all I sweare. (2606–8, 2613–14)

Though there has been no question about Kate's sexual fidelity, Henry also at this point describes her as a "proud slut" to convince Edward to stop begging him to allow Kate access (2617). As we saw in chapter 1, in the sixteenth century when a woman moved beyond her expected role, one of the ways to destroy her was to accuse her of sexual misconduct. And while there was never a suggestion about such behavior with Katherine Parr, after her death she also was so labeled. In an effort to justify the execution of her widower Thomas Seymour, on March 15, 1549, Hugh Latimer preached before Edward VI "one of the most viciously political sermons which survives from him," according to Diarmaid MacCulloch. In an extended biblical metaphor, he described the recently deceased Katherine Parr "as King David's whore Abishag."[24]

Only when Prince Edward promises to "pawne [his] princely word" that Kate will only speak sweetly to the king does Henry allow her to enter, banishing all else from the room but his son. Kate throws herself at Henry's feet, but this does no good:

> How now, what doe you weepe and kneele,
> Dus your black soule the gylte of conscience feele,
> Out, out, you're a traytor. (2626–28)

Unlike Katherine in Foxe, Rowley's Kate does not go right into submission at this point. Rather, she passionately argues that if she were indeed a traitor, then Henry was being far too merciful:

> A traytor. O then you are too mercifull,
> If I have treason in me, why rip ye not
> My ugly hart out with your weapons point,
> O my good Lord, If it have traytors blood,
> It will be black, deformd, and tenebrous,
> If not, from it will spring a scarlet fountaine,
> And spit defiance in their perjurde throates
> That have accusde me to your majesty. (2631–38)

Kate asks the king directly who has accused her, but Henry is loath to tell her only:

> Some probable effects my selfe can witnesse,
> Others our faithfull subjects can testifie:

---

24. MacCulloch, *Thomas Cranmer,* 408.

Have you not oft maintained arguments,
Even to our face against religion. (2647–50)

But then Henry comes to the real reason he has moved so furiously against
Kate. He is afraid that "in mine age, lame and halfe bed-rid," he will be
turned out into the kingdom, a highly pathetic version of King Lear, or else,
he tells Kate, "youle keepe me fast inough in prison" (2556–57). Kate then
recognizes that she must now not only proclaim her innocence but also move
into her submissive mode, sounding much more like Queen Katherine of the
Acts and Monuments:

Heaven on my fore-head write my worst intent
And let your hate against my life be bent
If ever thought of ill against our majestie,
Was harbord here...
...
What I did speake, was as my womans wit,
To hold our Argument could compasse it,
My puny schollership is helde too weake
To maintaine proofes about religion,
Alas I did it but to wast the time,
Knowing as then your grace was weake and sickly. (2659–62, 2667–72)

Henry is delighted: "Saist thou so, was it no otherwise" (2576). When Kate
assures him, "If I am false, heaven strike me sodainly," Henry apologizes and
makes his peace with his queen, explaining that he could hardly believe it
when he had been told she was a traitor, but "it was applied so hard to me. . . . I
tell ye, King Harry would be loath to die by treason now" (2578, 2681–82).

Henry then gives a long meandering speech that mixes his ill health, his
affection for Kate and desire to fondle her, and his anger at those who con-
spired against her:

I growe stiffe, my legges faile me first, but they stand furthest from
my hart, and that's still sound, I thanke my God, give me thy hand,
come kisse me Kate, so now ime friends againe, hurson knaves, crafty
varlets, make thee a traytor to oulde Harries life, well, well, ile meete
with some of them, Sfoute come sit on my knee Kate. Mother a
god he that says th'art false to me by Englands crowne ile hang him
presently. (2685–90)

Henry hardly presents himself well in this speech. Margot Heinemann penetratingly describes it as a "violent, pathetic, randy outburst of forgiveness."[25] But if Rowley's Henry is a dismal old man, fearful and easily manipulated, frightening because of what he can do but far from majestic, his Kate is a highly intelligent, articulate, courageous woman of faith. As Kim Noling points out, "Although Rowley ultimately does rein in Queen Katherine's independent spirit somewhat," his queen is still far more unwilling to present herself as some submissive, foolish woman than Foxe's was.[26] Still, she does know how to deprecate her "womans wit" and refers to her "weake" and "puny schollership" if this will save her life.

Taming Kate as Wife in *The Taming of the Shrew*

The method of using force and threats to subdue a wife that appeared in Foxe and was retold by Rowley also uneasily echoes with that other Kate, tamed by her "lord and husband" Petruchio. At her wedding, Kate expresses no intention of being tamed:

> Gentlemen, forward to the bridal dinner.
> I see a woman may be made a fool
> If she had not spirit to resist. (3.2.219–21)

But Petruchio will not allow his wife to show her spirit, certainly not after he has married her and thus has full legal control over her:

> She is my goods, my chattels, she is my house
> My household stuff, my field, my barn
> My horse, my ox, my ass, my anything (3.2.230–32)

Petruchio's comments would hardly have shocked an Elizabethan audience. As Sara Mendelson and Patricia Crawford point out, "Very often women were legally constructed as property and possessions."[27] Moreover, common law taught that husband and wife were one, and that one was the husband.

---

25. Heinemann, "God Help the Poor," 156.
26. Noling, "Woman's Wit and Woman's Will," 336.
27. Sara Mendelson and Patricia Crawford, *Women in Early Modern England* (Oxford: Oxford University Press, 1998), 98.

In terms of property, "that which the husband hath is his own," and "that which the wife hath is the husband's."[28]

Petruchio takes Kate away with him to a place where she has no relatives and where no one knows her. While an audience may well find their relationship amusing—Ruth Nevo called the play "unencumbered enjoyment"—Petruchio also deliberately starves Kate of food and sleep as a means to "curb her mad and headstrong humor."[29]

> She ate no meat today, nor none shall eat.
> Last night she slept not, nor tonight she shall not.
> . . .
>
> This is a way to kill a wife with kindness;
> And thus I'll curb her mad and headstrong humor.
> He that knows better how to tame a shrew,
> Now let him speak (4.1.185–86, 196–99)

Petruchio's plan works well. As Kate tells his servant, Grumio:

> But I, who never knew how to entreat
> Nor never needed that I should entreat
> Am starved for meat, giddy for lack of sleep,
> With oaths kept waking, and with brawling fed.
> And that which spites me more than all these wants,
> He does it under name of perfect love. (4.3.6–11)

Again, an audience might well find all this amusing, and indeed, Lynda Boose suggests that Shakespeare's wit is enough to make "Kate's humiliation seem wildly comic," but it may be less so when one considers all the cases of husbands who abuse their wives "out of love."[30] As a fifteenth-century Sienese book on marriage advised husbands:

> When you see your wife commit an offense, don't rush at her with insults and violent blows: rather first correct the wrong lovingly and pleasantly, and sweetly teach her not to do it again. . . . But if your wife is of a servile disposition and has a crude and shifty spirit, so that pleasant words have no effect, scold her sharply, bully, and terrify her. And

---

28. *The Law's Resolution of Women's Rights,* in *Half-humankind: Contexts and Texts of the Controversy about Women in England, 1540–1640,* ed. Katherine U. Henderson and Barbara F. McManus (Urbana: University of Illinois Press, 1985), 79.

29. Ruth Nevo, *Comic Transformations of Shakespeare* (London: Methuen, 1980), 38.

30. Lynda Boose, "Scolding Brides and Bridling Scolds: Taming the Woman's Unruly Member," in *Materialist Shakespeare,* ed. Ivo Kamps (London: Verso, 1995), 141.

if this still doesn't work... take up a stick and beat her soundly... not in rage, but out of charity and concern for her soul.[31]

This sentiment is echoed in William Whately's early-seventeenth-century marriage manual, *A Bride-bush*. While he agrees that it is better for a husband not to beat his wife, if "she give just cause, after much bearing and forebearing, and trying all other ways, in case of utmost necessity," he can indeed beat her, but should "exceed not measure."[32] This perspective was certainly not universal, and some authors of manuals, such as Thomas Gouge, were clearly opposed to wife beating; English law, however, was on the side of those who did provide "reasonable correction."[33] Scholars have found from examining evidence of the early modern period that "wife beating was rife among all social groups."[34]

Linda Bamber suggests that the play demonstrates a triumph "over the feminine," a point made even more strongly by the director Michael Bogdanov, who argues that *The Taming of the Shrew* is "a play about a male wish-fulfillment dream of revenge upon women. The humiliation to which Kate is subjected is what happens in a world ruled and dominated by men, where any woman who challenges male supremacy has to be smashed down by any means possible, until she is submissive, pliant... and comes when called."[35] Of course, this is exactly what we see Kate do at the end of the play.

And while Petruchio's servant Peter is certainly not being literal when he tells his co-worker Nathaniel, "He kills her in her own humour," Petruchio's treatment of Kate could certainly be harmful to her health. As Lena Orlin points out, "Kate's physical torture is intensified" during the time she is at his residence.[36]

An Elizabethan audience, of course, would have been aware of how common abuse of wives actually was. Sara Mendelson and Patricia Crawford tell us that "Married women experience a whole spectrum of mistreatment, ranging from verbal and psychological harassment and threats of violence, physical assault and attempted murder, to actual homicide. In some

31. Cherubino de Siena, *Regole della vita matrimoniale* (Bologna, 1888), pp. 12–14 in Frances and Joseph Gies, *Women in the Middle Ages* (New York: Harper and Row, 1978), 46–48.

32. William Whately, *A Bride-bush* (London, 1623), 107.

33. As stated in *The Law's Resolution of Women's Right* quoted in *Half-Humankind*, 79.

34. Mendelson and Crawford, *Women in Early Modern England*, 147.

35. Linda Bamber, *Comic Women, Tragic Men: A Study of Gender and Genre in Shakespeare* (Stanford: Stanford University Press, 1982), 32; and John Elsom, ed., *Is Shakespeare Still Our Contemporary?* (London: Routledge, 1989), 68–70.

36. Lena Cowen Orlin, "The Performance of Things in *The Taming of the Shrew*," in *The Taming of the Shrew: Critical Essays,* ed. Dana E. Aspinal (London: Routledge, 2002), 194.

matrimonial cases which have been preserved in church and secular court records, we can document an escalating spiral of mental and physical cruelty."[37] As Keith Thomas points out, while in theory accused witches in early modern England were not tortured to gain confessions, there were a number of cases where the accused, most of them women, were kept awake for days and starved in an effort to gain a confession.[38] Petruchio's treatment of Kate, while much less severe, echoes this horror.

There is a wide range of perspectives about Petruchio and his relationship with Kate.[39] Elizabeth Schafer has detailed a number of late-twentieth-century productions influenced by feminist critiques that present a tragic Kate and a brutish Petruchio.[40] But a number of modern critics, however, uncomfortable with a view of a Petruchio as a "slam-bang wife-beating type," argue instead, suggests Robert Heilman, that he is a "generous and affectionate fellow whose basic method is to bring out the best in his fiancée and wife by holding up before her an image both of what she is and what she can become."[41] Marianne L. Novy takes this position, arguing that "play and mutuality may be goals of taming" and that Petruchio's lessons have given Kate "an education in folly [that] has taught her how to live with relative comfort in a patriarchal culture."[42] Corrine Abate argues that Petruchio's wooing of Katherine is unconventional but loving, that he uses "tactics of positive reinforcement" that allow Katherine to create a positive private space in her marriage that was also, in turn, loving.[43] Anne Barton sees Petruchio "as a man who genuinely prizes Katherine, and, by exploiting an age-old and basic antagonism between the sexes, manoeuvres her into an understanding of his nature and also her own."[44] Ruth Nevo takes Barton's characterization even further, arguing that "only a very clever, very discerning man could bring off a psychodrama so instructive, liberating and therapeutic as Petruchio's."[45]

37. Mendelson and Crawford, *Women in Early Modern England,* 140.

38. Keith Thomas, *Religion and the Decline of Magic* (New York: Charles Scribner's Sons, 1971), 517.

39. For an excellent discussion of the different perspectives, see Frances E. Dolan, *The Taming of the Shrew: Texts and Contexts* (Boston: Bedford Books of St. Martin's Press, 1996), 18–24.

40. Elizabeth Schafer, ed., *The Taming of the Shrew: Shakespeare in Production* (Cambridge: Cambridge University Press, 2002), 36–44.

41. Robert Heilman, "The Taming Untamed, or, The Return of the Shrew," in *The Taming of the Shrew: Critical Essays,* ed. Aspinal, 46.

42. Marianne L. Novy, "Patriarchy and Play in *The Taming of the Shrew,*" in *William Shakespeare's* The Taming of the Shrew, ed. Harold Bloom (New York: Chelsea House, 1988), 17, 21.

43. Corrine S. Abate, "Neither a Tamer Nor a Shrew Be: A Defense of Petruchio and Katherine," in *Privacy, Domesticity, and Women in Early Modern England,* ed. Abate (Burlington, VT: Ashgate 2003), 31.

44. *The Riverside Shakespeare,* ed. G. Blakemore Evans (Boston: Houghton Mifflin, 1974), 106.

45. Nevo, *Comic Transformations,* 39. Fiona Shaw suggests that this was the way Jonathan Miller directed his version of *The Taming of the Shrew,* having Petruchio "very non-violently disorientate her

But I find it hard to perceive Petruchio as a therapist/lover or to discover any trace of generosity, affection, or playfulness in his treatment of Kate. Though the whips he has carried on stage in a number of productions are certainly not in the text, the abusiveness of his behavior is. My discussion of *The Taming of the Shrew* may be perhaps unrelenting in my treatment of Petruchio's behavior; this does not mean that I believe that this character, or the entire play for that matter, means that we can label Shakespeare as "sexist," a term I am uncomfortable using about a Renaissance dramatist in any case. Also, one can find an entire range of beliefs and behaviors in the characters of Shakespeare's plays; to my thinking, it is incorrect to read any of them as speaking "for" Shakespeare the playwright.

Shakespeare's Petruchio is not only concerned with taming Kate's body; even more concerning is the "taming" of her spirit. Another servant [Curtis] describes how Petruchio

> rails, and swears, and rates, that she, poor soul
> Knows not which way to stand, to look, to speak,
> And sits as one new risen from a dream. (4.1.172–74)

By bringing in food and then not allowing her to eat, by bringing her to bed and not allowing her to sleep, Petruchio is refining his cruelty to her by setting up expectations before he crushes them. His telling Kate that something is not what she believes it to be, and then forcing her to agree, creates in Kate a belief that her own perceptions do not matter or may even be incorrect. Knowing this is the only way to stop his abuse, Kate agrees to what Petruchio says:

> What you will have it named, even that it is,
> And so it shall be so for Katharine. (4.5.22–23)

But Petruchio confuses the matter further by telling Kate she is wrong when she agrees with him that an old man they encounter on the road is really a young girl.

---

by not accepting anything she says. Jonathan says that is what doctors do with aggressive children. I think he was translating the 'taming' of the shrew into 'therapy,' the realignment of the delinquent." Shaw was not happy with this interpretation: "That's a heavy imposition, because once you commit yourself to that statement, you could go a step further and have Petruchio in a white coat." Carol Rutter, *Clamorous Voices: Shakespeare's Women Today* (London: Women's Press, 1988), 6.

Why, how now, Kate? I hope thou art not mad.
This is a man, old, wrinkled, faded, withered,
And not a maiden, as thou sayst he is. (4.5.41–43)

Just as in Foxe, when King Henry did not want Katherine to argue with him over anything, Petruchio also desires Kate to agree with him no matter what he says. When they are on the road traveling to see her father, he threatens to abort the visit until she agrees:

Now by my mother's son, and that's myself,
It shall be moon, or star, or what I list,
Or ere I journey to your father's house. (4.5.6–8)

While Kate's situation is less serious than Katherine's was in disagreeing with her husband—Queen Katherine could have lost her life as a result—Kate potentially faces more abuse and isolation from her family.

By this time in the play, Kate has learned her lesson by her husband's treatment:

Be it moon, or sun, or what you please,
And if you please to call it a rush candle
Henceforth I vow it shall be so for me. (4.5.13–15)

While Novy suggests that in this interchange there is more play going on, in which Kate "replaces a language determined by the external world…with another determined by her relationship with Petruchio," I see something very different, and more disturbing, in this interchange.[46] In modern parlance, one might say that Petruchio is "gaslighting" Kate. This term for attempting to manipulate someone so that he or more likely *she* believes she is going crazy came in to use after the George Cukor film *Gaslight* in which the Victorian husband, greedy for his wife's wealth, attempts to convince her that she is going mad. Mysterious footsteps, objects that disappear and reappear suddenly, and gas lights that dim and flicker are all part of his plan. Petruchio's constant harangues that what Kate perceives is not accurate might well have the same result. In the same way, while some critics call Kate and Petruchio's interchange on the street where he demands, "Kiss me, Kate," as more play and private language, he is still threatening "Why, let's home again," when she refuses out of a sense of modesty (5.2.135, 140).

---

46. Novy, "Patriarchy and Play," 19.

Bianca as Educated Woman

In our discussion of The *Taming of the Shrew,* we have been concentrating on the parallels between Katherine and Kate, but I want to complicate the discussion further by suggesting that the Katherine who both reads and presents herself in the modest way of the ideal young woman (while still being true to herself) is also echoed by the other woman of *The Taming of the Shrew,* Kate's sister Bianca. Though often in staged and filmed presentations of *The Taming of the Shrew,* Bianca is shown as a simpering fool who has not an iota of studious intent but only uses her books to flirt, this is not necessarily the Bianca of the text.

While many of Shakespeare's women are literate—we think of Lady Macbeth reading her husband's letter, or Beatrice writing of her affection for Benedick—there are few characterizations of women studying. One that definitely presents this in the most tragic of modes is Lavinia, whose father Titus Andronicus says of her:

> But thou art deeper read and better skilled;
> Come and take choice of all my library,
> And so beguile thy sorrow. (4.1.33–35)

Lavinia, with neither tongue nor hands, manages to point out with her stumps the story of Philomel from Ovid's *Metamorphoses,* a book she obviously knows well enough that she can let her family know how she was ravished and mutilated.

Bianca's love of study has none of these tragic connotations. But though she is presented as the ideal feminine counterpart to the shrewish Kate, she is also from the beginning fascinated by her studies and music:

> My books and instruments shall be my company,
> On them to look and practice by myself. (1.1.82–3)

Her father Baptista recognizes this about her and approves. He is delighted to accept a "small packet of Greek and Latin books" (2.1.100) for his daughters and says specifically about Bianca:

> And for I know she taketh most delight
> In music, instruments, and poetry,
> Schoolmasters will I keep within my house. (1.1.92–94)

Indeed, her suitor Lucentio disguises himself as her tutor so that he can be near her. Though David Bevington describes the relationship between the two as "superficial," they spend much more time together than most courting couples, and Bianca is learned enough that she tells him her feelings for him in Latin (1.1.109). Indeed, though often described as "passive" (1.1.109), Bianca does inform Lucentio that she is no schoolboy liable to be whipped if he does not know the correct answer but rather she is learning for her own pleasure, which may well serve as a warning of how she will act when married:

> I am no breeching scholar in the schools;
> I'll not be tied to hours nor pointed times.
> But learn my lessons as I please myself. (3.1.18–20)

Bianca is an example of the new brand of teaching and learning fostered earlier in the century by Thomas More and Roger Ascham that discouraged use of corporal punishment and encouraged attempts to make education fun and engaging. Bianca so enjoys her studies that she has to be dragged away from them. A servant calls to her:

> Mistress, your father prays you leave your books
> And help to dress your sister's chamber up,
> You know tomorrow is the wedding day. (3.1.80–82)

"Come Kiss Me Kate"

At the end of the play, Petruchio, Lucentio, and Hortensio, the last recently married to a widow, wager on which of their wives is the most obedient, betting on their women as they might on their dogs or their horses.[47] As the widow also does, Bianca does not come when summoned, sending word that she is busy. After Kate comes and wins her husband his bet, she then brings the widow and her sister Bianca back with her. Petruchio demonstrates further how much he has tamed Kate:

> Katharine, that cap of yours becomes you not.
> Off with that bauble. Throw it underfoot. (5.2.127–28)

Kate at this moment is silent, but, as the stage directions inform us, "She obeys." As Susan Wabuda points out, "Woman's submission had its symbolic

---

47. A point made by Michael Bogdanov in Elsom, ed., *Is Shakespeare Still Our Contemporary?*, 71.

expression for all to see" in the cap on her head. "If a man should not cover his head because he was made in God's image, according to Paul, then a woman needed a covering." Many people of her own time argued that Margaret Clitherow, discussed in chapter 1 for her refusal to plead pregnancy, was unconcerned about the obedience she owed her Protestant husband. Margaret was well aware of this criticism, and before her execution, she sent her hat to her husband to acknowledge his authority.[48]

Onstage, Bianca may well show her disapproval of Kate's action even before she speaks. Novy suggests that the cap had become "a fool's toy" and that "Bianca's scorn for folly has modulated into a scorn for duty."[49] But we might well wonder about the meaning of duty and the reasons for obedience. Patient Griselda from *The Canterbury Tales* was held up as a model of wifely obedience in sixteenth-century England—she also agreed to, as she thought, the death of her children when Count Walter demanded it. Though Lucentio is distressed that he has lost his bet, Bianca's "What a foolish duty call you this?" is certainly a question worth pondering. Kate's final speech in *The Taming of the Shrew* resonates with Foxe's version of Katherine Parr's submission to her kingly husband. Kate tells the other women that

Thy husband is thy lord, thy life, thy keeper,
Thy head, thy sovereign . . .
. . .

And craves no other tribute at thy hands
But love, fair looks, and true obedience—
Too little payment for so great a debt.
Such duty as the subject owes the prince
Even such a woman oweth to her husband;
And when is froward, peevish, sullen, sour
And not obedient to his honest will
What is she but a foul contending rebel
And graceless traitor to her loving lord?
I am ashamed that women are so simple
To offer war where they should kneel for peace,
Or seek for rule, supremacy, and sway

48. Susan Wabuda, "Sanctified by the Believing Spouse: Women, Men, and the Marital Yoke in the Early Reformation," in *The Beginnings of English Protestantism,* ed. Peter Marshall and Alec Ryrie (Cambridge: Cambridge University Press, 2002), 112; and Claire Walker, "Clitherow, Margaret [St Margaret Clitherow] (1552/3–1586)," *Oxford Dictionary of National Biography* (Oxford: Oxford University Press, 2004).

49. Novy, "Patriarchy and Play," 22, 23.

When they are bound to serve, love, and obey.

. . .

Come, come, you forward and unable worms!
My mind hath been as big as one of yours,
My heart as great, my reason haply more,
To bandy word for word and frown for frown;
But I see our lances are but straws
Our strength as weak, our weakness past compare,
That seeming to be most which we indeed least are.
Then vail your stomachs, for it is no boot,
And place your hands below your husband's foot,
In token of which duty, if he please
My hand is ready; may it do him ease. (5.2.146–47, 152–64, 169–79)

While Juliet Dusinberre may well be correct that Kate's "speech steals the show," it is still a troubling one.[50] Scholars such as Nevill Coghill would argue that Kate is "generously and charmingly" making this speech for Petruchio, and "it is a total misconception to suppose that she has been bludgeoned into it."[51] Stephen Bretzius places Coghill in the "revisionist" school, suggesting that "for revisionist readers Kate's final speech simply humors Petruchio."[52] Ruth Nevo writes, "That Kate is in love by act 5 is, I believe, what the play invites us to perceive. . . . And indeed she may well be. The man she has married has humour and high spirits, intuition, patience, self-command and masterly intelligence."[53] Novy sees a Kate and Petruchio who have "exclusive dependence on each other." Kate's speech "presents their marriage as a private world, a joke that the rest of the characters miss, a game that excludes all but the two of them."[54] But it's a joke that a number of women, both then and now, might not find very humorous.

Some scholars argue for Kate's autonomy and spirited pleasure throughout the play, all the way to this last speech. Margie Burns proposes that Kate's final speech succeeds as "intentional though extemporaneous irony, along the lines of Katherine and Petruchio's game playing in Act 4 scene

50. Juliet Dusinberre, "The Taming of the Shrew: Women, Acting, and Power," *Studies in the Literary Imagination* 26 (1993): 80.

51. Nevil Coghill, "The Basis of Shakespearean Comedy," *Essays and Studies* (1950): p. 11 in *Shakespeare in Theory: The Postmodern Academy and the Early Modern Theater*, ed. Stephen Bretzius (Ann Arbor: University of Michigan Press, 1997), 57. I found Bretzius's discussion of different theoretical approaches to *The Taming of the Shrew* extremely helpful.

52. Bretzius, *Shakespeare in Theory*, 59.

53. Nevo, *Comic Transformations*, 50.

54. Novy, "Patriarchy and Play," 25.

five. . . . Like Katharina herself at every point in the play, the speech continuously displays strength and animation."[55] Camille Wells Slights sees the speech in not quite such an ironic turn but still reads the relationship between Kate and Petruchio as positive: "Petruchio certainly demands that Kate submit to his will, but we know, as she does, that he won't step on her hand."[56]

But I am not so sure that Kate's hand, or more importantly her sense of self, is all that safe. These are her last lines of the play. Petruchio's response to her lengthy speech of submission—"Why there's a wench! Come on, and kiss me Kate"—suggests that all is well between them, but really, we only have that from Petruchio's point of view (5.2.180). Earlier in the play, he pressures Kate to kiss him or face punishment; when she does not want to kiss him publicly on the street, he threatens to take her away without seeing her family. And this is almost exactly the same line that Henry says to Queen Kate in *When You See Me, You Know Me:* "Come kisse me Kate, so now ime friends againe." How good for Henry that he is now friends again with his wife, but he has just nearly had her killed. We are never shown how either Rowley's or Shakespeare's Kate really feel about the prospect of kissing a man who has such power over them.

Katherine Parr was clearly reluctant to marry Henry VIII; Kate did not wish to marry Petruchio. Both Foxe's Queen Katherine and Shakespeare's Kate had to make the marriage and then had to deal with the issue of male authority in the household and the dangers to them as a consequence of resisting that authority, though Katherine's dangers were actual in a way that Kate's certainly were not. Both, at the absolutely necessary time, make a powerful speech that is a strategic concession to the husband, one that pleases him into affectionate behavior. And with both, we are left questioning just how they figured out how to craft this submission and how much—or how little—did they really mean what they said. The actual Katherine Parr was a far more complex woman than the idealized version of her we see in Foxe; in some ways, both Kate and Bianca are her symbolic daughters. The shadow of this early-sixteenth-century queen consort, knowing that the wrong word might lead to her death, stands behind Kate as she makes this speech; she is a troubling reminder to audiences, both then and now, of what can happen to wives who are not "tamed."

---

55. Margie Burns, "The Ending of the Shrew," in *The Taming of the Shrew: Critical Essays,* ed. Aspinal, 88, 89.

56. Camille Wells Slights, *Shakespeare's Comic Commonwealths* (Toronto: University of Toronto Press, 1993), 52.

♨ CHAPTER 6

Shakespeare and the Women Writers of the Veneto

The secular education of women posed an even greater threat to the English household than Protestant Bible reading. Although Protestantism came to England from the continent, successive Tudor regimes soon made it seem more English than the Catholicism that it had replaced. In contrast, Renaissance humanism always retained its foreign aura. The humanist scholar trespassed frontiers that increasingly defined European identities. The risks were even higher when women aspired to humanist learning, since it exposed them not only to other cultures but to other standards of female behavior as well.

This chapter explores Bianca's humanist tutelage and Katherine's antihumanist taming as a commentary on the cultural and material conditions that allowed a flowering of women's intellectual life in the Italian Veneto. As an adaptation of Ludovico Ariosto's 1509 comedy *I suppositi, The Taming of the Shrew* provides a source for thinking through divergences between the experiences of sixteenth-century women living in England and Italy. It focuses on issues of inheritance and property ownership in which English customs differed from the Italian ones that Ariosto represented. These differences may account for a striking fact, that women wrote in greater numbers and across a wider range of genres in northern Italy than in England.

No inquiries into the past are more troubling than questions about comparative oppression.[1] Comparing *structures* of oppression might be relatively unproblematic. We can often determine whether the same restrictive practice occurred in two different societies at the same time or in the same society at two different periods of its history. During the sixteenth century, for example, Venetian and Paduan families often forced their younger daughters into convents to preserve assets for their older daughters' dowries.[2] That practice did not figure into women's lives in post-Reformation England because Henry VIII had closed all of the convents.

It is more difficult, however, to assess the consequences of such divergence. The moment we suggest that one practice may have had a liberating consequence, we risk overlooking how that supposed advantage may have been offset by factors that we have missed. We also run the complementary risk of ignoring the unexpectedly liberating consequences of a manifestly oppressive practice. Few things are more methodologically and even ethically risky than suggesting that one oppressed population suffered greater deprivations than another living under different historical circumstances.[3]

Early modern travel writers sometimes commented on the different conditions under which women lived in different countries. But most of these writers were men, and they seem never to have asked the question of whether women were happier or better off in one place than in another. I know of only one writer who seems to have felt that such differences had an impact on women's welfare: the Venetian nun Arcangela Tarabotti. In a treatise entitled *La tirannia paterna,* published posthumously in 1654, Tarabotti claimed that women north of the Alps were better off than women living in Venice: "In how many other kingdoms do women enjoy truly great liberty? In how many

---

1. On the methodological challenges posed by comparative history, and especially comparative women's history, see Cheryl Johnson-Odin and Margaret Strobel, "Conceptualizing the History of Women in Africa, Asia, Latin America, and the Caribbean, and the Middle East," *Journal of Women's History* 1 (1989): 31–62; Hilda Smith, "Are We Ready for a Comparative Historiography?" *Journal of Women's History* 1 (1989): 96–100. Ida Blom, "Global Women's History: Organizing Principles and Cross-Cultural Understanding," in *Writing Women's History: International Perspectives,* ed. Karen Offen et al. (Bloomington: Indiana University Press, 1991), 135–50; Offen, "Defining Feminism: A Comparative Historical Approach," in *Beyond Equality and Difference: Citizenship, Feminist Politics, and Female Subjectivity,* ed. Gisela Bock and Susan James (New York: Routledge, 1992), 79–88; and George Frederickson, "From Exceptionalism to Variability: Recent Developments in Cross-National Comparative History," *Journal of American History* 82 (1995): 587–604.

2. See Francesca Medioli, "Monacazioni forzate: donne ribelli al proprio destino," *Clio: Rivista trimestrali di studi storici* 30 (1994): 431–54; and Jutta Gisela Sperling, *Convents and the Body Politic in Late Renaissance Venice* (Chicago: University of Chicago Press, 1999).

3. See, for example, Levon Chorbajian and George Shirinian, eds., *Studies in Comparative Genocide* (London: St. Martin's Press, 1999); and Alex Alvarez, *Governments, Citizens, and Genocide: A Comparative and Interdisciplinary Approach* (Bloomington: Indiana University Press, 2001).

other cities do women perform public roles that are here exercised only by men? In France, Germany, and many northern provinces, women run households, handle money, and keep accounts of merchandise; even noblewomen shop in the marketplace for their families' needs."[4] Tarabotti focused these complaints about the exclusion of Venetian women from public life on the evil of forcing women to take the veil. This concern may have encouraged her belief that women outside Italy, specifically those in areas with large Protestant populations, were more fortunate than their Venetian counterparts.

But is that claim true? In writing about the sufferings endured by women forced to become nuns, Tarabotti spoke from her own experience. Her father had sent her to the convent when she was sixteen. We can only speculate about how much she really knew about life in other countries. It is unlikely, however, that she traveled as a girl, even more unlikely that she traveled once she had taken her vows. Her knowledge of "France, Germany, and many northern provinces" rested probably on conversations, possibly on books, and almost certainly on the hope that women were better off somewhere than they were in Italy. The comparison's polemical context suggests that Tarabotti was less interested in its truthfulness than in its rhetorical impact. An astute polemicist, she may have raised questions about the comparative indignities suffered by Venetian women to goad her male readers into reforming a corrupt system.

I do not want to suggest that Tarabotti was naive or wrong in asserting the advantages enjoyed by northern women over their Mediterranean sisters. I have raised these questions instead to make a point about a difficulty in the comparative study of women's history. Regardless of how precisely we identify differences in women's treatment in two different cultures, such findings still do not answer the question of where would it be better to have lived. After all, what precisely would have counted as "better"? The question of women's comparative welfare ultimately raises questions about what constitutes legitimate historical inquiry.

To get beyond this impasse, I want to recast the question in terms of literary as well as social history. From a literary perspective, one way of defining "better" would be approximate access to the same opportunities and venues for writing that were available to men. Within a sixteenth-century context, such access would depend on education and familiarity with the same canons of ancient and vernacular literatures. Women would need to have available time for writing, to be able to establish patronage relationships like those

---

4. Arcangela Tarabotti, *Paternal Tyranny,* trans. and ed. Letizia Panizza (Chicago: University of Chicago Press, 2004), 100.

that fostered male writers, to enjoy supportive mentorships, to circulate their manuscripts within coterie readerships, and even to have them published and printed. Perhaps above all, women would need to write across the range of genres undertaken by male writers: comedies, tragedies, prose romances, lyric poetry, the *romanzo,* even the epic.

Although no early modern society witnessed men and women writing in equal numbers, Italy had more women writers than England. This comparative advantage resulted in part from the earlier proliferation of humanist pedagogies throughout the major Italian cities. But it also arose from divergent relationships to property. That Italian women could inherit, own, and transmit property in ways that women in England could not may have encouraged at least some fathers to provide their daughters with a more worldly education. But in a more subtle way, it also may have given them a greater sense of entitlement to their own voices as writers.

The nature of extant evidence makes such a case difficult to prove using traditional historical methods. In lieu of a woman who had lived in both countries and could comment on differences between Italian and English society, we can turn to the traces of intercultural contact suggested by English adaptations of Italian sources. While literary scholars have often commented on these adaptations, they have limited their historicist interpretation to observing that Shakespeare shared a common Elizabethan ambivalence, even hostility, toward all things Italian.[5] I want to be more specific: English writers, in their frequent adaptations of Italian texts, confronted representations of alien social structures that they had to adapt for English audiences. Their departures from their Italian precedents are implicit comparative commentaries on the English and Italian social experience.

Reading *The Taming of the Shrew* against its Italian source reveals that Ariosto's *I suppositi* challenged Shakespeare with a glimpse into the conditions supporting a northern Italian Renaissance of women's writing. While Shakespeare may have read the work in Italian, he almost certainly knew it in George Gascoigne's 1566 translation, *Supposes.*[6] As Shakespeare's dialogue between text and Italian subtext builds toward its climax in Katherine/ Kate's concluding pronouncements on women's subjection, the play offers

---

5. See especially Robert C. Jones, "Italian Settings and the 'World' of Elizabethan Tragedy," *Studies in English Literature* 10 (1970): 251–68; G. K. Hunter, *Dramatic Identities and Cultural Traditions: Studies in Shakespeare and His Contemporaries* (Liverpool: University of Liverpool Press, 1978), 103–21; John Lievsay, *The Elizabethan Image of Italy* (Ithaca: Cornell University Press, 1964); Murray Levith, *Shakespeare's Italian Settings and Plays* (New York: St. Martin's, 1989); and Jack D'Amico, *Shakespeare and Italy: The City and the Stage* (Gainesville: University Press of Florida, 2001). For previous discussion of Shakespeare and Italy, see the sources cited in chapter 4, note 9.

6. For discussion of this problem, see Charles Ross, "Ariosto in Prose," in *Prose Studies: History, Theory, Criticism* 29 (2007): 336–46.

its readers insight into a paradox in Tarabotti's reflections on the advantages enjoyed by northern Italian women. If Italian women were more excluded from public life than their English sisters, why did they write in greater numbers and adopt more assertively anti-patriarchal language several decades before English women? Did something inherent in Italian oppression prompt women to vent their resentments in print? Or did something in English culture discourage women from following the Italian example even after the arrival of humanist education?

Tarabotti demonstrates how official attempts to cloister and silence Venetian women often backfired—by stimulating women's writing.[7] For over a hundred years before the 1654 publication of *La tirannia paterna,* women of the Veneto like Gaspara Stampa, Moderata Fonte, Veronica Franco, and Giulia Bigolina had challenged their subordination by reading, talking, writing, and publishing in almost every humanist genre and even by reading their works at public ceremonies.[8] Although other Italian women had written Petrarchan sonnets, Stampa used the genre to reflect on her career as a woman writer.[9] About the time of Elizabeth I's accession in England, Bigolina penned a pastoral romance entitled *Urania* that may have influenced Sir Philip Sidney, who spent ten months traveling back and forth between Venice and Padua in 1573–74.[10] Franco published a volume of *terza rima* verse epistles in 1575 and a collection of *Lettere familiari a diversi* in 1580.[11] Moderata Fonte emulated Boiardo and Ariosto by writing a chivalric romance entitled *Il Floridoro.*[12] In 1588, the Paduan actor-dramatist Isabella Andreini published her pastoral romance *Mirtilla,* which enjoyed multiple reprintings.[13]

---

7. See Virginia Cox, "The Single Self: Feminist Thought and the Marriage Market in Early Modern Venice," *Renaissance Quarterly* 48 (1995): 513–81.

8. See especially Ann Rosalind Jones, *The Currency of Eros: Women's Love Lyric in Europe, 1540–1620* (Bloomington: Indiana University Press, 1990); Margaret King and Albert Rabil, eds., *Her Immaculate Hand: Selected Works by and about the Women Humanists of Quattrocento Italy,* rev. ed., Medieval and Renaissance Texts and Studies, vol. 20 (Binghamton, NY: Center for Medieval and Early Renaissance Studies, 1983); Maria Ornella Marotti, *Italian Women Writers from the Renaissance to the Present: Revising the Canon* (University Park: Pennsylvania State University Press, 1996); and Letizia Panizza and Sharon Wood, *A History of Women's Writing in Italy* (Cambridge: Cambridge University Press, 2002).

9. See Jones's discussion of Stampa in *The Currency of Eros,* 118–41; and Gordon Braden, "Gaspara Stampa and the Gender of Petrarchism," *Texas Studies in Literature and Language* 38 (1996): 115–39.

10. See Valeria Finucci's introduction to her translation of Bigolina's *Urania: A Romance* (Chicago: University of Chicago Press, 2005), 1–35.

11. See Margaret F. Rosenthal, *The Honest Courtesan: Veronica Franco, Citizen and Writer in Sixteenth-Century Venice* (Chicago: University of Chicago Press, 1992).

12. Fonte, *Tredici canti del Floridoro,* ed. Valeria Finucci (Modena: Mucchi, 1995).

13. See Laura Anna Stortoni's introduction to Andreini in *Women Poets of the Italian Renaissance: Courtly Ladies and Courtesans,* trans. Stortoni and Mary Prentice Lillie, ed. Stortoni (New York: Italica, 1997), 221–23.

Attitudes toward women's learning were never unambiguously positive in any Italian city-state. Nevertheless, some of the most influential Italian humanists had advocated educating girls as well as boys from the dawn of the Renaissance, and their encouragement was a precondition of the cinquecento flourishing of women's culture in the Veneto. To varying degrees, Boccaccio, Antonio Cornazzano, Vespasiano da Bisticci, Agostino Stozzi, Bartolomeo Goggio, Galeazzo Flavio Capella, Castiglione, and Ariosto had championed women in *la querelle des femmes*, the pan-European debate over women's worth.[14] Many of them argued for the right of contemporary women to an education, and several explicitly championed women's writing.[15] In a tribute to Vittoria Colonna, Ariosto rejoiced that women were now writing in their own defense:

> Donne, io conchiudo in somma, ch'ogni etate
> molte ha di voi degne d'istoria avute;
> ma per invidia di scrittori state
> non sète dopo morte conosciute:
> il che più non sarà, poi che voi fate
> per voi stesse immortal vostra virtute. (*Orlando Furioso* 37.23)[16]

[Ladies, in sum, I conclude that each age has had many women worthy of history, but through the envy of writers you have not been known after your death. This will no longer be the case, since you yourselves are now making your own virtues immortal.]

Ariosto offers his own homage to Colonna and her peers to counter the "invidia" (envy) of previous male writers. But he also acknowledges the limitations of his project. Women will be able to redeem themselves from male slanders when they avail themselves more fully of the means of literary production.[17]

---

14. See Joan Kelly, *Women, History, and Theory* (Chicago: University of Chicago Press, 1984), 65–109; Constance Jordan, *Renaissance Feminism: Literary Texts and Political Models* (Ithaca: Cornell University Press, 1990); Margaret L. King, *Women of the Renaissance* (Chicago: University of Chicago Press, 1991), 181–87; and Pamela Joseph Benson, *The Invention of the Renaissance Woman: The Challenge of Female Independence in the Literature and Thought of Italy and England* (University Park: Pennsylvania State University Press, 1992).

15. See Benson, *Invention of the Renaissance Woman*, 33–64.

16. Ludovico Ariosto, *Orlando Furioso*, ed. Cesare Segre, 2 vols. (Milan: Mondadori, 1976). Translation mine.

17. The championship of women voiced in this passage is only one of the attitudes expressed in the *Furioso*. For a more extensive treatment of the poem's relationship to the *querelle*, see Deanna

Ariosto's appeal first appeared in 1532, and the Venetian women who wrote over the next few decades answered it in their literary activities and sometimes even in explicit statements. While imitating Ariosto in the *Floridoro,* for example, Moderata Fonte argued that the perceived differences in the abilities of men and women resulted from discriminatory education:

Se quando nasce una figliuola il padre
La ponesse col figlio a un'opra eguale,
Non saria nelle imprese alte, e leggiadre
Al frate inferior né disuguale,
O la ponesse in fra l'armate squadre
Seco o a imparar qualche arte liberale,
Ma perché in altri affar viene allevata,
Per l'educazion poco è stimata.[18]

[If, when a daughter is born, the father were to set her to do the same work as his son, she would not be inferior or unequal to her brother in noble and gracious undertakings. Or if he were to place her alongside him in an armed troop, or had her learn some liberal arts. But because she is brought up for other affairs, she is not seen as fit for education.]

Fonte developed this theme in *Il Merito delle Donne,* an imaginary conversation among seven women, each representing a different stage of life and expressing different attitudes toward men and marriage.[19]

The same Renaissance that carried humanist educational ideals to England also introduced the Italian debate over the merits of women. But as Benson and other scholars have noted, English champions of women's virtue departed from their Italian counterparts: writers like Thomas More, Richard Hyrde (the 1529 translator of Juan Luis Vives's *The Instruction of a Christen Woman*), and Edward More drew back from the radical social and political directions of Italian defenses. English writers treated female virtue as wholly distinct from masculine virtue and upheld the notion that good women were chaste, silent, and obedient. Only Robert Vaughan, the obscure author of

---

Shemek, "Of Women, Knights, Arms, and Love: The *Orlando Furioso* and Ariosto's *Querelle des Femmes.*" *MLN* 104, 1 (1989): 68–97.

18. Fonte, *Tredici canti del Floridoro,* 4.4. Translation mine.

19. Moderata Fonte, *The Worth of Women, Wherein Is Clearly Revealed Their Nobility and Their Superiority to Men,* ed. and trans. Virginia Cox (Chicago: University of Chicago Press, 1997). All references are to this translation and are cited in the text according to page number.

A Dyalogue Defensyve for Women (1542), followed Ariosto in urging women to take up their own cause in print (Benson, 157–81).

As ringing as Vaughan's apologia might be, it was a lone voice in Tudor England. This inattention to the potential significance of women's writing and, more generally, to their capacity for participation in public life parallels the comparative paucity of Tudor women's writing. The sixteenth century in England produced some remarkable women writers: Anne Askew, Anne Bacon, Mary Sidney, and Elizabeth Tudor. But as scholars have often noted, these women restricted themselves to religious rather than secular themes and genres.[20] Their piety was bound up with an official—although certainly complex and arguably compromised—submission to patriarchal norms. Even Queen Elizabeth adopted in her devotional writing the posture a simple "handmaid" of the Lord, "slight of age, and inferior in understanding of [His] law."[21] The first real flowering of secular women's writing happened after Elizabeth's death, when Lady Mary Wroth and Elizabeth Cary began writing in such conventionally masculine forms as sonnets, tragedies, and prose romances, a project that writers like Gaspara Stampa and Moderata Fonte had pioneered in Venice in the sixteenth century.

The earlier emergence and greater proliferation of non-religious women's writing in Italy depended on numerous factors.[22] Italy enjoyed a more fully developed urban commercial economy that valued learning as key to civic life. With its greater population and greater number of cities, Italy simply had more learned men than England. From time to time, some of this elite group felt that their daughters might benefit from the same humanist education that they gave their sons. A commitment to women's education was never widespread, but there were more Thomas Mores in Italy, so to speak, to encourage the occasional lucky daughter's intellect.

North of the Alps, humanism was bound up with Protestantism. In theory, the Protestant emphasis on literacy should have given English women an advantage. A protestanizing commitment to scripture played a role in the writing lives of such women as Marguerite d'Angoulême and her daughter Jeanne D'Albret in France and Anne Askew, Anne Bacon, and Mary Sidney in England. But the Reformation abolished one of the two institutions where women's artistic production had sometimes flourished

---

20. See Margaret Patterson Hannay, ed., *Silent But for the Word: Tudor Women as Patrons, Translators, and Writers of Religious Works* (Kent, OH: Kent State University Press, 1985).

21. *Elizabeth I: Collected Works,* ed. Leah S. Marcus et al. (Chicago: University of Chicago Press, 2000), 138.

22. See Patricia H. Labalme, "Venetian Women on Women: Three Early Modern Feminists," *Archivio veneto,* 5th series, vol. 117 (1981): 104–9.

in the Veneto: the convent. Although restrictions had become tighter by Tarabotti's day, sixteenth-century Venetian convents had been famous for soirées in which nuns performed their own plays and musical compositions for lay audiences.[23] English Protestantism also prevented the other institution that supported Italian women's writing—the courtesan's salon—from ever developing. In Venice, courtesans were independent businesswomen who cultivated a lifestyle compatible with their identities as companions of male aristocrats; they established a salon culture predating that of seventeenth-century France. As Margaret Rosenthal has noted, they entered "a world denied to most upper-class Renaissance women; the honest courtesan offered social and intellectual refinement in return for patronage. Playing music, singing, composing poetry, and presenting a sophisticated figure were the courtesan's necessary, marketable skills."[24]

One final factor contributed, elusively but significantly, to the proliferation of married women writers like Moderata Fonte and Giulia Bigolina in the Veneto. Venetian women owned one thing that English women did not: their dowries. Under English law, the dowry, or bride's portion, was a gift from a woman's father to her future husband. It became her husband's property, and he could do with it what he pleased. Common law stipulated that a third of his estate—the "dower"—was owed to his widow after his death, but this dower had nothing to do, at least in theory, with the original dowry. The dowry and the dower were completely separate. The same was true of the jointure, a prenuptial agreement to provide the wife with a certain level of support in the event of the husband's death, which gradually replaced the dower in ordinary legal practice.[25]

In Venice, by contrast, the dowry remained the property of the wife. During the marriage, the husband could do with it what he pleased. Upon his death, however, the dowry had to be paid back to the wife in full; she or her heirs could demand its return, down to the last ducat. Husbands went to great lengths to guarantee the return of their wives' dowries: they invested them in reliable government stocks, earmarked real estate for purposes of repayment, and even got their brothers to pledge repayment from their funds if

23. See Sperling, *Convents and the Body Politic*, 158–69.

24. Rosenthal, *Honest Courtesan*, 6.

25. See Maria L. Cioni, *Women and Law in Elizabethan England, with Particular Reference to the Court of Chancery* (New York: Garland, 1985); Amy Erickson, *Women and Property in Early Modern England* (London: Routledge, 1993); Susan Staves, *Married Women's Separate Property in England, 1660–1833* (Cambridge, MA: Harvard University Press, 1990). See also the essays collected in *Early Modern Conceptions of Property*, ed. John Brewer and Susan Staves (London: Routledge, 1995).

the husband himself were to die without sufficient resources.[26] The government supported these strategies in the courts and through legislation.[27]

In England, whatever a woman owed became her husband's upon marriage. In Venice, it remained the woman's, and she had rights to any property that she inherited after her marriage. By longstanding government statute, she could sell it or do anything else she wanted to do with it, without her husband's consent. It is hard to assess the impact of these legal distinctions on individual lives. English dowers and Venetian dowries, for example, served a common purpose of providing for the upkeep of widows after the death of their husbands. Both systems were insistently patriarchal, in many ways treating the widow's portion as a necessary evil that complicated an otherwise male transfer of property from fathers to sons. But the Venetian woman's right to her dowry gave her a degree of legal agency, and possibly the potential for greater independence, than an Englishwoman in a similar position. It provided a material reason for a greater investment in women's education, since a woman who might control property arguably needed to know more about worldly affairs than a woman who could not.

Would a visiting Englishwoman have confirmed Tarabotti's sense that she was better off because she did not fear the convent? Or would the visitor have envied the opportunity of at least some Venetian women to live in female communities? Would she have envied them their right to reclaim their dowries and to own inherited property? Extant sources encourage such questions, but they do not answer them. What is clear is that, given the opportunity to assess the experience of living in the Veneto and living in England, a Venetian or Paduan woman would have been more likely than her English counterpart to have written about those experiences. The same cultural complex that denied English women the rights to chattel and a recoverable dowry seems to have challenged their very ability to write in their own defense. No record makes this divergence clearer than Shakespeare's adaptations of Ariosto's play about a woman's right to a dowry, *I suppositi*.

Italian Dowries, Ariosto, and the Origins of Shakespeare

Although both *The Taming of the Shrew* and Ariosto's *I suppositi* exemplify the conventional New Comic concern with generational conflict and mistaken

---

26. Stanley Chojnacki, *Women and Men in Renaissance Venice: Twelve Essays on Patrician Society* (Baltimore: Johns Hopkins University Press, 2000), 95–111.

27. Chojnacki, *Women and Men,* 106.

identity, the plays differ in their attitudes toward women and property. *I suppositi* aligns its author with other champions of women in *la querelle des femmes.* The plot centers around a father's attempt to manipulate the Italian dowry system without regard for his daughter's later security. As in Tarabotti, dowry abuse synecdochally serves as a critique of women's disenfranchisement within Italian society. Ariosto's Damone, the original of Shakespeare's Minola, typifies the greedy father who cares more about his coffers than about his daughter Polinesta's happiness. Damone is so determined to profit from her marriage that he is willing to marry her off without giving her a dowry at all. Gascoigne's imprecise rendering of the Italian in the translation that Shakespeare probably used blurs the details of the bargain, but its general outlines are clear. Damone plans to retain the *"dote"* that should be paid to his daughter's future husband and even hopes to collect from him a *"sopradote,"* a bride price that no was longer common practice in Italy. As Erostrato, the original of Shakespeare's Lucentio, who is truly in love with Polinesta, complains:

> O, how covetousness doth blind the common sort of men! Damon, more desirous of the dower than mindful of his gentle and gallant daughter, hath determined to make him his son-in-law, who for his age may be his father-in-law, and hath greater respect to the abundance of goods than to his own natural child. He beareth well in mind to fill his purse, but he little remembreth that his daughter's purse shall be continually empty unless Master Doctor fill it with double duck eggs. (2.3)[28]

Erastrato's puzzling last line underscores Polinesta's predicament. "Double duck eggs" is Gascoigne's suggestive translation of the original *dioppioni*, or doubloons, a word that also had bawdy overtones in Italian.[29] The father is eager to fill his own purse but has forgotten that his own daughter's purse will be empty unless her prospective husband—a rich old doctor—provides for her.

The danger that Damone's avarice poses to his daughter cannot be overstated. The dowry that a father typically gave his daughter was not simply a courtesy or token of esteem. It provided for her security in case her husband

---

28. Gascogine's translation of Ariosto's *Supposes,* ed. Donald Beecher (Ottawa: Dovehouse Editions, 1999). All references are to this edition and are cited in the text.

29. "...salvo se non fa conto che questo vecchio gli pogna drento di li suoi dioppioni." Ariosto, *I suppositi,* in *Le commedie: con VIII tavole fuori testo,* ed. Michele Catalano (Bologna: Zanichelli, 1940), 1:110.

died, something all the more likely when the groom was old enough to be her father-in-law. Damone's actions threaten Polinesta not only with marriage to a man whom she detests but also with destitution upon his death. Cleandro, the geriatric doctor in question, promises a *sopradote* of two thousand ducats to Damone but says nothing about "putting doubloons" into Polinesta's purse. To make matters worse, Cleandro shows no interest in Polinesta for herself. He wants her to produce an heir to replace the son stolen by the Turks when they raided his native Otranto. The sexual overtones in Gascoigne's bizarre reference to putting "double duck eggs" in her purse hint that Cleandro may not be able to do that. One character even suggests that Cleandro prefers men and hopes that his future wife will encourage attractive youths to visit.

Ariosto thus centers his plot around an abusive marriage negotiation. Dowries were the only concession to women's needs in what was otherwise a deal between two men, the father and his prospective son-in-law.[30] They were expected to provide for the woman's welfare in the event of her husband's death. In the marriage negotiation that Ariosto imagines, even that concession disappears, and the deal between Damone and Cleandro appears as a naked transaction between men, a fact underscored by Cleandro's lack of sexual interest in Polinesta or any other woman.

Polinesta might be excluded from the negotiations between Damone and Cleandro, but she has resources. She has found her own preferred suitor in Erostrato, the heir of a wealthy Sicilian nobleman. Like Shakespeare's Lucentio, Erostrato gains access to Polinesta by disguising himself and entering into her father's household service. But unlike Shakespeare's more virtuous couple, Erostrato and Polinesta have sex long before their marriage. Damone finds out about their affair before he learns about Erostrato's secret identity and lashes out against the couple for having compromised Polinesta's marketability as a virgin. But the situation also brings Damone to a degree of self-knowledge about the folly of his avarice:

> O wife, my good wife, that now liest cold in the grave, now may I well bewail the want of thee and mourning now may I bemoan that I miss thee! If thou hadst lived—such was thy government of the least things that thou wouldst prudently have provided for the preservation of this pearl. (3.3)[31]

---

30. Susan Staves, *Married Women's Separate Property*, 228–29.

31. Gascoigne's translation departs enough from Ariosto to justify a more exact translation: *O cara moglie mia, adesso connosco la iattura che io feci, quando di te rimasi privo! Deh! Perché, già tre anni,*

In the play's only reference to Polinesta's deceased mother, Damone admits the limitations of his drive to maximize profits. The comic logic of the denouement rewards him for his penitence, since he still ends up with a rich son-in-law. Polinesta's marriage to Erostrato seems to provide the perfect reconciliation between love and money: she gets the man she wants, and Damone sees her married into wealth. Even Cleandro gets off the hook of marrying a woman of whom he now has "little need," since Erostrato's tricky servant turns out to be Cleandro's long lost son (5.10).

Despite the happy Plautine ending, however, Damone's selfishness leaves so bitter an impression that one character's concluding tribute, "How great is the tenderness of fathers toward their little children," could hardly be more ironic, at least in the Ariostan original: "Quanta è la tenerezza de' padri verso de figliuoli!" (*I suppositi* 1:160). Gascoigne, in fact, dampened the line by reversing it: "Behold the natural love of the child to the father" (5.10). In terms of conventional morality, Erostrato and Polinesta are guilty of fornication, fraud, and filial disobedience. Italian culture and European culture more broadly excoriated daughters who married against their parents' wishes or, worse yet, had illicit sex. But from Ariosto's ethical perspective, Damone's avarice—epitomized by his attempt to avoid paying Polinesta's dowry—so outweighs the young couples' offenses that the latter come off as mere peccadilloes. The Plautine championship of youthful spontaneity over senescent oppression underwrites a commentary on Italian marriage. Italian society might remain patriarchal, but fathers are still responsible for protecting their daughters. The dowry that Damone wanted so much to avoid paying would continue to mark a woman's dignity and her potential agency and independence as property owner.

I suppositi offered Shakespeare a model for transforming comic conventions into an exposé of women's vulnerabilities in the Italian property system. The play's progressive social implications should not be overestimated. Ariosto focused on abuse within the current system; he did not advocate overturning the system itself. At this stage in his career, Ariosto never broached the possibility of women assuming public leadership, nor did he ever suggest any objection to dowry practices that left women, even in the best circumstances, dependent on men. Polinesta hardly appears in the play. Everyone talks about her, but she does little talking herself. Nevertheless, in the context of the *querelle* over women's worth, Ariosto rendered visible indignities that

---

quando io potetti, non la maritai? ["Oh my dear wife! Now I recognize the damage I have done since I have been left without you! Alas! Why, three years ago, did I not marry her off when I could have?"] *Le commedie,* 1:121.

women suffered at the hands of tyrannical fathers and husbands. More daring yet, he implicitly sanctioned Polinesta's fornication as a means of resisting her father's negligence. Above all, he set an example for how other dramatists might advocate for women's interests in a patriarchal society.

Framing Ariosto: Christopher Sly Awakens to Italy

The Taming of the Shrew is Shakespeare's earliest use of an Italian source. Written before his adaptations of Ariosto in *Much Ado About Nothing* and of popular *novelle* in *The Merchant of Venice, Othello,* and *Measure for Measure,* it surpasses these later plays in its self-consciousness about the divergences between English and Italian cultures. From the moment Christopher Sly claims his descent from "Richard Conqueror," the play raises questions about the integrity of English life and its relationship to foreign influence (Induction.1). On one level, this play, which borrows a plot from an Italian adaptation of plays by Plautus and Terence, exemplifies humanist drama as a cultural force bridging temporal and geographic divergence.[32] But that is only part of the story. Shakespeare builds alienation techniques into his representation of Paduan life that remind the audience that it is, after all, an *English* rendition of that life by *English* actors. Petruchio and Hortensio, for example, first greet each other in Shakespeare's most extensive single passage of Italian:

> PETRUCHIO: Signior Hortensio, come you to part the fray?
>   *Con tutto il core, ben trovato,* may I say.
> HORTENSIO: *Alla nostra case ben venuto, molto honorato*
>   *signior mio Petrucio.* (1.2.23–26)

But Petruchio's servant Grumio exposes the illusion by insisting "'tis no matter, sir, what he 'leges in Latin" (28–29). By speaking actual Italian, Hortensio and Petruchio remind us that what we have heard up to this point has been English, spoken by English actors rather than authentic Paduans. Grumio's comment reminds us further that in 1590s London, Italian was as much a foreign, learned, and potentially affected language as Latin. These moments

---

32. See Beecher's discussion of Ariosto's debts to Terence and Plautus in the introduction to his edition of *Supposes,* 26–33. See also Richard Hosley, "The Formal Influence of Plautus and Terence," in *Elizabethan Theatre,* ed. John Russell Brown and Bernard Harris, Stratford-upon-Avon Studies 9 (London: Edward Arnold, 1966), 131–45; and Robert Miola, *Shakespeare and Classical Comedy: The Influence of Platus and Terence* (Oxford: Clarendon Press, 1994), 64–70.

of detachment from the action invite the audience to weigh the differences between indigenous norms and foreign influences, England and Italy, Shakespeare and Ariosto, in ways that link Shakespeare more to native English principles than to potentially destabilizing European ideas.[33]

The Taming of the Shrew centers its assertion of English values primarily around women's education. Shakespeare alters his Ariostan source in several ways, but above all, he links *I suppositi*'s concern with women's property to the matter of women's education that figured prominently in the English and Italian *querelle des femmes.*[34] He moves the story from Ariosto's Ferrara to Padua, the site of a university famous throughout Europe and notorious for its many Protestant students.[35] In *I suppositi,* Polinesta's lover poses as a household servant rather than a tutor, and she has no sister. By transforming him into a university student posing as a tutor initiating Bianca into humanist reading practices, Shakespeare associates education with resistance to a social code that, theoretically at least, allowed fathers to pick their daughters' future husbands. Literacy paves the way for the filial deception and disobedience that Shakespeare never endorses quite as enthusiastically as Arisoto does. Bianca's Italianate education contrasts with her sister's taming, an educational practice whose roots are as vernacular and anti-humanist as the folk ballads about wife-beating that scholars have long acknowledged as the Katherine plot's most likely source. Juxtaposing the two plots, this indigenous pedagogy checks the disruptive female behavior to which literary studies threaten to lead.

Before Shakespeare introduces his English adaptation of Ariosto, he frames it in the story of the trick played on Christopher Sly by the Hostess, an English Lord, and a band of English players. By sounding the themes of education, property, social mobility, gender, and foreign influence, this induction contextualizes the "Italian" action that follows. The metadramatic gaps that the frame opens among the audience members seated in a London theater, the schemers in a Warwickshire pub trying to convince Sly that he is a rich lord, and the players pretending to be Italian burghers and their tricky servants expose the impact of foreign cultural models on English society.

---

33. See Mayard Mack, "Engagement and Detachment in Shakespeare's Plays," in *Essays on Shakespeare and Elizabethan Drama in Honor of Hardin Craig,* ed. Richard Hosley (Columbia: University of Missouri Press, 1962), 275–96.

34. See Geoffrey Bullough, *Narrative and Dramatic Sources of Shakespeare* (London: Routledge and Kegan Paul, 1958), 1:111; Brian Morris, ed., *The New Arden The Taming of the Shrew* (London: Methuen, 1981), 12–50, 65–88; Beecher, "Introduction," *Supposes,* 70–76; and Fernando Cioni, "Shakespeare's Italian Intertexts: *The Taming of the/a Shrew,*" in *Shakespeare, Italy, and Intertextuality,* ed. Marrapodi, 118–28.

35. See Levith, 46–47.

Shakespeare questions the relationship between national identity and indigenous social hierarchies in the opening exchange between Sly and the Hostess, who is threatening to put him in the stocks:

> HOSTESS: A pair of stocks, you rogue!
> SLY: Y're a baggage, the Slys are no rogues.
>   Look in the chronicles; we came in with Richard
>   Conqueror. Therefore *paucas pallabris,* let the world
>   slide. Sessa! (2–6)

The Hostess may be a humble tavern keeper, but at least she has a job and can count on the local constable to enforce laws against vagrants like Sly. To counter this threat, Sly, at the lowest rung of society, claims a pedigree for himself that he hopes will invert his relationship with the Hostess and offset his disadvantages as a beggar. He informs her that he is, despite appearances, the scion of an elite Norman family that came over with the Conqueror. He then reinforces his assumed superiority by brushing off her threats with a motto she probably does not understand.

The joke, of course, is on Sly, since his knowledge of history and languages exposes his pretensions. The Conqueror was William, not Richard, and the Spanish phrase that Sly conflates with dim recollections of Latin should read "*paucas pallabras.*" As silly as his verbal blunders might be, however, Sly realizes that rank in English society has something to do with continental origins. Families like the Mowbrays, the Mortimers, the Nevilles, the Darcys, and the Devereux cherished their Norman origins. Although more recent arrivals like the Cromwells, Walsinghams, and Wyatts had Anglo-Saxon names, their rise depended in part on their mastery of Latin and other foreign languages that made them invaluable servants of a Crown eager to wean itself from its reliance on clerics and the older aristocracy. Sly's slips epitomize the failed social climber's predicament in all its ridiculousness. He recognizes the kind of knowledge that marks social boundaries, but he has not mastered it in ways that might let him actually cross them. But his failure does not invalidate the strategy. For almost a hundred years, commoners who had mastered the languages that Sly apes had begun to achieve honors of rank previously enjoyed chiefly by descendants of the Norman elite.

The botched allusion to William the Conqueror suggests the play's ambivalence toward this association of family honor with a foreign aura that impinges on England's dignity as a sovereign power. A country whose elite is descended from foreigners or affects the veneer of a foreign culture looks suspiciously like a country in some sense under foreign dominion. The *Chronicles* to which Sly appeals to prove his Norman descent are presumably the contemporary printed ones, like Hall's and Holinshed's, to which a tavern keeper might have access, and which Shakespeare, himself the son of a glover, used for over a dozen plays. As scholars like F. J. Levy, Annabel Patterson, and others have noted, these chronicles provided the basis for an emergent national identity.[36] Part of this new historiography was resentment of England's past subservience to the "Norman yoke," an attitude that could be mobilized by the middle ranks of society against everyone from civil lawyers to aristocrats and even the Crown. The more England conceived of itself as an independent nation, the more it resented subservience to the Continent.

Sly's errors cut both ways. They make him look ridiculous, like someone who does not have the pedigree that he claims. But they also cast an oblique aspersion on a system that perpetuates the Norman yoke in its penchant for the foreign. The bona fide Lord who devises the scheme that punishes Sly's affectation could not be more assertively English. We never learn his proper name, and that omission downplays the possibility that he might bear the Norman lineage that Sly claims. His dogs have distinctly Anglo-Saxon names: Merriman, Silver, Bellman, "Clowder with the deep-mouthed brach" (Ind.1.14). The Lord uses the English language's older, indigenously Germanic and monosyllabic vocabulary more than its later French accretions: "how like a swine he lies! / Grim death, how foul and loathsome is thine image!" (Ind.1.30–31). The Lord's prank exposes Sly's social climbing and foreign affectations at once. Sly begins to learn his lesson almost the moment everyone pretends that he is a nobleman. He not only admits but also strongly asserts the English identity he previously denied:

> I am Christophero Sly, call not me honor
> nor lordship. I ne'er drank sack in my life; and
> if you give me any conserves, give me conserves of
> beef...
>   ...Am not
> I Christopher Sly, old Sly's son of Burton-heath,
> by birth a peddler, by education a card-marker
> ...and now...a tinker? Ask Marian Hacker, the fat
> ale-wife of Wincot, if she know me not. (Ind.2.5–8, 18–22)

The Spanish-speaking pseudo-Norman yields to the beef-eating, ale-swilling Englishman from Burton-Heath who has acquaintances with names

36. F. J. Levy, *Tudor Historical Thought* (San Marino, CA. Huntington Library, 1967); and Annabel M. Patterson, *Reading Holinshed's* Chronicles (Chicago: University of Chicago Press, 1994).

like "Marian Hacker." The comedy aligns virtues like honesty and plainness with squarely local, English experience. A peddler-turned-tinker who renounces his foreign pretensions and admits that he is just Christopher Sly of Burton-Heath is well on his way to becoming a better, more integrated member of English society.

But this is only the beginning of the play, and the Lord exposes Sly even further to the risks posed by dalliance with foreign culture. This most English of lords has one prop—most likely of foreign, probably even Italian origin—to enlist in the scheme: a set of "wanton pictures" on such Ovidian themes as the metamorphoses of Io and Daphne and Venus's courtship of Adonis (Ind.1.47). These stories formed a part of the humanist educational canon, particularly as filtered through the moralizing of scoliasts like Pierre Bersuire, Georg Schuler, and Jacob Spanmüller.[37] But if the humanists' Ovid was supposed to inspire readers to embrace virtue, the Lord's "wanton pictures" rekindle Sly's fantasies of noble birth. Instead of explaining their sexual content as a vehicle for teaching higher ethical truths, the Lord foregrounds it as a foretaste of the pleasures that Sly assumes he will soon enjoy with his Lady, to the audience, a boy actor pretending to be his wife. The Ovidian trope of metamorphosis comes back to indict the humanist enterprise itself as a dubious means of advancement.[38] Sly starts speaking blank verse like the Lord himself, but he appears more ridiculous than ever when his newly refined language fails to disguise his vulgar appetites: "Well, bring our lady hither to our sight, / And once again a pot o' th' smallest ale" (Ind.2.74–75). His language has changed, but there is no metamorphosis. A tinker speaking blank verse is still a tinker, and the social mobility that might come with a humanist education leads only to an absurdity epitomized by his longing for a boy dressed as a lady.

Scholars have often seen the Induction's metadrama as reflecting Shakespeare's ambivalence toward theatricality.[39] But it also reflects his ambivalent sense of himself as someone whose social mobility would depend on his own French, Italian, "small Latin and less Greek." Shakespeare identifies himself with soundly English values by using the Sly plot to recall his own English

---

37. See Don Cameron Allen, *Mysteriously Meant: The Rediscovery of Pagan Symbolism and Allegorical Interpretation in the Renaissance* (Baltimore: Johns Hopkins University Press, 1970); and Leonard Barkan, *The Gods Made Flesh: Metamorphosis and the Pursuit of Paganism* (New Haven: Yale University Press, 1986).

38. See Jeanne Addison Roberts, "Horses and Hermaphrodites: Metamorphoses in *The Taming of the Shrew,*" *Shakespeare Quarterly* 34 (1983): 159–71.

39. See especially Anne Righter (Barton), *Shakespeare and the Idea of the Play* (London: Catto and Windus, 1962), 94–97.

origins. Burton-Heath, where Shakespeare's aunt lived, and Wincot, where there really was a family of Hackers, are Warwickshire villages just outside Stratford.[40] Sly's insistence on his common origins arguably constitutes Shakespeare's most direct and extensive allusion to his boyhood home. But by the early 1590s, the Stratford boy was fashioning a career that depended largely on transmuting foreign literary sources like Ariosto's *I suppositi*. As the story of Baptista Minola's two Paduan daughters unfolds, Shakespeare focuses his sense of Italian humanism's potential to destabilize categories of rank almost exclusively on the question of *women's* education. In the process, he created an identity for himself as England's greatest writer by reinforcing assumptions that made it difficult for English women to write at all.

From an Italian Education to an English Taming

As an adaptation of Ariosto, *The Taming of the Shrew* foregrounds two advantages that Venetian and Paduan women enjoyed over their English counterparts and that contributed to greater proliferation of women writers in Italy. As we have seen, northern Italian custom granted women a greater chance to own property, and Italian intellectuals were more enthusiastic than English ones about letting women have an education and write.[41] Shakespeare grapples with the connection between property and literacy in transforming his Italian source. *I suppositi* confronted him with a pro feminist discourse that, by the late sixteenth century, had been taken over and amplified by Moderata Fonte and other women writers. Shakespeare's handling of this Italian material suggests just how foreign and threatening these attitudes were for Englishmen of his generation, particularly when articulated by women.

The Taming of the Shrew engages *I suppositi* primarily to stigmatize it as a potentially dangerous influence to be domesticated before it could be performed before an English audience. This domestication involves both a rewriting of Ariosto's own story, the basis of the Bianca plot in Shakespeare, and its coupling with the story of Kate's humiliation, whose roots are English rather than Italian. As he wove the two plots together, he altered Ariosto's commentary on paternal authority. Ariosto centered his story around a bad Italian father whose avarice in withholding his daughter's dowry leads her to

---

40. Frances Dolan notes these local associations in annotations to her edition of *The Taming of the Shrew: Texts and Contexts* (Boston: Bedford Books of St. Martin's Press, 1996), 48.

41. See Benson, 209.

rebel. Shakespeare re-centers it around a good Italian father whose generosity toward his daughters, for whom he arranges favorable marriage settlements and access to tutors, leads to the same end: rebellion.[42] Whereas Ariosto's play indicted fathers who abused the Italian dowry system, Shakespeare's work raises questions about the system per se, which in his version leads to female misbehavior even when a father acts in his daughters' best interests. The misbehavior results in unwarranted female speech that challenges the prerogatives of fathers and husbands alike.[43]

Although Shakespeare translates Italian dowry practices into English terms, he emphasizes Minola's generosity by minimizing the liabilities to which widows were subject under English custom. If Minola were actually arranging his daughters' marriages in northern Italy, he would have given them dowries that they would have repossessed upon their husbands' deaths. If he were arranging them in England, the dowries would have become the husbands' property without any obligation to restore them. English common law provided for widows to receive a dower of one-third of their deceased husbands' estates. In contrast to Italian practice, this stipulation linked a widow's security to her husband's wealth at his death rather than to her father's generosity at her marriage. Like an adjustable-rate mortgage, the dower's eventual size was difficult to predict. Depending on how well the husband managed his estate, the dower could end up being larger or smaller than the bride price that she originally brought to the marriage.

Although Katherine's and Bianca's dowries will become their husbands' unentailed property, Shakespeare goes beyond English common law in ways that approximate, and arguably exaggerate, the legal and financial advantages enjoyed by women in Italy. First, Shakespeare conveniently denies Minola a male heir, so his property can be divided evenly between his two daughters. Since that considerable inheritance will become their husbands' legal possession, it puts Minola in the best possible position to bargain for a generous settlement in the event of their widowhood.

As scholars have noted, Shakespeare's imprecise use of the terms governing marriage makes it hard to understand just what Petruchio and Lucentio promise their future wives. At least in the case of Bianca, Lucentio seems to offer a jointure, a portion agreed on in advance between fathers and future husbands that barred the widow's right to the one-third dower guaranteed

---

42. See Lynda Boose, "The Father and the Bride in Shakespeare," *PMLA* 97 (1982): 325–47.

43. See especially Jane Kamensky, *Governing the Tongue: The Politics of Speech in Early New England* (Oxford: Oxford University Press, 1997); and Lynda Boose, "Scolding Brides and Bridling Scolds: Taming the Woman's Unruly Member," *Shakespeare Quarterly* 42 (1991): 179–213.

her under common law.[44] In a sense, Minola's bargain with Lucentio is on the cutting edge, since over the next two centuries, jointures tended to displace dowers in English legal practice. Historians continue to debate the significance of that shift, and no one can safely argue that the jointure necessarily improved women's position.[45] But in the agreements reached in *The Taming of the Shrew*, the advantage falls on Bianca's side. In offering her to the suitor "that can assure my daughter greatest dower," Minola precipitates a bidding campaign that would make her a wealthy widow in the event of her husband's death (2.1.336). The de facto auction seems to reduce Bianca herself to a kind of property. But within the conventions of early modern jointure customs, the scene places less emphasis on Minola's materialism than on his concern for his daughter's future.

Minola shows the same concern for Katherine's future in his negotiations with Petruchio. Sokol and Sokol have argued that the terms of their agreement sound more like a dower than a jointure, but regardless of its precise legal nature, the deal is highly favorable to Katherine:

And for that dowry, I'll assure her of
Her widowhood, be it that she survive me,
In all my lands and leases whatsoever. (2.1.123–25)[46]

Although this may mean a dower guaranteeing one-third of a large estate, the syntax is fuzzy enough to make it sound almost as if Petruchio will leave her everything. The main point is unmistakable: both Katherine and Bianca will have enormous wealth in the demographically likely event that they outlive their husbands. Shakespeare reinforces this impression by omitting any reference to the issue that limited widows' portions in historical practice: male heirs. This conspicuous omission allows Shakespeare to present Minola in an almost untenably favorable light as a father who puts his daughters' security above every other consideration and bargains hard to achieve it.

Several factors—Minola's lack of a son, the apparent scale of every party's estate, and their common failure to consider future male heirs—convey a general impression of the daughters' rich and independent fortune. The marriage negotiations have a hyperbolic aspect that has made them seem

---

44. See B. J. Sokol and Mary Sokol, *Shakespeare, Law, and Marriage* (Cambridge: Cambridge University Press, 2003), 178–79, 182–84. See also Ann Jennalie Cook, *Making a Match: Courtship in Shakespeare and His Society* (Princeton: Princeton University Press, 1991), 261.

45. See Staves, *Married Women's Separate Property*, 95–130.

46. Sokol and Sokol, *Shakespeare, Law, and Marriage*, 180–82.

implausible to historicist critics.[47] Few women in early modern Europe controlled the wealth that promises to come to Bianca and Katherine. But this implausibility itself yields the play to further historicist analysis. Shakespeare may not offer an accurate picture of either English or Italian marriage arrangements, but he does create a powerful fantasy of what an Italian marriage might be. That fantasy suggests a sixteenth-century Englishman's sense of Padua as a place where women might control the kind of wealth that would underwrite significant free agency.

Yet another instance of Minola's generosity, his commitment to his daughters' education, promises to support that agency even further:

> And for I know she taketh most delight
> In music, instruments, and poetry,
> Schoolmasters will I keep within my house,
> Fit to instruct her youth. (1.1.92–95)

On one level, Minola presumably fosters Bianca in the arts to increase her value on the marriage market. But the same was probably true of the fathers of women like Moderata Fonte, Gaspara Stampa, and the formidable Elena Cornaro, who had important careers as writers and intellectuals.[48] Once again, Shakespeare casts Minola, in contrast to his Ariostan original, as the epitome of a generous Italian father providing for his daughters' welfare.

As a crowning touch, Shakespeare suggests that Minola cares just as much about his daughters' feelings. Even after obtaining Petruchio's consent to a settlement, he insists that he will only sign a contract "when the special thing is well obtain'd, / That is, her love; for that is all in all" (2.1.128–29). In an era when, according to the historian's old adage, the only people who could afford to marry for love were those with no property to settle, Minola's stipulation marks a rare concession to the claims of a woman's heart. His line contrasts noticeably with what seems to be his later willingness to award "Biancha's love" to the highest bidder. But no one in the play suggests that he loves Bianca less than Katherine, and Katherine herself accuses him of preferring Bianca. When Minola discusses Bianca's marriage to Lucentio, the man she actually loves, he emphasizes the couple's mutual affection as a strong

---

47. See Ann Cook, "Wooing and Wedding: Shakespeare's Dramatic Distortion of the Customs of His Time," in *Shakespeare's Art from a Comparative Perspective,* ed. Wendell M. Aycock (Lubbock: Texas Tech Press, 1981), 83–101. See also Cook, *Making a Match: Courtship in Shakespeare and His Society* (Princeton: Princeton University Press, 1991).

48. See Jane Howard Guernsey, *The Lady Cornaro: Pride and Prodigy in Renaissance Venice* (Clinton Corners, NY: Attic Studio Press, 1999).

argument for their union. Even Minola's insistence that Bianca must wait to get married until Katherine has found a husband comes off less as paternal tyranny than as a concession to Katherine's claim as his elder daughter and, more significantly, as a way of encouraging Bianca's suitors to help him find a match for her seemingly matchless sister.

In contrast to *I suppositi, The Taming of the Shrew* is not about a father who abuses the Italian dowry system to enrich his own coffers. But if Ariosto endorsed the system while lamenting individual instances of abuse, Shakespeare questions the wisdom of according women the freedom to which Italian wealth and education might lead. In Ariosto, Damone's tyranny makes Polinesta's fornication almost acceptable as a means of thwarting her father's determination to marry her to an unworthy husband. In Shakespeare, Bianca is no fornicator, but her deception of her father associates her increasingly with her wayward sister. Whereas Polinesta hardly appears in *I suppositi,* much of *The Taming of the Shrew* focuses on Bianca's scuffles with Katherine, her education at the hands of her disguised tutors, and her growing interest in Lucentio. Bianca's education is entirely a Shakespearean addition. In Ariosto, Erostrato disguises himself as a household servant rather than as a tutor, and we learn nothing about Polinesta's learning. In Shakespeare, Bianca uses her training to conduct her own marital negotiations in counterpoint to those her father is conducting with her official suitors. Eventually it contributes to her independence from male authority, an independence that Shakespeare presents as anything but unambiguously positive.

As the play opens, Bianca appears to be just what her sister Katherine and her own Italian model Polinesta are not, a daughter obedient to her father's will. While Katherine bludgeons her music teacher with her lute, Bianca submits to her father's choices for her education: "Sir, to your pleasure humbly I subscribe; / My books and instruments shall be my company" (1.1.82–83). This is not much of a submission, however, since Minola soon informs us that Bianca herself enjoys her musical and humanistic studies (92–93). The tension between Minola's view of her education as a concession to her interests and Bianca's description of it as a concession to his will serves as a prelude to the intertexual complexities that follow. The more Shakespeare distances Minola from Damone by presenting him as a father sensitive to his daughter's wishes, the more he identifies Bianca with Polinesta as a daughter willing to dupe her father.

The primary medium for that deception becomes the humanist tutorial sessions in which her love for poetry and music leads directly to her love for Lucentio. In his eagerness to educate his daughters and to satisfy their taste for the arts, Minola fails to limit the syllabus. When the poetry that

Lucentio teaches Bianca turns out to be Ovid's *Heroides* and *Ars Amatoria,* the grounds are set for her seduction. The scene reinforces the suspicions about Ovid's impact on impressionable minds that were raised earlier by the Lord's "wanton pictures." As Patricia B. Phillippy has noted, the texts are not only erotically suggestive, but the *Heroides* in particular, a set of letters addressed by mythological women to men who have abandoned them, creates an opportunity for women to protest patriarchal conventions.[49] In the letter that Lucentio parses with Bianca in their first love scene, for example, Penelope's complaint about Ulysses' delays indicts the Homeric double standard that praises Penelope for her chastity while ignoring Ulysses' adulteries. Bianca's brush with classical education provides her with literary role models and quickens her capacity for rhetoric and debate. But the models turn out to be women who assert themselves against men, and Bianca soon creates a place for her own agency in a society where fathers and husbands are presumed to have total authority over their wives and daughters.

Critics have responded in divergent, and often antithetical, ways to Shakespeare's characterization of Bianca, her education, her rhetorical sophistication, and her relationships to her father and future husband.[50] As a display of her intelligence and wit, her exchanges with Lucentio anticipate the repartee of later comic heroines. The play's Plautine underpinnings invite our sympathies with tricky young people, even though their actions violate the obedience that children owed their parents in traditional Christian discourse. At the same time, Bianca's challenge to her father's authority carries suggestions of women's rebelliousness that are not contained within the logic of comic convention. As Lucentio himself discovers, fostering women's native ingenuity might lead them to claim more independence than the men in their lives might ultimately want to give them. Plautine precedent underwrote a daughter's resistance to an oppressive father, but it did not accommodate a wife's rebellion against her newlywed husband. As a less genial Venetian father would later respond to the son-in-law whom his daughter had courted without his knowledge, "Look to her, Moor, if thou hast eyes to see; / She has deceiv'd her father, and may thee" (*Othello* 1.3.292–93).[51]

---

49. See Phillippy, "'Loytering in Love': Ovid's *Heroides,* Hospitality, and Humanist Education in *The Taming of the Shrew,*" *Criticism* 40 (1998): 27–53.

50. For an alternative interpretation of Bianca's humanist training, see Leah Marcus, "The Shakespearean Editor as Shrew-Tamer," *English Literary Renaissance* 22 (1992): 177–200. See also Phillippy, "Loytering in Love," 52n69.

51. See Wayne Rebhorn, "Petruchio's 'Rope Tricks': *The Taming of the Shrew* and the Renaissance Discourse of Rhetoric," *Modern Philology* 92 (1995): 294–327.

These ambivalences involving Bianca are inseparable from the play's response to Italian educational and literary culture. The texts that Bianca reads with Lucentio and that encourage her to resist the conventional gender roles are part of the same legacy that produced the Elizabethan cultural elite. The London theater was arguably the primary channel through which that culture was disseminated to a wider, even marginally literate, public. Most people attending the play could not read Ariosto, much less Ovid, in the original. But the experience of seeing an Englished *I suppositi* brought them into a kind of contact with Italy, complete with Italian humanism and provocative ideas about the status of women. *The Taming of the Shrew* measures both the excitement and the anxiety that accompanied the acquisition of humanist learning.

While the Bianca plot transforms *I suppositi* into a tale about the seductions of an Italianizing educational program, the Katherine plot offers in its place an English model of taming upstart wives. While Ariosto provided the model for Lucentio's courtship of Bianca, Petruchio's taming of Katherine derives from a native tradition of jest books and ballads like "A Merry Jest of a Shrewd and Curst Wife Lapped in Morel's Skin for Her Good Behavior" (ca. 1550). Lynda Boose, Frances Dolan, and others have shown how deeply the Katherine plot is implicated in an English folk culture that "tamed" obstreperous women by parading them in animal skins, forcing them to wear bridles, and dunking them in "cucking" stools.[52] By juxtaposing a story with local roots with one imported from Italy, Shakespeare nationalizes the contest between divergent educational traditions as a contest between English and Italian authority.

The characters in both the Bianca and the Katherine plots, of course, are all supposed to be Italian. But some are more Italian than others. Shakespeare qualifies Petruchio's Italian identity through a series of alienation effects that make him seem more like an English country squire than a Veronese urbanite. As we have seen, the metadramatic jokes about his initial lines of actual Italian remind us that the original Petruchio was not really Italian but an English actor and, in a still more complicated way, an English character caught up in an Italian comedy. His "Englishness" becomes even more apparent in his resistance to Italian urban life, his association with a country seat out in the middle of nowhere, and in his non-Ariostan attitudes toward women. The Italian that he speaks for one line is for him an emphatically

---

52. See Boose, "Scolding Brides and Bridling Scolds"; and Dolan's introduction to her edition of *The Taming of the Shrew*, 8–23.

foreign language, one associated with a continental urbanity that he repudiates throughout the play.

As the agent of an English educational program, Petruchio sets out to domesticate Katherine not only by making her an obedient wife but also by making her more English. In the Folio text, the concluding "a" in the first several references to "Katherina" underscores her Italianness. But in first describing her to Petruchio, Hortensio changes "Katherina" to "Katherine" and embeds her alliteratively within a context of English associations under the title "Katherine the curst" (1.2.128). Petruchio then carries the anglicization one step forward by calling her "Kate" despite her objections:

> PETRUCHIO: Good morrow, Kate, for that's your name, I hear.
> KATHERINA: Well you have heard, but something hard of hearing:
>   They call me Katherine that do talk of me.
> PETRUCHIO: You lie, in faith, for you are call'd plain Kate,
>   And bonny Kate, and sometimes Kate the curst;
>   But Kate, the prettiest Kate in Christendom,
>   Kate of Kate-Hall, my super-dainty Kate,
>   For dainties are all Kates.... (2.1.182–89)

Calling her by an English diminutive, Petruchio places Katherine in a web of demeaning verbal associations culminating with the identification of her as a "dainty" to be consumed or as a piece of property to be possessed.[53]

The contrast between Bianca's Italian education under Lucentio and Katherine's English training under Petruchio could not be more pronounced. While one pedagogy heightens a woman's independence and teaches her the language to resist patriarchal restriction, the other inscribes her fully within the patriarchal order. In the play's most emphatic turn against Ariosto and Italian social practices, Petruchio focuses Katherine's taming on the attribute that may have most distinguished actual Paduan and Venetian women of her social class from their English counterparts: the right to own property. In *I suppositi,* Damone learns just how mistaken he was to deny his daughter the dowry that, at least in northern Italian practice, would remain her legal possession. As we have seen, Shakespeare revises Ariosto by replacing the avaricious Damone with the generous Minola, who provides his daughters the dowries that Polinesta was denied. But English dowries did not work in the same way that Italians ones did. As Petruchio's incessant punning continually reminds us, English women could not hold property because they

---

53. See Natasha Korda, "Household Kates: Domesticating Commodities in *The Taming of the Shrew,*" *Shakespeare Quarterly* 47 (1996): 116–18.

were themselves properties, or household "cates." Petruchio makes the case brutally clear when he carries Katherine off to his country house without even letting her attend her own wedding reception:

She is my goods, my chattels; she is my house,
My household stuff, my field, my barn,
My horse, my ox, my ass, my any thing. (3.2.230–32)

The strategy of reducing Katherine to a possession by reminding her that she cannot own anything reaches a climax in the scenes where Petruchio turns away the haberdasher and tailor who have made Katherine the attire that she wants to wear.[54] The point of Petruchio's taking over the household decisions that one might think of as his wife's prerogative is painfully obvious. Under the English principle of coverture, Katherine owns nothing, not even the clothes on her own back.

Katherine's domestication is arguably complete when she yields not only to Petruchio's authority over her but also to his ownership of her, her most personal possessions, her words, and, depending on the interpretation of her last speeches, her thoughts.[55] The scene in which Petruchio schools Katherine to call the moon the sun and the old man a "young budding virgin" parallels the earlier one in which Lucentio teaches Bianca to express her thoughts and feelings by parsing Ovid (4.5.37). But whereas Lucentio taught Bianca to violate the trust that bound her as a daughter to her father, Petruchio teaches Kate to suppress thoughts that run counter to the duty that she owes her husband. Lucentio, of course, gets more than he bargained for. Bianca's refusal in the last scene to obey his summons suggests that the humanist education he helped her to attain may grant her an independence that limits his own authority. Petruchio, in contrast, gets exactly what he wanted: a woman so obedient to his authority that she suppresses whatever rebellious instincts she might harbor. In its reinforcement of the social structure, English schooling seems safer all around.

---

54. Korda, "Household Kates," 125–28.

55. Few points in Shakespearean interpretation are more controversial than the question of how fully Katherine submits to Petruchio's authority. See Margie Burns, "The Ending of The Shrew," Shakespeare Studies 18 (1986): 41–64; Robert B. Heilman, "The Taming Untamed, or, The Return of the Shrew," Modern Language Quarterly 27 (1966): 147–61; Coppélia Kahn, Man's Estate: Masculine Identity in Shakespeare (Berkeley: University of California Press, 1981); Karen Newman, "Renaissance Family Politics and Shakespeare's The Taming of the Shrew," in Renaissance Historicism: Selections from English Literary Renaissance, ed. Arthur F. Kinney and Dan S. Collins (Amherst: University of Massachusetts Press, 1987), 131–45; Lena Orlin, "The Performance of Things in The Taming of the Shrew," Yearbook of English Studies 23 (1993): 167–88; and Korda, "Household Kates," 130–31.

Perhaps no other moment in Shakespeare provides a more compelling occasion to consider the question of women's relative status in England and Italy
than Katherine's notorious last speech urging women's total subjection:

> Thy husband is thy lord, thy life, thy keeper,
> Thy head, thy sovereign; one that cares for thee,
> And for thy maintenance; commits his body
> To painful labor, both by sea and land;
> To watch the night in storms, the day in cold,
> Whilst thou li'st warm at home, secure and safe. (5.1.146–51)

Katherine has mastered the arts of rhetoric, but under Petruchio's English
pedagogical regime, she uses them to defend the patriarchal establishment. In
urging women to obey their husbands, she builds her speech around *topoi* that
would have been familiar to readers of Ludovico Ariosto, Moderata Fonte,
and others who participated in the Renaissance *querelle des femmes*. They are,
in fact, the same arguments that Fonte's female interlocutors refute in *Il Merito
delle Donne*. At several points in Fonte's dialogue, for example, the women debate the pseudo-Aristotelian argument that sovereignty within the household
compensates men for the labors they endure by land and sea to provide for
their families. The newlywed Helena gives this argument a Venetian twist by
insisting that the expense of keeping up their wives justifies men's right to
use and invest their wives' dowries: "Dowries are paid to husbands because
when a man marries, he is shouldering a great burden" (113).

But if Shakespeare borrows some arguments from the *querelle*, he suppresses others supporting women's right to greater independence from their
fathers and husbands. In Fonte's *Il Merito delle Donne*, for example, Helena's
attempt to defend men because they work hard to support their wives meets
resistance:

> "You've got it all wrong," Corinna retorted. "On the contrary, the
> woman when she marries has to take on the expense of children and
> other worries; she's more in need of acquiring money than giving it
> away. Because if she were alone, without a husband, she could live like
> a queen on her dowry." (113)

In another passage, Corinna turns the pseudo-Aristotelian argument on its
head. Instead of underwriting male sovereignty, men's labors in the world
demonstrate their subjection: "For don't we see that men's rightful task is
to go out to work and wear themselves out trying to accumulate wealth, as

though they were our factors or stewards, so that we can remain at home like the lady of the house directing their work and enjoying the profit of their labors" (59). She and other speakers back up this claim by emphasizing women's greater virtue and their resistance to the passions that are often men's downfall.

Shakespeare too stages a debate over male sovereignty in the final scene of *The Taming of the Shrew*. But Fonte's dialogue and intellectual exchange solely among Italian women yields instead to a brawl before men, one that proves the greater effectiveness of Katherine's training over Bianca's education. Bianca may have learned to defy men's authority, but for all her reading of Ovid's *Heroides,* she seems incapable of defending that position on rationally compelling grounds. Rather mysteriously, the lute-cracking Katherine ends up as the play's only compelling female rhetor, while Bianca and the Widow seem at best peevish in their comparative silence. In contrast to the lively exchanges in *Il Merito delle Donne,* no one answers Katherine's pseudo-Aristotelian claim that a husband's "painful labor, both by sea and land" authorizes his position as wife's "lord," "life," "keeper," "head," and "sovereign" (5.2.149, 146–47).

We have little way of knowing how Shakespeare might have responded to Katherine's speech in a conclusion to the Christopher Sly plot, since no such conclusion appears in the 1623 Folio that is the play's only authoritative text. But a quarto entitled *The Taming of a Shrew* appeared in 1594 that parallels Shakespeare's text and concludes the Sly plot. Without arguing about the relationship between the two texts, I note that Sly seems to have survived his heavily mediated encounter with Ariosto and *la querelle des femmes* without absorbing any pro-feminist attitudes.[56] For him, the play's didactic value could not be clearer: "I know now how to tame a shrew /...I'll to my / Wife presently and tame her too" (180, 184–85). Nothing could have been farther from Ariosto's apparent polemic considerations in *I suppositi.*

I began this essay by noting the difficulty of drawing comparisons between the experience of women in Italy and England, particularly when so few women traveled between the two countries. Of those who did, not one recorded her impressions in a text that has come down to us in our efforts to recover the voices of early modern women writers. But if women did not travel in large numbers between Italy and England, ideas about women did. There are enough extant English responses to the *querelle*—including Katherine's last speech in *The Taming of the Shrew*—to suggest wide familiarity

---

56. See Marcus, *Unediting the Renaissance: Shakespeare, Marlowe, Milton* (London: Routledge, 1996), 100–131.

with a tradition of women that often included, at least in its Italian versions, an advocacy of women's writing. A writer as familiar as Ariosto had suggested that women would correct the distortions of male-authored history when they asserted their own views in print. As an adaptation of Ariosto, *The Taming of the Shrew* suggests an English reaction against the more radical implications of the vision that he shared with many of his compatriots. Especially in Venice and its domains, that vision bore fruit in the writings of Veronica Franco, Moderata Fonte, Gaspara Stampa, and many other women writers. Within a century, it inspired the neo-Aristotelian disputations of Elena Cornaro, a Venetian woman who received her doctorate from the University of Padua in 1678. In England, however, the first real flowering of secular women's writing—and especially women's writing that challenged patriarchal norms—would take several more decades. And no English woman would take a university degree until the nineteenth century.

Afterword

As far as we know the playwright William Shakespeare never left his country. Yet many of his plays are set in foreign realms, and in many others a number of his characters are foreigners. As we have seen in this study, diplomatic international relations, life in other countries, and foreigners of a variety of description were of great interest to Shakespeare. But Shakespeare did not have to travel to experience the lives of foreigners or life in foreign realms. We know that Shakespeare read voraciously but also that there were many foreigners in early modern London, even more when we realize that, according to the Oxford English Dictionary, in the late sixteenth century the term *foreigner* had a wide range of meanings. Someone "foreign" was not only someone from another country but also someone not of the family or household, someone from far away, someone concerned with matters far away. It could also mean an outsider, someone unfamiliar or strange. Foreigners of all these stripes were ones that Shakespeare may have known and used as inspiration as he wrote *1 Henry VI, The Taming of the Shrew,* and *The Merchant of Venice.*

At the time when Shakespeare was writing his plays, London was the third-largest city in Europe. "Foreigners" flocked to London, whether visitors from other countries including merchants and skilled craftspeople, religious refugees fleeing their homeland, or strangers coming from the countryside perhaps to lose themselves or to create new identities in the city. The public theaters into which Londoners crowded allowed them to see presented on stage encounters and conflicts with those who were considered "foreign." Yet while there were clearly strong strands of xenophobia in late Elizabethan culture, Jean Howard points out that "it was countered, especially in London, by a competing cosmopolitanism more tolerant of difference and more inclined to look beyond the boundaries of the nation-state with something other than contempt or fear."[1]

Each of these sets of paired chapters examined different aspects of foreignness, whether foreigners, outsiders, strangers, foreign worlds, worlds outside England, or strange worlds within. By looking at these plays, *1 Henry VI, The Merchant of Venice,* and *The Taming of the Shrew,* separately we can understand more about many different meanings of *foreign;* by looking at them together we can learn much more about those outsiders, those arrivals from abroad as well as those who embodied difference from England's territories, both in Shakespeare's plays and in the Elizabethan cultural imagination more generally. Our double readings of each play and the ways our chapters interact with each other provide multiple perspectives on the central themes of the foreign.

But it is not only Shakespeare's characters who inhabit foreign worlds—as we discussed in the introduction, scholars also sometimes inhabit different—even hostile—worlds depending on their disciplines. All too often, historians and literary scholars come to distrust each other as their work intersects, each side maintaining that it has so much to teach the other—if the other side would only listen! The alienation some characters feel in Shakespeare's foreign worlds mirrors the alienation some academics feel within and beyond their disciplines.

As we stated in the introduction, we first met at an interdisciplinary conference, talked intently, and realized how much a historian who uses literature as a cultural source and a literary critic who reads a wide range of texts within a historical context have to say to each other. The more often we met and talked, the more we realized that we could not only learn from each other but also find a creative and new way to work. Having completed this project together, we are even more committed to the most thorough investigation of all aspects of the early modern past that our shared skills can produce, sharing our interests and learning from each other. Portia asks, "Which is the merchant here? And which the Jew?" As we discussed, that question served as our lodestar as we began the quest that resulted in this book. We emphasize that

---

1. Jean E. Howard, *Theater of a City: The Places of London Comedy, 1598–1642* (Philadelphia: University of Pennsylvania Press, 2007), 9.

our study is not being presented as a categorical imperative for our discipline; we are certainly not suggesting that all early modern scholars should do what we have done. Rather, we hope that this work can demonstrate the value of trying to eliminate the defensiveness that too often comes to the fore when literature scholars confront historians and vice versa. Instead of assuming that there are huge differences that must be overcome, it may be more helpful to concentrate on common projects and interests.

We are not claiming that the merchant and the Jew are interchangeable, that no one could not tell which one was Shylock and which Antonio. Nor are we arguing that the work of the literary scholar and the historian, however interdisciplinary their training, interests, and sympathies are, are completely comparable. But if the merchant and the Jew's modern analogues, the literary scholar and the historian, can bring together a confluence of approach and method as well as a respect for the differences inherent in their approaches as well as the similarities, the foreign worlds will be home to all of us.

✎ INDEX